The End of Phenomenology

lived experience
does not portray
the world as it is
"mind independent"
we do experience
non-mind dependent
phenomena

Speculative Realism

Series Editor: Graham Harman

Since its first appearance at a London colloquium in 2007, the Speculative Realism movement has taken continental philosophy by storm. Opposing the formerly ubiquitous modern dogma that philosophy can speak only of the human-world relation rather than the world itself, Speculative Realism defends the autonomy of the world from human access, but in a spirit of imaginative audacity.

Editorial Advisory Board

Jane Bennett   Iain Hamilton Grant
Nathan Brown   Myra Hird
Levi Bryant   Adrian Johnston
Patricia Clough   Eileen A. Joy
Mark Fisher

Books available

Quentin Meillassoux: Philosophy in the Making by Graham Harman

Onto-Cartography: An Ontology of Machines and Media by Levi R. Bryant

Form and Object: A Treatise on Things by Tristan Garcia, translated by Mark Allan Ohm and Jon Cogburn

Adventures in Transcendental Materialism: Dialogues with Contemporary Thinkers by Adrian Johnston

The End of Phenomenology: Metaphysics and the New Realism by Tom Sparrow

Forthcoming series titles

Romantic Realities: Speculative Realism and British Romanticism by Evan Gottlieb

Fields of Sense: A New Realist Ontology by Markus Gabriel

After Quietism: Analytic Philosophies of Immanence and the New Metaphysics by Jon Cogburn

Infrastructure by Graham Harman

Visit the Speculative Realism website at www.euppublishing.com/series/specr

For Dan Selcer, who taught me the meaning of method in philosophy.

© Tom Sparrow, 2014

Edinburgh University Press Ltd
The Tun - Holyrood Road, 12(2f) Jackson's Entry, Edinburgh EH8 8PJ

www.euppublishing.com

Typeset in 11/13 Adobe Sabon
by IDSUK (DataConnection) Ltd

A CIP record for this book is available from the British Library

ISBN 978 0 7486 8482 3 (hardback)
ISBN 978 0 7486 8484 7 (webready PDF)
ISBN 978 0 7486 8483 0 (paperback)
ISBN 978 0 7486 8485 4 (epub)

The End of Phenomenology

Metaphysics and the New Realism

Tom Sparrow

EDINBURGH
University Press

Contents

Series Editor's Preface

Tom Sparrow's *The End of Phenomenology: Metaphysics and the New Realism* is as bold a book as its title and subtitle suggest. Granted, it is not rare in today's continental philosophy to hear critiques of phenomenology in the name of realism. But such complaints too often resound from the grisly chambers of scientism, where everyone is in a terrible hurry to snuff out the "manifest" or "folk" images of consciousness through brash nihilistic claims about the explanatory powers of neuroscience. Premature dances are held on the grave of phenomenology before even the most basic lessons have been learned from it. By contrast, Sparrow has done his homework within the phenomenological guild. He holds a PhD from Duquesne University in Pittsburgh, one of America's most storied doctoral programs in phenomenology. A profound respect for such thinkers as Husserl, Levinas, and Merleau-Ponty is visible throughout Sparrow's work. Though he speaks bluntly of "the end of phenomenology," his tone is neither arrogant nor dismissive. Instead, he is filled with optimism that traditional phenomenology can and must be transformed into a new lineage of realist metaphysics.

Until recently, Sparrow was a relatively unknown younger scholar. This immediately changed with the publication of his innovative debut book *Levinas Unhinged* (Zero Books, 2013). Levinas scholarship has largely been exhausted by two approaches that might be called "Right" and "Left" Levinasianism. The Right Levinasians take him mostly for an ethical and religious philosopher, impeccably pious in his calls to respect the Other, and guided by a single divine infinity shining forth in the human face and its command that Thou Shalt Not Kill. The Left Levinasians, hostile to objective ethical codes and filled with outright contempt for religion, can hardly conceal their annoyance with this first group. But rather than offer a fresh alternative, they generally reduce Levinas to a mere appendage to the supposedly mightier thinker Jacques Derrida. Sparrow, following in the footsteps of Alphonso Lingis, is one of the few commentators on Levinas to find fresh paths irreducible to those of the two aforementioned groups. *Levinas Unhinged* is an endlessly fresh and challenging work that has established Sparrow as one of the most promising new voices in continental thought.

Another book by Sparrow, *Plastic Bodies: Rebuilding Sensation After Phenomenology*, is forthcoming from Open Humanities Press in late 2014. In manuscript form this book made an impression on Cathérine Malabou, the leading philosopher of plasticity, who has written a generous preface to accompany it. While the subtitle of Sparrow's book again proclaims friction with mainstream phenomenology, it draws deeply from the wells of Merleau-Ponty and Levinas in arguing for *sensation* rather than cognition as the basic material of subjectivity. Here as in the first book, Sparrow combines erudition with an unusual power of original formulation. More generally, he consolidates the strong authorial voice that already rang clear in *Levinas Unhinged*.

That brings us to the present book, possibly his most important so far. The opening sentence of the Preface already captures one's attention: "At some point during the writing of my doctoral thesis I became obsessed with phenomenological method and frustrated by its professed practitioners." Obsessed with the method, frustrated by its practitioners. This is typical of Sparrow: his urge to recover an inner kernel of promise from phenomenology without retaining the tedious methodological concerns and tacit antirealism that were encrusted onto the movement from its earliest years. As Sparrow candidly recognizes, "it is ultimately necessary to close the door on phenomenology as an approach to realism." Despite phenomenology's thick carnal descriptions of blackbirds, fountain pens, bread, cigarettes, and burning churches, it cannot even match Heidegger's insights into a deeper withdrawal of real entities from consciousness – much less tell us anything about the interaction of nonhuman objects.

This is the point where Sparrow makes common cause with one prominent recent movement: "Speculative realism signals the end of phenomenology." But for Sparrow this is less a dramatic recent event than a lingering death that began long ago. No mainstream phenomenologist will be pleased by his verdict that "what we … witness in Husserl's faithful followers is a kind of living death of phenomenology: so many phenomenologists walking the earth believing themselves to be the living embodiment of their master's program, yet practicing a philosophy that has either died or never existed at all." What entitles Sparrow to such a harsh judgment? I do think he is entitled to it, even though my passion for phenomenology equals Sparrow's own. The early death of phenomenology stemmed from its systematic avoidance of the realism vs. antirealism debate. In Husserl we find a marked tendency to portray this debate as a "pseudo-problem," as if phenomenology were a "third way" somehow beyond this apparently vulgar and well-worn question. Admittedly, the same tendency can be found in Heidegger, though the withdrawal of being behind presence in this thinker at least opens a path to a frankly realist position. But Husserl claims that phenomenology is even beyond idealism, since we are always already immersed in a world of objects: loving them, hating them, mocking them, taking them seriously. Yet these intentional objects, as they are known, exist only as correlates of a thinker. They have no autonomous status, and Husserl insists on the absurdity of imagining that any object might not be the potential or actual correlate of some act of thought. In this way, Husserl makes a radical claim about reality that Sparrow rightly rejects: all reality is either thought or the correlate of thought. And if that is not full-blown idealism, then nothing is.

My view is that the *primary* mission of philosophy is neither scholarship, nor flattery of God, nor flattery of the political Left, nor flattery of natural science, nor flattery of one's academic tribe. Instead, philosophy's mission is to produce fresh conceptual alternatives that outflank the grinding intellectual trench wars of the present, whatever they might be. In view of the present-day tendencies in continental thought either to pursue a bloodless old-fashioned phenomenology or to denounce phenomenology with shallow and hectoring lessons on the structure of the brain, few innovations can be more important than Sparrow's attempt to transform phenomenology from within.

Graham Harman
Ankara
November 2013

Preface

At some point during the writing of my doctoral thesis I became obsessed with phenomenological method and frustrated by its professed practitioners. As I read through Merleau-Ponty's corpus I often found him saying things that seemed to me unspeakable for a phenomenologist. His remarks gnawed at me because I am of the view that a philosophical method is supposed to *regulate* a philosopher's metaphysical commitments, that is, what a philosopher is authorized to *claim* about existence. If this is the purpose of method, I reasoned, then Merleau-Ponty's method should prohibit him from holding some of his avowed views or else he has no method at all, despite identifying himself as a phenomenologist. While struggling to remain focused on my fundamental argument I found myself perpetually tempted down digressive paths by the myriad *metaphysical* claims made by Merleau-Ponty and other phenomenologists whose method of investigation, I believe, confines them to a kind of disavowed antirealism which is unsupported, if not contested, by their practice of description. Today I still think this is true.

At that time, however, chasing these intuitions too far would have deferred indefinitely the completion of my degree, which is why one of my committee members implored me to exorcise my critical demons at a later date in a pamphlet-style polemic called, perhaps, *Against Phenomenology*. The spirit of that polemic haunts the pages of the Introduction and first two chapters of this book, although not merely for the sake of unleashing frustration or hurling glib criticism at phenomenology just for being phenomenology. Its purpose is to clarify the relation between phenomenology and metaphysical realism, and to prepare a contrast with the philosophical movement that has come to be known as

speculative realism (SR).[1] Speculative realism's relation to phenomenology – which varies widely from thinker to thinker – is the
focus of the remaining chapters.

My suspicion about the reach of phenomenology was intensified by an encounter with a slightly older new approach in
continental philosophy: the object-oriented philosophy (OOP)
developed by Graham Harman. In April 2005 I was finishing my
first year of doctoral studies in philosophy at Duquesne University
in Pittsburgh. At the invitation of the same committee member
who suggested I put off the present project until after the completion of my PhD, Harman was in town to deliver a lecture and
run a workshop on his current research in object-oriented philosophy (now often referred to as object-oriented ontology or OOO),
which has since become the most prolific species of speculative
realism. Harman, who would become one of the original four par-
ticipants – along with Quentin Meillassoux, Iain Hamilton Grant,
and Ray Brassier – at the landmark colloquium on speculative realism held at Goldsmiths, University of London in April 2007, delivered a paper on Leibniz and facilitated a small-group discussion
of Heidegger and the "volcanic structure of objects." Harman's
talks and presentation style intrigued me, so I picked up his books
Tool-Being: Heidegger and the Metaphysics of Objects and *Gue-
rilla Metaphysics: Phenomenology and the Carpentry of Things*.
Not until I began serious work on my dissertation prospectus did
I realize that Harman, and especially his discussion in *Guerrilla*

---

[1] It is now common to qualify the use of this term, "speculative realism,"
and call into question its very existence or announce its nascent demise.
It is increasingly common to denounce it as a mere Internet trend or blog
phenomenon. While it may be difficult to identify the red thread running
through all of those philosophies that answer to the name of speculative
realism, it is not impossible. Moreover, it would be wrong to denigrate
these philosophies for their links to blogging, open access publishing,
and para-academic practices, all of which are virtues of the movement
and increasingly vital to the future of the humanities. Before too long it
will be plainly evident that calling these links vices is simply reactionary, a conservative attempt to safeguard the institutional power of the
traditional academy and its scholarly appendages. Indeed, the practices
of speculative realism mark its timeliness as much as its potential to alter
the institution of philosophy.

Metaphysics of the "carnal phenomenologists" (Merleau-Ponty, Levinas, and Lingis), would be an invaluable ally in my study of phenomenology. More specifically, he would give me an alternative route to the things themselves, one decidedly realist in persuasion. Not only did his work offer an innovative approach to Heidegger, it presented the work of Husserl, Merleau-Ponty, and Levinas in a fresh light that I found lacking in the critical literature on phenomenology. It took Alphonso Lingis seriously as a philosopher. It confirmed many of my suspicions about what phenomenology can and cannot accomplish. Finally, it approached the work of deconstruction and poststructuralism in a way that made me realize their ascendancy in continental philosophy was waning, that their hegemony was not inevitable, and that new paths of research were opening up. Speculative realism was one of those paths.

While phenomenology offers clues to the new directions in realism that have taken hold after the "speculative turn" in continental philosophy, it is ultimately necessary to close the door on phenomenology as an approach to realism. Speculative realism signals the end of phenomenology. The present book is an attempt to explain why Harman and the other speculative realists are not and cannot be phenomenologists, as well as how the methods of speculative realism fulfill the promise of phenomenological realism. If phenomenology harkened us to the things themselves, speculative realism actually delivers them.

My title, *The End of Phenomenology*, bears a double meaning. It first implies that speculative realism, as noted, brings phenomenology to a close, either as the fulfillment of the hope of phenomenology or as the displacement of phenomenology as the beacon of realism in the continental tradition. Second, it suggests that phenomenology has perhaps already come to an end; or, to borrow some of phenomenology's own language, that it has always already come to an end. If this is the case, there are many who have failed to recognize it. I will argue that phenomenology really began and ended with Husserl; or, rather, that his famed perpetual return to the beginning of phenomenology was at the same time a perpetual ending of phenomenology. If he could never settle on what phenomenology should become, it is not clear that it ever was anything at all. What we then witness in Husserl's faithful followers is a kind of living death of phenomenology: so many phenomenologists walking the earth believing themselves to be the living embodiment of their master's program, yet practicing a philosophy that has either died or never existed at all. So, in addition to working out the relationship between speculative realism and phenomenology, I hope also to contribute to our understanding of the current state of phenomenology.

This book accomplishes two things. First, it interrogates phenomenology to see if it qualifies as realist in any sense. Second, it examines several of the primary speculative realists to identify the extent to which their work engages and disengages phenomenology. Some figures, Harman for instance, draw quite heavily from phenomenology, while others, like Grant and Jane Bennett, engage phenomenology only peripherally. Uniting these two investigations is the thesis that, for much of the twentieth century, it was phenomenology that promised to satisfy the desire for realism among continental thinkers, but now it is clear that phenomenology cannot deliver realism as commonly understood. Speculative realism returns us to the real without qualification and without twisting the meaning of realism. This return, however, is not unified and does not follow a singular method. It is as diverse as its many practitioners. But I hope to provide here an account of the coherence that underlies its diversity and to indicate the options opened by those working in the field.

There should be little doubt that speculative realism has taken hold in continental philosophy. Not only have numerous books appeared under its aegis, but conferences, workshops and colloquia continue to stage discussions of the topic. A major university press, Edinburgh, has initiated a series devoted to work in speculative realism; several journals have emerged to further critical discussion of it; university fellowships have been offered to research it; and senior members of the continental establishment are engaging it in their published work.[2] This is all in addition to the international network of blogs and para-academic events that have come to be associated with the new realism.[3]

Whereas many call themselves phenomenologists, there are few who explicitly identify their work as speculative realism. Harman is the glaring exception to this rule. The other three

---

[2] For example, John Caputo, *The Insistence of God: A Theology of Perhaps* (Bloomington: Indiana University Press, 2013).

[3] This and more is catalogued in Graham Harman, "The Current State of Speculative Realism," *Speculations* IV (2013): 22.

Goldsmiths realists have, in one way or another, distanced themselves from the label. More are flocking to it. Labels aside, what we are witnessing is not only a resurgence of realism in the continental tradition, but a "lively realism vs. antirealism debate"[4] that was strategically avoided – dismissed as tired or conservative or passé – prior to the emergence of speculative realism. Think of how much effort phenomenology has put into fending off the language of realism and antirealism! In the following chapters I discuss in some detail all four of the Goldsmiths realists, as well as several notable figures who have accepted Meillassoux's critique of "correlationism" – and, by extension, critique of phenomenology – and aligned themselves with Harman's object-oriented philosophy.

To prepare this ground I first provide an account of phenomenology's philosophical objective and the method it proposes to reach it. The Introduction and first two chapters are critical and written with defenders of phenomenological realism in mind. They are written especially with consideration for those who believe that phenomenology can disclose something about the divine, God, or radical alterity. The remaining chapters are less critical, more introductory, and written for readers familiar with phenomenology but curious to know how speculative realism purports to move beyond the method of Husserl, Heidegger, and Merleau-Ponty.

The Introduction asks a sincere, simple question that still begs for an answer after a century of asking: *What is phenomenology?* Some phenomenologists explain the incorrigibility of this question by pointing out, like a philosophy professor teaching Plato to newcomers, the inherently philosophical nature of the question and the problem of giving a satisfactory definition. I suggest that the question has no answer because the idea of phenomenology lacks a coherent center. In phenomenological parlance: it has no *eidos*. The absent center results from a failure on the part of phenomenology to adequately clarify its method, scope, and metaphysical commitments. Ultimately, I reject the idea that such clarification is unnecessary on the grounds that clarification is critical to determining what phenomenology can do and assessing whether or not its practitioners are doing it well.

---

[4] Harman, "The Current State of Speculative Realism," 22.

Chapters 1 and 2, respectively, make the case that phenomenology holds metaphysical commitments despite itself and that phenomenology can only underwrite a rhetoric of realism, not metaphysical realism. This forces us to distinguish between phenomenology and phenomenologists. Just because a phenomenologist says something, this does not mean that what is said is a phenomenological statement or authorized by phenomenological method. These two terms, phenomenology and phenomenologist, are often run together and lead to the erroneous belief that phenomenology is whatever a phenomenologist says or does. The fact that Merleau-Ponty is someone who describes the day's weather does not entail that his descriptions are part of the phenomenological canon. The question remains: what *would* make them phenomenological? For this we need a coherent definition of phenomenology. Moreover, just because Merleau-Ponty provides us with a characteristically rich and evocative description of the day's weather, then adds that he sincerely believes in the autonomous, mind-independent reality of meteorological events, this does not entail that phenomenology authorizes him to make realist commitments. What I try to show is that, if there is any realism in phenomenology, it is the product of a sophisticated "rhetoric of concreteness." If a phenomenologist like Merleau-Ponty commits to some form of metaphysical realism ("weather events will continue to exist when humanity goes extinct!"), this commitment is speculative and, as speculative, nonphenomenological. The same applies to the claims of transcendence made by members of phenomenology's "theological turn," two responses to which – one conservative (held by Dominique Janicaud), one progressive (held by Lee Braver) – I discuss to close Chapter 2.

Chapter 3 spells out what Meillassoux means by correlationism, sketches it weak and strong forms, and examines some of its entailments. It builds the case against realist phenomenology by arguing that phenomenology is in principle strong correlationism and, as such, prohibited from making realist metaphysical commitments. Additionally, it shows how Meillassoux works through strong correlationism to arrive at his own position, which he names "speculative materialism."

Chapter 4 is devoted to Harman's object-oriented philosophy, in particular its emergence and departure from phenomenology. Phenomenology is a perfect example of what Harman calls the "philosophy of access." These are philosophies that privilege the human/world correlation and as such dull, or "undermine," the realist edge of claims about what exists. Discontented with the philosophy of access, Harman taps the resources of Husserl, Heidegger, and the carnal phenomenologists to construct a nonphenomenological philosophy of objects. His work paves the way for a new wave of speculative realism, explored in the follow-up chapter.

Chapter 5 provides a synoptic account of the remaining Goldsmiths speculative realists, Brassier and Grant, and several established figures of the second wave of speculative realism, namely, Levi Bryant, Ian Bogost, Timothy Morton, and Jane Bennett. The chapter does not provide a detailed account of their views, nor criticize their positions. It is meant to signpost future directions in SR and OOO, and to give a rough idea of how these directions rub elbows with, modify, or sever themselves from phenomenology. In the same vein, the Conclusion of the book summarizes what I take to be the many ends of phenomenology and its strongest means of resisting death.

Even though this book is written for a general audience, one faction of which are readers well-versed in phenomenology but unfamiliar with speculative realism, I do not introduce or discuss speculative realism as though the reader is completely ignorant of it. Even today, nearly seven years since its inauguration, many authors (whether in published articles or conference papers) begin by explaining what speculative realism is before launching into the criticism that makes up the substance of their text. What I have done here is weave together my presentations of speculative realism and phenomenology so that readers familiar with one camp will readily discern the import of the other. With any luck this will minimize the fatigue that inevitably results from reading a book whose exposition of old terrain is a necessary stepping stone to new territory.

This book was made possible by several invaluable persons, especially Graham Harman and the editorial and design team of Carol Macdonald, Tim Clark, Jenny Daly, and Rebecca Mackenzie at Edinburgh University Press. Dan Selcer planted the seed for the book and opened my eyes to the necessity of thinking about method in philosophy. If I have applied his lesson poorly, the fault is entirely my own. Likewise, my perspective was crafted by conversations with Fred Evans, Rich Findler, Adam Hutchinson, Laura McMahon, Leon Niemoczynski, Tom Rockmore, and George

Yancy. Two anonymous readers for Edinburgh University Press wisely suggested I reframe the book, and I thank them not only for their suggestion but also for bolstering my courage to write. Without the patience, understanding, and affection of Cierra Clark my daily struggle with writing would have been much less bearable. Many thanks to all of you.

I cannot even for an instant imagine an object in itself.

Maurice Merleau-Ponty,
"The Primacy of Perception"

*And that's why I love those guys from the Goldsmiths panel
last April ... They are realists without being boring.
Why are realists in philosophy always so boring?
Not these guys.*

Graham Harman,
email to the author et al.,
24 November 2007

Introduction

Once Again, What is Phenomenology?

The Question of Method

While not all variants of speculative realism borrow from the literature of phenomenology, all of them do share the phenomenological aspiration to engage reality on its own terms. It is this aspiration – coupled with a longstanding belief in the naiveté of such an aspiration – that provokes the question of method. Is this actually achievable? How do we get there? Which school – phenomenology or speculative realism – is best equipped to put us in touch with the real? Neither? Both? On the face of it both steer continental philosophy onto the road out of Kantian idealism and into what Quentin Meillassoux has called "the great outdoors" of realism. Throughout the twentieth century phenomenology promised to get us "back to the things themselves," that is, back in touch with the world of lived experience *as it is lived*. But what phenomenology actually delivers is a subtler version of the Kantian world for-us, not the world of real or material things as they are in themselves. Phenomenology does not get us to the noumenal, it instead keeps us chained to the phenomenal, where we have been all along. Despite appearances, only speculative realism can actually get us out of Kant's shadow. This requires a radically different method than the one introduced by Husserl and modified by his descendents. For anyone searching for a realist alternative to the Kantian program, phenomenology appears as a dead-end that leaves its practitioners gesturing toward the outside without ever actually stepping out of the house. This introduction explores the problem with defining the method of phenomenology as well as the rhetoric of "concreteness" that gives phenomenology the feel of realism without actually delivering a realist metaphysics.

It would be inaccurate to claim that either phenomenology or speculative realism adheres to a standard, univocal method.[1] The various figures gathered under the speculative realist label deploy disparate methodologies, although each in their own way attempts to overcome the antirealist hegemony in continental philosophy. Toward this end they share a willingness to speculate about things metaphysical and, some more than others, to construct original ontologies. This compels them to reach beyond the finite limits of perception, historicity, and language. Another thing shared by the multiple variants of speculative realism is a rejection of the ontological primacy of the correlation between thought and being. Not all of them reject the legitimacy of the correlation as such, but all do agree that there is much more to the real than what appears within human consciousness. There is, however, much disagreement about just how to characterize the real. Phenomenology, by contrast, is exclusively committed to investigating only those dimensions of human experience that take shape within the correlation between thought and being. To be sure, it explicitly focuses philosophy's lens on what is evidenced within this correlation.[2] Although each phenomenologist assumes this task in their own idiosyncratic way, each one is bound to the method of phenomenology which, however it is construed, eschews metaphysical speculation. Unlike speculative realism, phenomenology purports to practice something called phenomenology, while few, if any, speculative realists pledge their allegiance to a speculative realist methodology.

Despite their resolution to speak only of what is *evidenced* – that is, intuitively given and identified *as* this or that – in the correlation between consciousness and world, it is not difficult to find a phenomenologist making metaphysical assertions. Even Husserl and Heidegger make metaphysical claims that are not legitimated by phenomenological evidence. Phenomenologically speaking, they are illegitimate precisely because phenomenology is supposed to be metaphysically neutral on the existence of the things of the world. This is the meaning of the methodological device known as phenomenological "*epoché*" (suspension, bracketing), which is Husserl's analogue to the radical methodological doubt implemented by Descartes in the *Meditations*. The *epoché* does not force the phenomenologist to actually doubt the existence of the world as it appears to consciousness, but merely prevents her from making any judgment about the existence of things.[3] As such it cannot be metaphysically realist. Such assertions, I suggest, are akin to non sequiturs in the sense that they do not follow from, and are not supported by, the phenomenological method. Just as the empiricist method deployed by Hume in a text like "Of Miracles" could not justify his commitment to the existence of miracles, phenomenology cannot justify commitments to what is not disclosed phenomenologically.[4] And much of what realism is committed to is never disclosed phenomenologically. This is not to say that a transcendental phenomenologist is not permitted to hold realist commitments. What I mean is that those commitments are not the *product* of the phenomenological method or phenomenological description. Phenomenology, I contend, must lead necessarily to either antirealism or metaphysical agnosticism. It therefore cannot be realist because its method prohibits the kind of speculation required for grounding realism in philosophical argument. This kind of speculation we get in speculative realism.

Husserl founded the phenomenological movement by perpetually writing, rewriting, and beginning to write books and lectures that would define the precise principles of the phenomenological method and conform it to "rigorous science." It is now commonplace to point to this constant rewriting and rethinking to epitomize Husserl's work in essence or to characterize phenomenology's approach to philosophy.[5] It is often regarded as one of its virtues. Even today the critical edge of phenomenology is lauded as a "perpetual self-rejuvenation, for which [phenomenology] is ready to ransom all the prestige attached to a mature, tried-and-tested doctrine."[6] Husserl was never satisfied with the presentation, which means that would-be phenomenologists are left without a definitive statement of how properly to conduct a phenomenological investigation. They are likewise without a proper understanding of how far phenomenology can take us toward solving the classical problems of philosophy. This is no doubt a crucial reason for the methodological disparity among phenomenologists. Nevertheless, it must be possible to establish at least what Husserl considered the necessary elements of phenomenological method, however minimal these elements may be. Without these is it possible to know how to practice phenomenology? If the method of phenomenology is uncertain, it is difficult to see how its results could be reliable, let alone rigorously scientific. As Husserl writes, only a "positive criticism of principles of method" can give us "confidence in the possibility of a scientific philosophy."[7] If Husserl saw this clearly, his followers remain less concerned about securing the integrity of their method. Many since Husserl have asked about the meaning of phenomenology. Still no consensus exists. Methodologically speaking, this is phenomenology's fateful, perhaps fatal, vice.

Husserl's descendents, often the most prominent, rarely take his efforts to establish the science of phenomenology as seriously as he did. As Dermot Moran has noted, following Paul Ricoeur, "phenomenology is the story of the deviations from Husserl; the history of phenomenology is the history of Husserlian heresies."[8] Husserl's followers interpret and apply phenomenology as they wish, often preferring to reroute it down a less scientific, more existential path. It is generally reconceived as the philosophy that dispenses with abstractions in order to get us back in touch with what it is like to live and think in the real world. Some, including Heidegger and Merleau-Ponty, downplay or outright reject the idea of phenomenology as a strict philosophical method. But if it is not a method, then what is it? More than forty years after Husserl published his *Logical Investigations* (1900–1), Merleau-Ponty expressed wonder that this question was still unanswered, so he took the opportunity to once again redefine phenomenology, as Heidegger and others had done before him. In the preface to *Phenomenology of Perception* he decides that phenomenology is not really a method, but instead a *style* of philosophy: "the opinion of the responsible philosopher must be that *phenomenology can be practised and identified as a manner or style of thinking*, that it existed as a movement before arriving at complete awareness of itself as a philosophy."[9] If it does not render meaningless the allegiance to phenomenology, an interpretation like this definitely calls into question the integrity of the phenomenologist's method, even as it insists that "phenomenology is accessible only through a phenomenological method."[10] It basically casts phenomenology's net too wide and does little to prevent us from gathering a whole range of philosophers and nonphilosophers under the umbrella of phenomenology, whether they self-identify as phenomenologists or not. It allows someone like Moran to count Hannah Arendt amongst the important figures in the phenomenological movement, despite the fact that Arendt "exhibited no particular interest in the phenomenological method and contributed nothing to the theory of phenomenology."[11]

For Moran it is enough that Arendt's work "can be fruitfully understood as a species of phenomenology."[12] This is only possible, however, because Moran vaguely and typically defines phenomenology as an "anti-traditional style of philosophising, which emphasises the attempt to get to the truth of matters, to describe *phenomena*, in the broadest sense as whatever appears in the manner in which it appears, that is as it manifests itself to consciousness, to the experiencer."[13] Vagueness of this sort does not help us to understand what makes phenomenology unique and, in fact, seems to implicate more than one school of philosophy as well as some other fields of inquiry, like ethnography. Moran's definition (along with many others) has a post hoc ring to it, and seems motivated in part by a desire to have the definition apply to anyone who has been called a phenomenologist as well as many who have not. On this definition we could call Melville a phenomenologist of whaling, Thoreau a phenomenologist of walking, or Foucault a phenomenologist of power. A post hoc definition cannot satisfy the demands of method, which needs to be worked out prior to the study it is meant to guide.

Nearly all of the major phenomenologists see phenomenology as a method, which means they see it as directed by a certain set of principles or attitudes that circumscribe its practice. This view is shared by Husserl, Heidegger, Merleau-Ponty, Sartre, Levinas, Ricoeur, Marion, and many others. Even in their disagreement about what precisely is entailed in it, they recognize that liberties cannot be taken when trying to pin down a philosophical method without compromising the very integrity of that method. A method is supposed to rein in spurious conjecture and speculative impulse, not send out search parties in every possible direction. Absent a clear method we are not unlike, as Descartes says, "someone who is consumed with such a senseless desire to discover treasure that he continually roams the streets to see if he can find any that a passer-by might have dropped."[14] A trustworthy method is necessary if we wish to be more than fortunate in our philosophical investigations.

What exactly is a method? Descartes gives the following definition in Rule Four of the *Rules for the Direction of the Mind*.

This is not the only possible definition, but it comes from the philosopher who provides Husserl with his model of methodological reflection and is presumably sufficient for the moment:

> By "a method" I mean reliable rules which are easy to apply, and such that if one follows them exactly, one will never take what is false to be true or fruitlessly expend one's mental efforts, but will gradually and constantly increase one's knowledge till one arrives at a true understanding of everything within one's capacity.[15]

In one sense a method is about conserving energy, ensuring efficiency, guaranteeing accuracy, and growing knowledge. In another sense method is about restricting what can and cannot be said, what counts as a legitimate statement and what does not. When John Watson, for example, lays down the methodological guidelines of behaviorism he explicitly puts the domain of introspection out of play from the behaviorist standpoint.[16] This is why we would, and should, be suspicious if Watson were to begin talking about mental life the way that, say, William James does. It is precisely the prohibition against this kind of talk that not only defines Watson's method, but also provokes someone like James or Merleau-Ponty to devise a new approach to account for the complexity of human behavior, one that allows him to *say* more about mental life than the behaviorist allows. This is one way to think about method: as a device that enables its adherents to make statements that are not authorized for nonadherents. And to be clear, it is neither authority nor power that authorizes these statements. It is the method itself. A method opens up a new domain of speech and is precisely what guarantees the legitimacy of that speech. Husserl was no foreigner to Cartesian method, which clearly instructs us to order our thoughts and stick to our principles when attempting to extract the truth of experience. For the phenomenologist, not unlike Descartes himself, legitimacy is garnered by the fulfillment of an intention in experience underwritten by the certainty or givenness of subjectivity.

Husserl's phenomenology develops in response to a perceived crisis in the sciences and philosophy. The crisis is the result of a certain "corruption" of existence, of the "spirit" of humanity in early twentieth-century Europe. The corrupting force, according to Husserl, is what he calls the "exteriorization" of reason in the naturalistic objectivism that dominates the science of his day.

Naturalism attempts to subject every domain of existence to the rigor of mathematical science, and ideally limit the sayable to the language of mathematics.[17] At the heart of this crisis is the Cartesian conviction that everything, including human consciousness, can be quantified and thereby understood – the dream of a *mathesis universalis*. Phenomenological method, for Husserl, is supposed to resolve this crisis by humbling the tendencies of naturalism and calling radically into question the presuppositions of objectivist sciences and philosophy. Phenomenology is the antidote, then, to the kind of naturalism that "alienates" the immortal human spirit by reducing it to third-person natural knowledge.[18] But this antidote cannot be administered without first neutralizing the philosophical foundation of dualistic naturalism, namely the view that both nature and spirit are realities (*Realitäten*) in the same sense. For Husserl, only spirit is truly real in the sense of autonomous, in itself, and for itself. Nature, by contrast, is the product of the spirit that studies it.[19] Only once the neutralization of naïve naturalism is accomplished can the essence of spirit be reclaimed from the clutches of barbaric naturalism. Transcendental phenomenology is the only method equipped for the scientific study of spirit and the legitimation of statements about nature, spirit (the ego, consciousness), and their internal relation.

In an exposition of the meaning of the phrase "to the matters [things] themselves," found in the 1925 lecture course *History of the Concept of Time*, Heidegger attempts to pinpoint the meaning of method. He is obviously attempting to characterize phenomenology. As someone grappling with the prospect of phenomenology as a method, he helps us get a handle on what Husserl was up to in his attempt to burrow beneath the method of naturalism which, in his view, brought about the crisis to which phenomenology is the only philosophical response. For Heidegger, method is one of the basic components of what he calls a principle of research. It is the "principle of developing the way of dealing with [a subject matter]..."[20] It is clear that for Heidegger the "way of dealing" with "the matters themselves," which is the most general object of phenomenological research, is *not* via a constructive or speculative route. This way is "groundless."[21] A grounded approach is one that is "autochthonously demonstrative" and which "lay[s] the foundation" for this demonstration. For phenomenology the demonstrable is what is evidenced in the phenomena themselves, not what is deduced from the idea of the things themselves or from the idea of phenomenology. Phenomenology is not a deductive method, but, as it were, an *adductive* method in the sense that it is committed to adducing the matters themselves through concrete experience. The matters themselves are the source of the method, as it were. This principle of research is not plucked out of thin air, Heidegger insists, but is something gleaned "from its concretion in the research work" itself.[22] For Husserl as well as Heidegger (this is examined in more detail in Chapter 2), by focusing on the "concrete" things themselves we are led back into the ground of experience, we lay open the foundation of experience, and are ultimately referred to the dimension of *intentionality*. Intentionality forms the subject matter of phenomenological research or, in Heidegger's words, "Phenomenology is the analytic description of intentionality in its apriori."[23] Phenomenology is a transcendental investigation into the ground of the matters themselves as they give themselves. It is thus a "'*methodological*' term, inasmuch as it is only used to designate the mode of experience, apprehension, and determination of that which is thematized in philosophy."[24]

Heidegger eventually drops, or turns away from, all intensive study of this conception of method. There is more than a little irony in the fact that Husserl worked tirelessly to crystallize a method that would avoid needless philosophical toil, only to come up short and have his project pushed ahead in spirit, but nowhere near the letter. Few today see phenomenology as a scientific endeavor and only some as a propaedeutic to science. It is no longer apparent how phenomenology is to be carried out, or how it differs from, say, thick empirical description or poetic embellishment. This is not to say that phenomenology can be reduced to mere rhetoric, or to claim that phenomenology has never achieved a coherent approach to philosophical problems, but to suggest that perhaps its meaning has proliferated beyond coherence, rendering phenomenology such a diluted term that any activity could qualify as "phenomenological" in nature.

Many practices and inquiries are called phenomenological, but, like "game" (to take Wittgenstein's example), a refined definition that covers them all seems to be lacking. This may not seem like a problem. It may sound like a naïve Socratic worry. In response, it is tempting to insist that phenomenology is better regarded as a family resemblance term. This would permit the practice of phenomenology to be as diverse as the worlds it aims to unveil. It would permit the inclusion of Wittgenstein, Ryle, Austin, Cavell, McDowell, and Putnam in the canon of phenomenology, for, after all, each of them bear a "methodological affinity" with Husserl, Heidegger, and Merleau-Ponty. Simon Glendinning argues for this in *In the Name of Phenomenology*, as does François-David Sebbah and the authors of *The New Phenomenology*.[25] Phenomenology, Glendinning says, is more about the method (the "how") than it is about the content (the "what"). It is not a set of doctrines, it is about paying closer attention to the appearances that present themselves to subjective experience. How is this done? He does not really say. He prefers to keep the definition "skeletal" to avoid drawing too much attention to particular texts.[26] Nevertheless, he enumerates three possible answers to the question of phenomenology's content, including: 1) phenomenology is the legitimate heir to what used to be called philosophy; 2) phenomenology is the philosophical answer to modern scientific naturalism; 3) phenomenology is a "work of convincing words" that allows us to retrieve a radical understanding of ourselves and our place in the world.[27]

Instead of a singular definition of phenomenology, now we have three different definitions, none of which spell out the methodological principles of phenomenology. Socrates would not be pleased. The latter two formulations characterize phenomenology as basically an ideological reply to the worldview of technoscientific rationality and culture. These capture the historical spirit of Husserl's motivation for founding phenomenology, but they do not clarify the nature of phenomenology as a philosophical practice. As for the first definition, it is fair enough to call phenomenology the future of philosophy after modernity — this is what Husserl explicitly does in *Cartesian Meditations* — but, once again, it does not specify what it takes to do phenomenology. Glendinning's distillation of phenomenology is symptomatic, as well as emblematic, of the way phenomenology has been dissociated from its method. Today, anything is called phenomenology so long as it involves some kind of subjective description of experience.

Note also that Glendinning's formulations do not represent phenomenology as fundamentally concerned with intuiting essences (eidetic intuition) or elaborating the essential structures of consciousness or intentionality.[28] These days there is deep disagreement about how important this kind of "essentialism" is to the phenomenological project. It is often ridiculed as merely a symptom of Husserl's latent modernism or idealism. But it is still used to identify the work of phenomenology in individual thinkers. Whenever a philosopher pays especially close attention to a particular region of experience, and attempts to lay out the essential features of that region, this practice is often identified as phenomenology. The working assumption here is that *this* is what phenomenology does/is. When Moran calls Arendt a phenomenologist of public space or publicness, he no doubt means that her work is remarkably attuned to public life and more than capable of extracting the essential features of it. Nevertheless, as Dan Zahavi points out, "this interest in essential structures is so widespread and common in the history of philosophy that it is nonsensical to take is as a defining feature of phenomenology."[29] If phenomenology is about intuiting essences (*Wesenschau*) as opposed to establishing facts, or empirical evidence,[30] then it still remains to be asked how these essences are to be seen. It is arguable that Husserl was the only person who believed in and sought them with anything like methodological rigor.

If there is no singular methodological thread linking the practice of phenomenology, then what does link it? If Merleau-Ponty is right to call phenomenology a *style* of thinking, then it must be that style which allows the practitioner to, as Raymond Aron put it to Sartre, "talk about this cocktail and make a philosophy out of it."[31] Now, anyone could talk about a cocktail. William James, to be sure, could talk philosophically about a cocktail. But he is not considered a phenomenologist, although the case has been made for his inclusion in the movement,[32] and no doubt it is his literary style that affiliates him with phenomenology. His inclusion, however, really disrupts the narrative because so much of his work predates Husserl's inaugural *Logical Investigations*. And pointing to his style does not get us any closer to understanding what phenomenology as a philosophical practice requires. It simply leads us to ask what it is about a description of the world that makes it phenomenological, if it is not the description's concern for the essential structure of intentional experience. For every philosophical description we must provide some criteria that would enable us to differentiate the phenomenological from the nonphenomenological, and at this point it is not clear that this can be done. As Heidegger writes: "*Phenomenological* signifies everything that belongs to such a way of exhibiting phenomena and phenomenal structures, everything that becomes thematic in this kind of research. The *unphenomenological* would be everything that does not satisfy this kind of research, its conceptuality and its methods of demonstration."[33] It is not even clear that such a circumscription is desirable or even useful. At any rate, the burden of proof lies on the shoulders of anyone who holds that phenomenology actually exists as a coherent approach.

Philosophers in the Anglo-American tradition can be heard calling phenomenology an enterprise "as moribund as logical positivism,"[34] while countless figures writing in the wake of deconstruction treat it with the kind of contempt Heideggerians reserve for Platonic ontotheology and Cartesian substance ontology. This attitude fails to appreciate the continuing vitality of phenomenology: many phenomenology journals remain active; numerous international conferences are held each year; scholarly societies continue to convene annually. The theological turn taken by figures like Marion, Henry, Levinas, and so forth – all of whom were sharply chastised by Dominique Janicaud in *Phenomenology and the "Theological Turn"*[35] – remains a fertile site of phenomenological research. Ideologically it is quite invested in phenomenology's recovery (in the wake of what Glendinning calls "the modernist predicament") of lived experience in every one of its dimensions, particularly the religious. Phenomenology continues as a viable research strategy for social scientists disaffected by more positivistic, quantitative models. Perhaps the most promising program is charted by people like Francisco Varela, Evan Thompson, Dan Zahavi, Shaun Gallagher, and others: this is the attempt to naturalize phenomenology or otherwise synthesize it with the hard sciences, a project which seems more than a little paradoxical insofar as phenomenology is originally constituted by a suspension of the natural sciences and the naïve metaphysical attitude they presuppose. At this point it remains unclear whether the naturalization of phenomenology would signal the abolition of the ideology motivating the theological turn or instead solidify with hard facts the justification of that ideology. In any event we will not determine here if this marriage is methodologically misguided or not. It should be noted instead that the proliferation of such attempts testifies – against those who would proclaim phenomenology a moribund program – to the health of phenomenological research. This is not to say that many people working in phenomenology do not take its promise for granted or sugarcoat its apparent incoherence.

If phenomenology has indeed not been abandoned, then what does it mean to speak of the end of phenomenology? I mean to suggest a few things. First, phenomenology has become so diffuse that its methodology seems no longer relevant to its practice. Ever since Heidegger the project of realizing phenomenology as a rigorous science complete with a worked out method of investigation has been abandoned. This is already evident in *Being and Time*. In this respect phenomenology began and ended with Husserl. Second, insofar as phenomenology lives on today, we must ask what it seeks to accomplish. Does it have a clear *telos*? What end does it have in view? Third, if phenomenologists are still eager to get philosophers "back to the things themselves," I suggest that this task has a new, better-equipped vanguard. Speculative realism, which mines and adapts the resources of phenomenology, has taken up phenomenology's call to get us back to reality, but without distracting us from the demand for metaphysical accountability. Speculative realism's intensive engagements with metaphysics reveal the weakness of phenomenology for the project of realism. Phenomenology forsakes metaphysical realism in favor of a timid "realism" of phenomena that is nothing more than a modified version of idealism, Kantianism by another name. It is commonplace, as I will show in the following chapter, for phenomenologists to pay homage to realism, but not without qualifying their allegiance with scare quotes. What they call the "real" or "realism" is what is given in "concrete" lived experience. To speak of concrete experience, then, amounts to speaking about the real as it appears to a human observer, not as the real is in itself.

What I hope to accomplish in this book is a circumscription of the promise of contemporary phenomenological research while at the same time showing that speculative realism is better equipped to achieve some of phenomenology's philosophical ends. I will suggest that phenomenology should give up on realism and package itself instead as a formidable idealism. My purpose is quite specific: to demonstrate that, while phenomenologists are often keen to present themselves as thinkers committed to the reality, if not materiality (Henry), of the world they describe, phenomenology is a poor conduit for delivering metaphysical realism. On the contrary, phenomenology is a brilliant vehicle for antirealism in the Kantian vein,[36] and if phenomenology is going to thrive in the contemporary philosophical milieu, it might do well to enthusiastically embrace its antirealist potential rather than disavowing it. This is a prospect that will inevitably appear unattractive to the adherents of the theological turn, but it is, I think, the best live option. So, when this book proclaims the end of phenomenology, it means that phenomenology *as a method for realists* has worn itself out. Phenomenology, if it means anything, is simply not a method that can commit itself to the human-independent reality of bodies, objects, qualities, properties, material, or events.

This position will no doubt sound counterintuitive to anyone who has found in phenomenology an ally of the philosophy of embodiment. Even as early as Husserl, but especially after Merleau-Ponty, the body is situated at the center of the phenomenological standpoint. Given the embodied character of our experience, our embeddedness in the lifeworld assumes priority over dispassionate theoretical analysis and the quest for an objective perspective or view from nowhere. If practice always comes before theory, the story goes, then the ideal objects of theory cannot be detached from the living, breathing *Umwelt* that supports the practice of thinking. This priority is again and again underscored by the phenomenologist, often as a way to remind the reader that this is real, tangible life we are talking about, not some docile mental construction or aloof realm of innocuous abstract entities. The phenomenologist is no armchair spectator! From all of this we are meant to infer – are explicitly told on occasion – that there is a world out there that precedes our existence and, especially, our thought. It is *much more* than a construction; it exceeds the finitude of human life and thought. Into this reality we are thrown; it receives us because it is always already there, awaiting our birth and outliving our death. Phenomenology, then, is replete with a *rhetoric of concreteness* that testifies to its realism. This rhetoric should not blind us to the fact that phenomenology remains a poor choice for metaphysical realists precisely because its method prohibits the phenomenologist from actually committing to a reality outside human thought.

It is certainly difficult to deny that phenomenology represents a fresh start in philosophy. It is arguably as radical as the critical philosophy initiated by Kant, even though Husserl and his adherents borrow quite a bit from Kantian transcendental philosophy, including its suspension of metaphysical speculation. Much of its radicality, however, is embedded in the realist rhetoric that forms a fundamental part of the poetics phenomenology deploys to supplement its methodological constraints. Next I lay out these constraints so that my understanding of what phenomenology is, or must be, is transparent. These constraints I take to be both minimal and essential to phenomenological practice. Phenomenology's rhetoric of realism forms the focus of the next chapter.

Minimal Conditions for the End of Metaphysics

This book does not intend to police the doors of phenomenology for the sake of safeguarding the purity of the school. Nor will it lament the recession of rigor in phenomenological texts. I am not trying exhaustively to specify the sufficient conditions of phenomenological practice, nor am I trying to enumerate the criteria that qualify something as evidence in the phenomenological sense. What I maintain is that for a philosophical description, study, or conclusion to count as phenomenological – that is, to mark it as something other than everyday description, empirical study, or speculative metaphysics – that description must take place from within some form of methodological *reduction* that shifts the focus of description to the transcendental, or at least quasi-transcendental, level.[37] This is what differentiates the mundane from the philosophical as far as description goes. Since Husserl several types of reduction are commonly identified, most notably the *epoché*, phenomenological, transcendental, and eidetic reductions.

Whether or not these reductions are genuinely multiple or just variations on a singular reduction, entailed in each of them is a suspension or bracketing of what Husserl calls the "natural attitude," a view which includes either an uncritical or critical belief in the reality of the external world. As Heidegger interprets it, in explicit contrast to its "substantive intent," the reduction is what leads us from objectively present beings (the ontic) to being itself (the transcendental).[38] He therefore puts the reduction to ontological use, rather than using it as an epistemological or skeptical tool after the manner of Descartes. Merleau-Ponty famously proclaims in the preface to the *Phenomenology of Perception* that the basic lesson of the reduction is that a complete reduction is impossible because of the incorrigibility of the real world. Like Cartesian doubt, this suspension does not lead us into positive disbelief in the world's existence. It instead requires us to withhold any belief, which is to say, neutralize our *commitment* to either the reality or unreality of the perceived world. As such, the reduction is a prohibition against metaphysics. This, I think, is the absolute minimum condition of phenomenology. Without a suspension of the natural attitude and its attendant realism; without a strict commitment to phenomena as they appear to consciousness as the sole arbiter of truth; and without refraining from committing to anything that does not give itself phenomenally to consciousness, phenomenology cannot maintain its methodological integrity. Either phenomenology is a method whose basic principle includes a suspension of metaphysical commitments – precisely because the metaphysical status of phenomena is not revealed by the phenomena themselves, but is at best hinted at by their resistance or apparent transcendence of human consciousness – or it is simply a name applied to a style of doing philosophy that has no coherent method for establishing the legitimacy of its results.

For phenomenology to be phenomenology it must enact at the very least a suspension of the natural attitude and its concomitant metaphysics. This suspension requires the phenomenologist to confine his or her investigations to the much-derided subject/object correlation. As Dan Zahavi puts it, "The *reduction* [in contrast to the *epoché*] is the term for our thematization of the correlation between subjectivity and world."[39] It is this confinement that lends phenomenology its transcendental flavor. More than mere description, phenomenology means to describe the transcendental dimension of experience as it unfolds within experience itself. It is therefore more basic than the empirical. Without at least some attention to the transcendental, whether this is interpreted as the uncovering of consciousness's essential structures (Husserl) or the return to prereflective experience (Merleau-Ponty), it becomes nearly impossible to see the philosophical value or understand the institutional influence of phenomenological description.[40] Otherwise put, phenomenology must *at least* adhere to Husserl's "principle of principles" (*Ideas* §24), which dictates that direct intuition is the origin of knowledge and to be respected as its own authority, and necessarily entails the view (hereafter referred to as "correlationism")[41] that subject and object, consciousness and phenomena, thought and being are inseparable binary pairs. The rejection of correlationism, as we will see, is a foundational brick in the edifice of speculative realism. If phenomenology must commit itself to correlationism, and it seems it must, then speculative realism's commitment to the reality of things can be read as anti-phenomenological.

The importance of the phenomenological reduction[42] for twentieth-century continental philosophy cannot be overstated. It is a driving force behind the numerous attempts to overcome metaphysics and crucial to conceiving the end of metaphysics announced by Heidegger, Derrida, and everyone else sympathetic to deconstruction. It is therefore partly responsible for the "linguistic turn" taken by continental philosophers in the wake of phenomenology and deconstruction. And insofar as the resurgent speculative impulse witnessed in contemporary continental theory represents a direct confrontation with the linguistic turn's desire to overcome metaphysics, it is important to see that the phenomenological reduction is the first step toward the end of metaphysics.[43] As John Sallis has shown, Husserl's *epoché* is nothing other than the installment of the phenomenologist within the correlation of consciousness and being, otherwise known by phenomenology as intentionality or immanence.[44] The *epoché* enacts a reduction of transcendent being to immanent presence, and converts real objects into "irreal" or "intentional" objects by neutralizing their existence. As Sallis puts it,

> the ἐποχή [*epoché*] takes the form of neutrality-modification, neutralizing whatever real existence the object might otherwise be taken to possess, especially that unanalyzed objective existence that things in the world are naturally taken to have. By undergoing the reduction brought by the ἐποχή, objects come to be taken as *being* precisely insofar as they *present* themselves in an intentional experience – that is, as *being* precisely insofar as they are *intentionally present*.[45]

From the phenomenological standpoint objects cease to exist in the usual sense of the term. They take on a new, mitigated form of reality as intentional objects, "real" insofar as they are intended or thematized. They assume an "internal reality" within the subject/object correlation, which means that if we wish to call Husserlian phenomenology – or any phenomenology that performs the *epoché* or phenomenological reduction – a realism, as Zahavi writes, "it has to be emphasized that it is a realism based on experience. It is an experiential realism or an internal realism not unlike the one espoused by Hilary Putnam, having no affinities with a metaphysical realism."[46]

If phenomenology is nothing without the reduction – and here I am in agreement with Leonard Lawlor and Eugen Fink, who make "the reduction absolutely necessary for phenomenological research"[47] – then it is necessarily complicit with the end of metaphysics. (Ironically, as we will see in Chapter 3, it is also complicit in legitimating dogmatism, irrationalism, and fideism.) It is the reduction that initiates the return to the things themselves and which, as Sallis notes, "decisively exceeds the history of metaphysics, exceeds it in precisely such a way as to realize its intent and be thus its end."[48] If metaphysics is an attempt to either identify or align thought and being, or to render present to thought that which is as it is, then phenomenology accomplishes this end. But it does so at the cost of reducing the reality of being, by rendering being dependent on human consciousness. It empties being of real transcendence.

It is true that phenomenology is replete with accounts of the excesses of being (I am thinking here of Marion's "saturated phenomenon" and Levinas's wholly Other, as well as Merleau-Ponty's claim about the impossibility of bracketing the world), but we must ask if these excesses are genuine evidence of a reality beyond consciousness or merely an excess *of consciousness*, an internal or intentional excess.[49] Here I side with Alexander Schnell when he argues that the excesses of phenomenology (which Husserl calls the "potentialities" of the ego's "I can" and "I do") are always internal to intentionality, not evidence of the autonomous reality of what appears in the phenomena. I do not, however, endorse Schnell's claim that a closer look at "phenomenological metaphysics" can illuminate the speculative nature of phenomenology, mostly because I take "phenomenological metaphysics" to be an oxymoron. Sallis claims that phenomenology itself is capable at times of clarifying that which exceeds the subject/object correlation. He also claims that phenomenology adheres to certain "positings that exceed phenomenology" which cannot be accounted for from within the phenomenological standpoint.[50] In the next chapter I will argue that, while many phenomenologists affirm a reality that exceeds the subject/object correlation and claim to find evidence for this reality within the phenomenological standpoint, it is necessary to qualify their affirmations as nonphenomenological or speculative to flag their metaphysical nature.

It seems that phenomenology is forced into a choice: either it can prepare the groundwork for the end of metaphysics or it can make itself compatible with metaphysical realism. It cannot be both things at once. If it chooses to bring metaphysics to an end, then it forecloses the possibility of a realist phenomenology. If it allows a return of metaphysics in order to accommodate certain theological or other aspirations, then it can no longer be the harbinger of metaphysics' demise. How it conceives itself methodologically will inevitably betray its preference for one side of this dilemma or the other.

The Return of Metaphysics and the Speculative Difference

Today it is still believed that phenomenology can get us back in touch with the real. Since, we are told, realism is just as outdated as idealism, and both of them are "in principle absurd" (Husserl),[51] the closest thing to realism that we have on offer is phenomenology. That is, phenomenology, when properly disengaged from Husserl's brand of Kantianism and converted to *existential* phenomenology, is the closest we can get to an encounter with the real. This is a myth. The belief that phenomenology gets us realism instead of a modified form of idealism, or correlationism, results from a misunderstanding of the internal relation between the method and metaphysics of phenomenology. No matter how it is interpreted phenomenology can only align itself with antirealism.

So what do the various materialisms and realisms associated with the "speculative turn" in continental philosophy have that phenomenology does not? In a word: *speculation* – that activity denounced by Kantian critical philosophy and explicitly prohibited by phenomenology. It is commonplace nowadays to point to the rejection or radicalization of correlationism as the move that marks a philosophical position as speculative in the new sense. This is commonplace for good reason: the antirealism entailed in correlationism, which has oriented continental philosophy at least since Kant[52] and quite self-consciously in the twentieth century, is precisely what is spurned by those working in the new metaphysics. We can, however, characterize the new metaphysics – speculative realism included – in a different way, in terms of its commitments. If phenomenology is committed to metaphysical neutrality and to a species of correlationism that legitimates only those statements that are evidenced from within the subject/object correlate (that is, within the reduction), then the new metaphysics

begins with a commitment to the existence of a nonhuman reality outside the subject/object correlate. It then dedicates itself to
thinking, describing, demonstrating, and unleashing that reality.
Speculative philosophy, moreover, does not restrict itself methodologically to a particular region of research as phenomenology
does. Whatever one may think of the arguments for realism, it
cannot be said that they put themselves a priori in the bind that
phenomenology does. This does not mean that anything goes, but
that the range of metaphysical commitments up for grabs is much
wider than it is for correlationist philosophies. It is less about
limitation, more about proliferation.

As the editors of *The Speculative Turn* note, the proliferation
of speculative philosophy in recent years may be unnerving to
some. Is this the return of dogmatic, ungrounded, free-floating
knowledge claims? Has the Kantian lesson withered away, leaving us just where we were before the 1780s? Are we asking for
another "crisis in philosophy" like the one Husserl felt compelled
to remedy? In a sense, the speculative turn is the response to a
crisis in philosophy: namely, the antirealist reduction of reality
to human reality and the anthropocentrism that, for instance,
fuels the current climate crisis. Anthropocentrism and humanism
are two of the chief enemies of the new metaphysics. In a less
alarmist tone, the speculative turn is not a rejection of the critical philosophy, but "a recognition of [its] inherent limitations.
Speculation in this sense aims 'beyond' the critical and linguistic
turns. As such, it recuperates the pre-critical sense of 'speculation'
as a concern with the Absolute, while also taking into account the
undeniable progress that is due to the labour of critique."[53] And
in an unexpected twist, it is also a critical response to the kind of
dogmatism we find in phenomenology's theological turn.

Does this mean that speculative realism has its own critical
method? The short answer is no. What then legitimates its speculative claims? What the various adherents of speculative realism
share is a set of commitments, the most significant of which I have
already mentioned. These commitments, and their results, form
the subject matter of Chapters 3 to 5. In addition to its commitment to speculation and the autonomous reality of the nonhuman world, the new metaphysics affirms several other things, to
different degrees, depending on the thinker under consideration.
These include, but are not limited to: some kind of disavowal of
correlationism; an expansion of the concept of agency; a critique

of humanism and anthropocentrism; a renewed faith in the power of reason to exceed the bounds of perception; a blending of fiction and fact; the generation of metaphysical systems; a taste for the weird, the strange, the uncanny; an object-oriented perspective.[54]

Someone might be tempted to point out a contradiction in my account of speculative realism. "But wait!," they will say. "You're effectively saying that 'speculative realism' is a family resemblance term, but you've just finished arguing that 'phenomenology' cannot be seen as a family resemblance term because that doesn't help us identify any particular philosophy as phenomenology." To this I would respond: the difference is that no speculative realist claims that speculative realism is a school of thought, a method, a unified movement, or a radical way of practicing philosophy. It is, on the contrary, a loose confederation of thinkers each of whom is committed to a kind of speculation that refuses to draw the limits of the real within the immanence of human consciousness. Its purpose, as I understand it, is to clear the ground for new advances in the thinking of reality. This is, after all, the end of philosophy. If you ask how to spot a speculative realist in the wild, the best way to do so is to ask them about correlationism. If that term means something to them and they indicate a desire to witness correlationism's demise, then there is a good chance you have found a speculative realist.

Notes

1. Paul Ennis notes on the first page of *Continental Realism* (Winchester: Zero Books, 2011) that "there is no such thing as continental [speculative] realism as a method." Louis Morelle asserts that the "only agreed upon reference point" for speculative realism is what Meillassoux calls "correlationism." While in part true, a critique of correlationism is not the only shared attribute among speculative realists. I try to identify a few more. See Morelle, "Speculative Realism: After Finitude, and Beyond?" *Speculations* III (2012), 242.

2. Dan Zahavi, *Husserl's Phenomenology* (Stanford: Stanford University Press, 2003), 46. In *Cartesian Meditations* Husserl says that the "first methodological principle" of phenomenology is to accept only those judgments derived from evidence, where "evidence" is understood as an "experiencing" or "mental seeing" of what one

intends. Edmund Husserl, *Cartesian Meditations: An Introduction to Phenomenology*, trans. Dorion Cairns (The Hague: Martinus Nijhoff, 1969), §5.

3. See Edmund Husserl, *Ideas: General Introduction to a Pure Phenomenology*, trans. W.R. Boyce Gibson (New York: Collier, 1962), §32.

4. On the inescapability of ontological commitments see Manuel DeLanda, "Ontological Commitments," *Speculations* IV (2013), 71–3.

5. Moran identifies Husserl as a "self-styled radical beginner," while Merleau-Ponty recapitulates Husserl's sentiment when he conceives philosophy as an "ever-renewed experiment in making its own beginning." See Dermot Moran, *Introduction to Phenomenology* (London: Routledge, 2000), 2, and Maurice Merleau-Ponty, *Phenomenology of Perception*, trans. Colin Smith (London: Routledge, 1962), xiv.

6. Michael Marder, "The Pulse of Phenomenology," *Parrhesia* 14 (2012), 16.

7. Edmund Husserl, "Philosophy as Rigorous Science," in *Phenomenology and the Crisis of Philosophy*, trans. Quentin Lauer (New York: Harper & Row, 1965), 78.

8. Moran, *Introduction to Phenomenology*, 2–3.

9. Merleau-Ponty, *Phenomenology of Perception*, viii, italics modified.

10. Merleau-Ponty, *Phenomenology of Perception*, viii.

11. Moran, *Introduction to Phenomenology*, 189.

12. Moran, *Introduction to Phenomenology*, 287.

13. Moran, *Introduction to Phenomenology*, 4.

14. René Descartes, *Rules for the Direction of the Mind*, in *The Philosophical Writings of Descartes*, vol. 1, trans. John Cottingham et al. (Cambridge: Cambridge University Press), 371.

15. Descartes, *Rules*, 371–2.

16. John B. Watson, "Psychology as the Behaviorist Views It," *Psychological Review* 20 (1913), 158–77.

17. Husserl, "Philosophy and the Crisis of European Man," in *Phenomenology and the Crisis of Philosophy*, 191. See also Heidegger's account of Husserl's critique of naturalism in *Introduction to Phenomenological Research*, trans. Daniel O. Dahlstrom (Bloomington: Indiana University Press, 2005), 47–8.

18. Husserl, "Philosophy and the Crisis of European Man," 192.

19. Husserl, "Philosophy and the Crisis of European Man," 188–9.

20. Martin Heidegger, *History of the Concept of Time*, trans. Theodore Kisiel (Bloomington: Indiana University Press, 1992), 76, italics removed.

21. Heidegger, *History of the Concept of Time*, 76.

22. Heidegger, *History of the Concept of Time*, 77, italics removed.

23. Heidegger, *History of the Concept of Time*, 79, italics removed.

24. Heidegger, *History of the Concept of Time*, 85.

25. Simon Glendinning, *In the Name of Phenomenology* (London: Routledge, 2007), 6; François-David Sebbah, *Testing the Limit: Derrida, Henry, Levinas and the Phenomenological Tradition*, trans. Stephen Barker (Stanford: Stanford University Press, 2012), 6; J. Aaron Simmons and Bruce Ellis Benson, *The New Phenomenology: A Philosophical Introduction* (London: Bloomsbury, 2013), Introduction.

26. Glendinning, *In the Name of Phenomenology*, 7.

27. Glendinning, *In the Name of Phenomenology*, 6, 14, 27.

28. This theme spans nearly all of Husserl's work, especially after the "transcendental turn" taken post-*Logical Investigations* (1900–1) and is evinced in works like *The Idea of Phenomenology* (lectures delivered in 1907), *Ideas* (1913), and *Cartesian Meditations* (lectures delivered in 1929). Late works like *The Crisis of European Sciences and Transcendental Phenomenology* (1936) continue the search for essences, notably the essence of the "lifeworld" (*Lebenswelt*).

29. Zahavi, *Husserl's Phenomenology*, 37. Thanks to Paul Ennis, who helped clarify this point for me.

30. Husserl, "Philosophy as Rigorous Science," 116: "Phenomenology can recognize with objective validity only essences and essential relations, and thereby it can accomplish and decisively accomplish whatever is necessary for a correct understanding of all empirical cognition and of all cognition whatsoever…"

31. The encounter between Sartre and Aron is recounted in Simone de Beauvoir's *La force de l'âge*, cited in Ethan Kleinberg, *Generation Existential: Heidegger's Philosophy in France, 1927–1961* (Ithaca: Cornell University Press, 2007), 116.

32. Two books called *William James and Phenomenology* exist, one by Bruce Wilshire (Bloomington: Indiana University Press, 1968) and the other by James M. Edie (Bloomington: Indiana University Press, 1987).

33. Heidegger, *History of the Concept of Time*, 86.

34. Brian Leiter, "On Pluralism in Philosophy Departments, Once Again," *Leiter Reports: A Philosophy Blog*, March 4, 2007, available at <http://leiterreports.typepad.com/blog/2007/03/on_pluralism_in.html> (accessed October 7, 2013).

35. Dominique Janicaud et al., *Phenomenology and the "Theological Turn": The French Debate* (New York: Fordham University Press, 2000).

36. In *Kant and Phenomenology* (Chicago: University of Chicago Press, 2011), Tom Rockmore makes a compelling case for phenomenology as a viable constructivist (antirealist) approach to epistemology. This, I think, is the most promising future for phenomenology.

37. As Husserl says in *Cartesian Meditations*, 32: "It must be continually borne in mind that all transcendental-phenomenological research is inseparable from undeviating observance of the transcendental reduction, which must not be confounded with the abstractive restricting of anthropological research to purely psychic life."

38. Martin Heidegger, *The Basic Problems of Phenomenology*, trans. Albert Hofstadter (Bloomington: Indiana University Press, 1982), 21.

39. Zahavi, *Husserl's Phenomenology*, 46.

40. On the importance of transcendental phenomenology for the pervasive discussion and implementation of "meaning" in continental philosophy, see Steven Galt Crowell, *Husserl, Heidegger, and the Space of Meaning: Paths Toward Transcendental Phenomenology* (Evanston: Northwestern University Press, 2001).

41. I flesh out this concept, forged by Quentin Meillassoux, in Chapter 3. Here it is enough to cite *After Finitude: An Essay on the Necessity of Contingency*, trans. Ray Brassier (London: Continuum, 2008), 5: Correlationism is "the idea according to which we only ever have access to the correlation between thinking and being, and never to either term considered apart from the other."

42. This reduction, first introduced in *The Idea of Phenomenology*, is meant to exclude consideration of the transcendent existence of the world and its contents. It effectively restricts phenomenology to consideration of what is immanent to consciousness, just as the *epoché* introduced in *Ideas* effectively neutralizes ("reduces") our natural/naïve belief in objective reality.

43. As the editors of *The Speculative Turn* indicate in their introduction, the speculative turn in contemporary philosophy is not

only philosophically, but also rhetorically, a "deliberate counterpoint to the now tiresome 'Linguistic Turn'." Levi Bryant et al.,
eds., *The Speculative Turn: Continental Materialism and Realism*
(Melbourne: re.press, 2011), 1.

44. Immanence in the phenomenological sense means that subject,
object, and contemplation of the object by the subject are "*really*
[*reell*] included in one another," as Heidegger says, explicating Husserl's *Ideas*. Put otherwise, immanence means that consciousness
and object form an indivisible unity within lived experience, and
it is this unity that is the locus of phenomenological investigation.
Heidegger, *History of the Concept of Time*, 96–7. For a critique of
this construal of immanence, see Gilles Deleuze, *Pure Immanence:
Essays on a Life*, trans. Anne Boyman (New York: Zone Books,
2005).

45. John Sallis, *Delimitations: Phenomenology and the End of Metaphysics*, second edition, expanded (Bloomington: Indiana University Press, 1995), 208.

46. Zahavi, *Husserl's Phenomenology*, 71.

47. Leonard Lawlor, *Thinking Through French Philosophy: The Being
of the Question* (Bloomington: Indiana University Press, 2003),
149. Lawlor follows Eugen Fink, "Die Phänomenologische Philoso-
phie E. Husserl in der Gegenwärtigen Kritik," *Kantstudien* 38, no.
3/4 (1933). Lawlor takes from Fink the idea that phenomenology
comes to an end as soon as the reduction is abandoned. Without the
reduction phenomenology turns into dogmatism.

48. Sallis, *Delimitations*, 208.

49. Alexander Schnell, "Speculative Foundations of Phenomenology,"
trans. Mary Beth Mader, *Continental Philosophy Review* 45, no. 3
(2012), 461–79.

50. Sallis, *Delimitations*, 208–9.

51. Husserl, *Ideas*, Author's Preface to the English edition, 12.

52. As Bryant et al. see it, the "correlationist turn" originates "in
Immanuel Kant's critical philosophy, which famously abjured the
possibility of ever knowing a noumenal realm beyond human access
… This effacement of the noumenal continues with phenomenol-
ogy, as ontology becomes explicitly linked with a reduction to the
phenomenal realm." *The Speculative Turn*, 4. See also Lee Braver,
A Thing of This World: A History of Continental Anti-Realism
(Evanston: Northwestern University Press, 2007).

53. Bryant et al., *The Speculative Turn*, 3.

54. As Graham Harman has pointed out, it is necessary to keep SR and OOP separate, even though they tend to merge together in the discussion. For the sake of clarity, I am understanding speculative realism as an umbrella term under which falls object-oriented philosophy (most often associated with Harman's position). Graham Harman, "Brief SR/OOO Tutorial," in *Bells and Whistles* (Winchester: Zero Books, 2013).

"Realism" in Phenomenology

Method and Metaphysics

Phenomenology believes that its method immunizes it from metaphysics. Which is to say, when phenomenology is operating within the reduction it is supposed to be metaphysically neutral. But this is only partly true. Its method, I contend, inevitably aligns it with antirealism. This can be gleaned by looking at the methodological statements of Husserl, Heidegger, and Merleau-Ponty. Husserl increasingly embraces antirealism throughout his career by referring to phenomenology as transcendental idealism. Merleau-Ponty tries to mitigate his method's antirealism by radically redefining phenomenology, while Heidegger, already in *Being and Time*, seems only nominally committed to phenomenology as a method. When he is, it sounds like antirealism.

Much ink has been spilled after Husserl trying to show that phenomenology need not necessarily end in antirealism. This chapter attempts to show how the phenomenological method, rather than maintaining its intended metaphysical neutrality, actually forecloses metaphysical realism as it bolsters transcendental idealism. Endemic to this foreclosure is an evolution of the phenomenological method itself. This evolution is marked by a gradual slackening of the strictures of the method or, otherwise put, increasing inattention to the injunction that phenomenology must become rigorous science. It is arguably Merleau-Ponty who, by designating phenomenology as a style of philosophy, does the most to reset the meaning of the method and open it to the diversity of interpretations avowed today. In the first part of this chapter I signpost the evolution of phenomenological method as it is conceived by Husserl, Heidegger, and Merleau-Ponty. The second part assesses two divergent responses to the diversification of the method: 1) the conservative reading given by Dominique Janicaud and 2) the transgressive reading nascent in the work of

Lee Braver. While both responses tell us something useful about the relation between phenomenology and realism, neither, I suggest, are adequate accounts of the relation.

Husserl

Husserl is a philosopher often ridiculed. A personal example should suffice to support this claim. While sitting for my comprehensive exam in graduate school, the examiner charged with interrogating my knowledge of contemporary philosophy asked point blank if I could "see essences." He was, I knew well, asking whether Husserl was a man preoccupied with an untenable task, a man perpetually searching for a way to see things that are, frankly, nonexistent. Ordinarily my examiner has a much more charitable, although critical, reading of Husserl's project, but the anecdote shows how simple it is to caricature Husserl in order to dismiss his life's work. It is just as easy to see his incessant revision of phenomenology as a chronic inability to get his project off the ground in a way that would guarantee rigorous results.[1] Despite his indecision and questionable ideals, it is indisputable that Husserl exerted a tremendous influence on twentieth-century philosophy that is perhaps only now beginning to wane. That influence can be summarized as a suspension, even if not the end, of metaphysics. Or better, if we take his mature philosophy as a guide, what Husserl bequeaths to philosophy is a renewal of transcendental idealism as a method of philosophical inquiry, one that owes just as much to Descartes as it does to Kant and Hegel. Whether it is in an early text like *The Idea of Phenomenology* or later texts like *Cartesian Meditations, Ideas* I, or even *The Crisis of the European Sciences*, the phenomenological method is aligned with metaphysical idealism.

Zahavi claims that all phenomenologists are committed to the thesis that "the world is not something that simply exists," but something that appears, "and the structure of this appearance is conditioned and made possible by subjectivity." If he is right, then phenomenology as such involves "a rejection of a realistic and naturalistic objectivism that claims that the nature of meaning, truth, and reality can be understood without taking subjectivity into account."[2] The following examples, which are hopefully more representative than selective, support Zahavi's view and establish the affinity between phenomenology and idealism.

In his summary of the 1907 lectures published as *The Idea of Phenomenology*, Husserl raises the question of how cognition is supposed to "get at" the way things are in themselves. He understands this to be an epistemological problem, and certainly not a problem that troubles "*natural thinking* in science and everyday life."[3] Can the theory of knowledge figure out if it is possible for the mind to accurately represent the world, or if skepticism is true? Once these questions are resolved, only then can a critique of metaphysics begin. In short, "the critique of cognition in this sense is the condition of the possibility of metaphysics."[4] Husserl here echoes Kant's *modus operandi* in the *Critique of Pure Reason*, although instead of referring us to Kant he admits that the "Cartesian method of doubt provides the starting point" for the critique of cognition for which phenomenology is the method. As with Descartes, Husserl proposes to delimit the certain and the uncertain, clear and obscure knowledge. This involves first and foremost a reduction of the scope of the theory of knowledge to what is given immanently to consciousness, or what is immanently apprehended. In the early stages of critique only the "adequately self-given" can be used. "Therefore," writes Husserl, "I must accomplish a *phenomenological reduction: I must exclude all that is transcendently posited.*"[5]

The purpose of the phenomenological reduction – which is here first introduced into phenomenology's lexicon – is to ensure that the phenomenologist carries out their study of the possibility of scientific cognition at the level of immanence, that they fixate on the phenomenon of consciousness, and neither assume nor assert the theses of naturalism. Naturalism presupposes that its objects of study (natural events, physical laws) enjoy an existence that transcends scientific observation. It does not interrogate the conditions of these objects. Since phenomenology wants to determine how it is *possible* for science to cognize transcendent objects, if it is possible, it must restrict its investigation to what is immanent to consciousness because this provides the only phenomenologically accessible foundation for cognition. Toward this end, "everything transcendent (that which is not given to me immanently) is to be assigned the index zero, i.e., its existence, its validity is not to be assumed as such."[6]

The more radical aspect of the phenomenological orientation is that it abandons the question of how cognition can "get at," or know, an object that transcends it. The proper object of phenomenological study is the "pure phenomenon," that which is not taken as something real, but as something that is immanent to consciousness, which itself is not to be taken as real. The new question that Husserl broaches is: "How can the pure phenomenon of cognition reach something which is not immanent to it? How can the absolute self-givenness of cognition reach something not self-given and how is this reaching to be understood?"[7]

Husserl goes on to argue that phenomenology is capable of "seeing" essences, which is to say, universals. He is a realist about universals, but in an idiosyncratic sense. The universal is only given, purely or impurely, immanently; it is "given in evidence (*Evidenz*) within the stream of consciousness," but "in the genuine (*reellen*) sense it is transcendent."[8] He means to say that the universal is something instantiated in particular phenomena, but must not be seen as something that resides only in this or that particular phenomenon. Consciousness is able to intuit, or extract, the universal from particular phenomena through the process of "eidetic abstraction." It is in this sense that the universal transcends consciousness, but Husserl does not assign a metaphysical reality to this transcendence. Universals do not exist in a realm of Platonic forms. Instead, he encourages us to see the universal, essences, as immanently transcendent. The universal is given immanently, but *as transcendent*. This redefinition of transcendence results from the shift of perspective inaugurated by the phenomenological reduction, which "means not the exclusion of the genuinely transcendent ... but the exclusion of the transcendent as such as something to be accepted as existent, i.e., everything that is not evident givenness in its true sense, that is not absolutely given to pure 'seeing'."[9] The phenomenological field, therefore, deals only with the *meaning* of the given, not with the given – whether God, the ego, mathematics, natural laws, matter, and so forth – as really existing or metaphysically real. Husserl reassures us that while all objective matters are "held in abeyance" under the phenomenological reduction, nevertheless "all that remains as it is."[10] Reality is unaffected by the reduction. The phenomenologist simply refuses to affirm the autonomy of this reality. Every epistemological investigation must begin with this refusal.[11]

Everyday and natural-scientific consciousness posits, or at least presumes, the transcendence of what is immanently presented to the phenomenologist within the reduction. Husserl calls this kind of positing "nonsensical," by which he means something like unjustified or lacking evidence. This does not mean, however, that it is nonsensical to talk about transcendence altogether. It is only nonsensical if transcendence is not found within the immanent sphere of the reduction. And, as we have seen, it is possible to find evidence of the transcendence of essences (universals) within the reduction. Not quite a Platonist, Husserl is wont to establish that essences are not merely nominal or psychological, which is why he says that their transcendence is "constituted within immediate intuition" but not reducible to a constitutive act of consciousness.[12]

Essences, then, are real in the sense that they are neither subjective, the product of psychology, nor mere appearances. They are dictated by the constitution of the object in view, not the constitution of the subject viewing. They gain their transcendence, or their reality, from their object, which itself "is not a real part of the phenomenon" and does not exist in consciousness the way a toy exists in a toy chest. Objects present themselves as *appearances* that "in a certain sense create objects for the ego in their changing and highly peculiar structure."[13] The objects of consciousness, then, do not give unambiguous evidence of their mind-independent transcendence, although they might suggest it. They present themselves *as* transcendent and with what Merleau-Ponty calls an irreducible "opacity,"[14] but their reference beyond the phenomenal is always itself phenomenal. Surprisingly, this does not prevent Husserl from claiming that things can still exist without being perceived.[15]

Husserl's claim that objects and essences are constituted within the reduction as well as his choice of "transcendental idealism" as a name for his mature philosophy support the charge that his phenomenology is fundamentally idealist. As he writes in *Cartesian Meditations*: "Every imaginable sense, every imaginable being, whether the latter is called immanent or transcendent, falls within the domain of transcendental subjectivity, as the subjectivity that constitutes sense and being."[16] This position is increasingly emphasized after the introduction of the phenomenological reduction in *The Idea of Phenomenology*. But, as Heidegger reiterates, "'Constituting' does not mean producing in the sense of making and fabricating; it means *letting the entity be seen in its objectivity*."[17] Heidegger's qualification encourages us to interpret constitution as a tool of realism, an instrument that allows entities to show themselves as they are independent of the machinations of perception or cognition. At the same time, however, it subtly recapitulates a distinction that it ostensibly means to overcome, namely, the phenomenal/noumenal distinction. It does so by suggesting that there is a way that the objects of experience are, independent of experience, and it is constitution that lets them display this objectivity.

Husserl thus deploys constitution not to argue that subjectivity is responsible for the appearance of the world, but to suggest that the mind is not merely a reflection or receptor of the world's content. Just as Kant established that the mind is the condition for the possibility of experience but not the sole source of experience, Husserl is at pains to show that the world's appearance requires subjectivity, but subjectivity is not the sufficient condition for the world's manifestation.[18] He is not exactly a subjective idealist. Subjectivity is what allows objects to appear as the "changing and highly peculiar" entities they are. In this respect Husserl is very close to Kant's constructivist solution to the problem of knowledge, which, as Tom Rockmore frames it, reduces the apparent world to the phenomenal world, thereby dropping the assumption that there is a world in itself that gives itself through appearances but never directly.[19] The effect of this Hegelian/Nietzschean reduction, as Rockmore sees it, is the neutralization of the correspondence theory of truth as well as the causal theory of perception which regards our perception of objects as caused by the effect of those objects on our perceptual apparatus.[20] Despite this neutralization, argues Rockmore, Husserl inconsistently appeals to the transcendent world of objects as an empirical reality that cannot simply be dismissed: "[Constitution] presupposes a distinction between the object, which is not part of the reduced phenomenon, namely, what is directly, or immanently given, and what is given – roughly, a distinction between appearance and mind-independent external object."[21] Husserl, to avoid the Kantian constructivism he disavows, must commit to some form of metaphysical realism. And yet, as soon as he makes this commitment he has transgressed the boundaries of the subject/object correlation which he insists is the proper field and foundation of phenomenological investigation. This must be taken as a constrained but unjustified breach of method.

Karl Ameriks defends Husserl against the charge of idealism, arguing that Husserl offers us instead a novel version of metaphysical realism. Ameriks' thesis in "Husserl's Realism" only stands up, however, if we accept the claim that the world as it appears to us *just is* the world as it is in itself. This common phenomenological thesis trades on a move that is rightly rejected by speculative realism, namely, the reduction of metaphysical realism to epistemological realism. Or, as the phenomenologist would put it, the reduction of our natural faith in transcendence to the pure evidence of consciousness. Or, as we might put it (with Hegel in mind), the reduction of the thing in itself to the thing as phenomenon. However it is construed, the resolute metaphysical realist cannot remain silent when the phenomenologist concludes that the real is nothing more than what appears as real for us within the subject/object correlation. This is a counterfeit realism.

Ameriks addresses the supposed idealism of two Husserlian concepts: correlation and constitution. His strategy for dealing with these concepts exemplifies what he takes realism to mean in Husserl. It is fairly easy to show that the subject/object correlation, or the correlation of thought and being, does not necessarily entail idealism. Constitution, on the other hand, is a bit trickier. By saying that things are always correlated with consciousness, Husserl means that things are never simply reducible to consciousness, but neither are they knowable apart from consciousness. Their reality always evades or exceeds immanence, and to posit their mind-independence "would be unjustified and without motivation."[22] Husserl's focus on the subject/object correlation is, fundamentally, an avoidance of unmotivated speculation and itself motivated by the reduction of the natural standpoint for epistemological purposes.

Constitution, as we have seen, suggests that the world exists, but that it only means something because humans bestow sense on it. Constitution is a meaning-giving act, not an existence-bestowing act. In Ameriks' view, Husserlian constitution means that the things of the world constitute *themselves* for consciousness. So when we see Husserlian constitution as a kind of mental fabrication, we see it precisely backwards.

> Things constitute themselves in consciousness in the sense that that is where they display their form and meaning. For each thing we know, there are, according to Husserl, certain constitutive forms. These are accessible only through experience, and as experience becomes appropriately articulated we can say that things are constituted or take on meaning within it.[23]

A number of things are established in this passage. First, that things exhibit their form and meaning in consciousness. This is such a straightforward point that few people would dispute it. It does not establish, however, that their being is evidenced in consciousness. Second, it says that when we *know* something as it appears to consciousness, then we know its constitutive form, and we can only know its constitutive form though our experience of it. Again, this is a point about what we know about things, not about the mind-independent being of those things. It is, moreover, almost tautological insofar as it is saying something like the following: "Experience is required to know what things are like when they are experienced."[24] Third, Ameriks makes an implicit claim to the effect that there is a way that things are over and beyond mere appearances, but it takes an "appropriately articulated" experience to apprehend them. This is what Husserl is referring to when he talks about seeing essences, and what Merleau-Ponty has in mind when he argues that for any object or work of art there is an optimum distance from which to perceive its identity with maximum richness and clarity.[25]

We might say that for Husserl objects are experienced in two ways: essentially and inessentially. Only the properly trained phenomenologist is able to see them essentially, that is, as properly constituted. Everyday consciousness does not properly constitute objects, and therefore it cannot see them as they really are. Ameriks maintains that Husserl's epistemology here is "idealistic rather than crudely empiricistic," but he does not see this as "incompatible with believing that what is objectively true corresponds to and is correlated with experience but is not a part of it."[26] While the nonexistence of things is, therefore, "logically possible" because their absolute being is never immanently present to consciousness (at risk of contradiction), it is absurd to hold that the objects of experience do not exist because so much phenomenological evidence suggests otherwise. By the same token, it is absurd to assert that they exist mind-independently because the evidence for this is lacking, if not impossible to gather. The paradox of a realist phenomenology is that it cannot justify (nor disqualify) its realism using phenomenological evidence.

In sum, neither Husserl's rejection of the thing in itself nor his claim that a "world outside our own" is absurd force him, according to Ameriks, to abandon realism. It is simply necessary for us to see that his transcendental idealism does not end in subjectivism, nor does it logically foreclose the possibility that a world in itself does in fact exist. Indeed, as Ameriks concludes, "his metaphysical position is definitely not idealistic and not even neutral. He says the world's existence, though not 'immediately apodictic', nonetheless is 'empirically indubitable', and it is apodictic for him that given harmonious experiences it becomes absurd to deny an external world."[27] This, it seems to me, does not establish Husserl as a realist. Instead, it establishes that phenomenology cannot disprove the truth of metaphysical realism any better than it can provide evidence for it. Fair enough. Since evidence is the gold standard of phenomenological truth, metaphysical realism must be regarded as a groundless thesis. If it is true that Husserl's position is not metaphysically neutral, it does not, however, lean toward realism. It leans toward idealism, even absolute idealism, in its steadfast commitment to the inescapability of correlationism.

Even if Ameriks were to establish the realism of Husserlian phenomenology, his interpretation of constitution and correlation only works to confirm the presence of a skeptical fideism in Husserl's position. Fideism, as Meillassoux diagnoses it, is the dangerous, and today victorious, practical consequence entailed in correlationism. From the rationalist and realist perspective it is objectionable because it insists on the finitude of human reason and forecloses any knowledge of the in itself. It is true that a marked skepticism about knowledge of the in itself attends the contemporary closure of metaphysics, and this opens the door to all manner of mysticism, fanaticism, and irrationalism regarding the determinate existence of the in itself. "Fideism," writes Meillassoux, "invariably consists in a sceptical argument directed against the pretension of metaphysics, and of reason more generally, to be able to access an absolute truth capable of shoring up (or a fortiori, of denigrating) the value of faith."[28] After all, if, according to correlationism, nothing can be rationally stated about the in itself ("the absolute"), then it would be irrational to claim the truth or falsity of any statements, faith-based or otherwise, about the in itself. Philosophical speculation and fanatical dogmatism regarding the absolute must admit to being nothing more than mere belief, and as such outside the scope of rational criticism. In Meillassoux's view, "In leaving the realm of metaphysics, the absolute seems to have been fragmented into a multiplicity of beliefs that have become indifferent, all of them equally legitimate from the viewpoint of knowledge, and this simply by virtue of the fact that they themselves claim to be nothing *but* beliefs."[29]

Husserl, for his part, reaffirms the epistemological limit drawn by the Kantian critique in order to assert the logical possibility of the transcendent world, the thinkability of the in itself, and to argue against the "absurdity" of confidently dismissing the existence of transcendent reality. Here he leans away from Hegel and toward Kant again. He never claims to have established the truth of this reality's existence, just its possibility (or the absurdity of asserting its impossibility). Once the limit of human access to the in itself is solidified and metaphysics suspended, religious discourse about the in itself gains the same legitimacy as rational philosophical discourse. The end of metaphysics, as recent decades have shown, brings with it the forceful return of the religious and a new set of tools for legitimating this return.[30]

Whether or not Husserl's idea of constitution entails a construction of the object analogous to Kantian idealism, or a muted form of "realism" that simply enables the thing itself to appear as itself, it is clear that Husserlian phenomenology enacts a form correlationism. And, despite their attempts to disavow the primacy of the subject/object correlation, his followers are committed to correlationism insofar as they are committed to the primacy of the phenomenological, or the world reduced to phenomena as they give themselves to human perception and judgment. Zahavi concisely identifies correlationism (although he does not call it by name) as the idea that "subjectivity and world cannot be understood in separation from each other." He quotes Merleau-Ponty to elaborate the point:

> The world is inseparable from the subject, but from a subject which is nothing but a project of the world, and the subject is inseparable from the world, but from a world which the subject itself projects. The subject is a being-in-the-world and the world remains "subjective" since its texture and articulations are traced out by the subject's movement of transcendence.[31]

Meillassoux specifies that the kind of correlationism defended by phenomenology is *strong* correlationism, by which he means the view that the in itself is neither knowable nor thinkable. If Ameriks is right about Husserl, however, then the latter represents a *weak* form of correlationism, or the (Kantian) view that the in itself is thinkable but not knowable.[32] This would mean that it is Husserl's followers (Heidegger, in Meillassoux's view) who transform phenomenology into the strong form of correlationism, thus draining phenomenology of whatever shard of realism may have remained in the master's work. From this perspective, transcendence can only be evidenced within immanence, which means that absolute transcendence can never be affirmed by the phenomenologist for whom absolute transcendence is never given absolutely.

The suspension of the natural attitude, the *epoché*, which I am arguing is essential to phenomenology, drives a correlationist wedge between the world as it is represented in consciousness and the world as it stands outside of consciousness. A phenomenologist may insist that phenomenal/noumenal dualism is dissolved by Husserl (or Hegel) and remains so after him, but the metaphysical realist will see this precisely as an *evasion* of realism, not as an attractive recasting of realism's meaning. For the speculative philosopher who wants to affirm and speak of the reality of objects in the ordinary or material sense, "intentional objects" (objects whose transcendence is only demonstrable immanently) will not suffice, even if they do offer a quasi-realist retort to classical empiricism.

Intentional objects are objects in the sense that they make up the "objective" side of the subject/object correlation. They give themselves through their various appearances as transcendent unities, even though this unity is always only judged transcendent from within immanence. They are what intentionality takes to be objective, what it "means," as Husserl puts it, even though their absolute transcendence remains phenomenologically unconfirmed. Intentional objects gain both their meaning and their being from consciousness. Consciousness is never empty; it is always of something. As Husserl puts it in *Cartesian Meditations*, "Each *cogito*, each conscious process ... *"means"* *something or other* and bears in itself, in this manner peculiar to the *meant*, its particular *cogitatum*."[33] And in *Ideas* he specifies that, "Whilst the thing is the intentional unity, that which we are conscious of as one and self-identical within the continuously ordered flow of perceptual patterns as they pass off the one into the other, these patterns themselves have always their *definite descriptive nature (Bestand)*, which is *essentially* correlated with that unity."[34] Rockmore contends, and I incline in this direction, that none of this amounts to evidence that intentional objects are actual objects with independent lives all their own. As he puts it, "Brave talk about immanence in transcendence, claims that objects are experienced as transcendent to appearances, cannot be demonstrated."[35]

Heidegger

There is a palpable sense in which the early Heidegger abandons phenomenology, even prior to *Being and Time* (1927), while at the same time endorsing it as the proper method of his fundamental ontology. When Heidegger is exposing his students at the Universities of Marburg and Freiburg to phenomenology in the 1920s, in texts such as *Introduction to Phenomenological Research* (1923–4), *History of the Concept of Time* (1925), and *The Basic Problems of Phenomenology* (1927), he has already reinterpreted Husserl's method and shifted the focus of phenomenology from the study of consciousness to the question of the meaning of being.

Heidegger is already on his way to presenting phenomenology in a significantly revised form, as he does in the methodological introduction to *Being and Time* (§7). That is, he is deliberate in casting phenomenology less as a technical device made up of a discrete set of practices, including the various reductions, free imaginative variation, eidetic seeing, and so on, and more as the simple disposition proper to philosophical inquiry as such. "Philosophy is," he writes, "universal phenomenological ontology."[36] Interpreting Husserl's maxim "To the things themselves!" he writes that phenomenology means "to let that which shows itself be seen from itself in the very way in which it shows itself from itself."[37] What else is the philosophical quest for truth but the attempt to access the way things are without distortion?

One way of preventing, or at least mitigating distortion, is to first examine the instrument or means of access to truth. This is part and parcel of the transcendental project of Husserl and Heidegger as much as it is for Kant. Whereas Kant carries out a critique of reason, however, Husserl and Heidegger turn their attention to the structure of intentionality. In the 1925 *History of the Concept of Time* Heidegger is still reaffirming Husserl's idea of phenomenology as *"the analytic description of intentionality in its apriori.*"[38] But by 1927 Heidegger has already given up this view, first, by displacing emphasis onto the historicality of Dasein and, second, by claiming that phenomenology does not designate its object of study, but rather *how* one is supposed to access the object of study. For Heidegger, this "object" is the being of entities, which "does not become accessible like a being," as he says in *The Basic Problems of Phenomenology.*[39] Phenomenology is the way to ontology; or, rather, ontology is only possible as phenomenology.[40] "*For us,*" says Heidegger, "phenomenological reduction means leading phenomenological vision back from the apprehension of a being ... to the understanding of the being of this being."[41] Being, on Heidegger's reading, has largely remained hidden in the history of philosophy. It has for a long time been disguised by metaphysics, which is to say, being has typically been understood as the supreme or ultimate entity (God, substance, the One) upon which all other entities depend. Ontology, in other words, has for the most part been an ontotheology. Luckily, phenomenology provides the means to disclose being and allow it to manifest itself truly, without the distortion of metaphysics or ontotheology. Phenomenology, after all, is supposed to be a presuppositionless science. But, as Heidegger will make clear from the very beginning of *Being and Time*, this ideal of neutrality is complicated by the fact that ontology is always carried out and must proceed by way of an entity, Dasein, that is "ontologico-ontically distinctive" from other entities. It is distinctive, as we know, because it is the only entity whose existence or meaning is a question for it. That is, Dasein is the self-reflexive entity. Its understanding of itself and its world is always mediated by its history, never direct or unmediated. This compels Dasein, and consequently Heidegger, to question phenomenology's ideal of becoming a presuppositionless science.

Phenomenology is never merely a matter of description; it is always a problem of interpretation, or hermeneutics.[42] And since Dasein maintains an "ontological priority over every other entity," its existence represents the condition of possibility for the manifestation of being. This means that the truth of being is always at the same time a truth about Dasein's interpretation of being, a "transcendental knowledge" of the "*transcendens*" that is being. The disclosure of being, otherwise called phenomenological truth, is necessarily fused with a hermeneutic analysis of Dasein.[43]

Heidegger provides a substantial revision of phenomenology. In a certain respect he makes a significant turn away from it and signals an imminent break with Husserl's program altogether. Heidegger is unconcerned with the epistemological potential of phenomenology, its capacity to see or know the essence of objects. Indeed, Heidegger's object of study – being and the structure of being (and time) – lies "beyond every entity," which means beyond the profiles, perspectives, adumbrations, and intentional objects that occupy Husserl's world. Importantly, the reduction is no longer central to phenomenology. Heidegger gives up on the dream of philosophy without presuppositions and asserts instead the *necessity* of presuppositions.[44] And furthermore, Heidegger's fusion of Dasein and being, phenomenology and ontology, guarantees that his method will not aim at establishing the transcendent reality of objects, but instead will reveal the utter bankruptcy of our traditional belief in the independent existence of this reality. Realism is predicated on a false presupposition, namely, that the world of objects exists as present-at-hand, objectively independent of Dasein's access to them, and that Dasein exists as an isolated subject or cogito. Given this assessment, it is curious that Heidegger asserts that entities exist independent of Dasein's disclosure of them.[45] He certainly does not provide the evidence to support this claim.

Ontology can only be carried out as phenomenology, which means that the meaning of being can only be disclosed insofar as it appears or manifests itself to the phenomenologist. Heidegger thus aligns himself with antirealism about being. As Braver puts it, referencing *History of the Concept of Time*, "Phenomena are what are; the way we experience the world is the way it is. This is why Heidegger identifies phenomenology, the study of our experience of the world, with ontology, the study of the world as it is, indeed, we can go ahead and say as it is in-itself."[46] Braver calls Heidegger the "zenith" of continental antirealism. Even if it is true that Heidegger moves away from this antirealism in his later work, as Braver also argues, it remains true that in his phenomenological period Heidegger's ontology is packaged as an antidote to realism in its epistemological as well as metaphysical forms.

It is common to mark Heidegger's turn away from phenomenological ontology somewhere in the 1930s. The turn is signaled by increased attention to the language used to express being, to poetry and the event of saying. The turn is interpreted, in James

Risser's words, as a "shift in emphasis from an analysis of the being of Dasein to an analysis of the event of being itself that occurs in the 'there' (*Da*) of Dasein."[47] This is not to say that Heidegger changes his basic question after *Being and Time*, nor does he abandon the view that being can only be thought through Dasein. Even in later works like the *Contributions to Philosophy* Heidegger remains committed to the view that the meaning of being is always a "question of human being who speaks being." This is not a commitment to any established idealism, however, even if it is an affirmation of the view that, divorced from Dasein, being qua being is unthinkable. As he attempts to make clear in his response to Jean Beaufret, the "Letter on Humanism," Heideggerian ontology is not a metaphysics of subjectivity any more than the meaning of being is an accomplishment of human understanding.[48]

Just as important as his emphatic turn toward language is the methodological shift enacted early on in *Being and Time* and discussed in lectures delivered the same year his magnum opus was published. While on the one hand Heidegger cites phenomenology as the only method suitable for his investigation,[49] precisely because it does not descend from any metaphysical standpoint but rather justifies such standpoints; on the other hand, his entire investigation departs from a basic metaphysical distinction: the "ontological difference," or the distinction between being and beings.[50] This is the hinge upon which Heidegger's ontology swings, and it is arguably – Heidegger admits this – a distinction that cannot be established phenomenologically, but must be assumed at the outset or culled from the language we use to talk about beings.[51] Given this basic assumption, alongside his jettisoning of the reduction as essential to phenomenological method, we have to ask if Heidegger is a phenomenologist in any rigorous sense. Would it not be more accurate to say that his fundamental ontology only nominally aligns itself with phenomenology, while engaging hermeneutics as a method more intensively? Are hermeneutics and phenomenology necessarily intertwined, as Gadamer, Ricoeur, and countless others seem to believe? Admittedly, in a certain respect *Being and Time* delineates the end of phenomenology as a descriptive method, while carrying forward phenomenology as a species of impure epistemology, or hermeneutics, which is fulfilled in the work of Gadamer.[52] John Caputo is then right to say that, for Husserl, "phenomenology ought to have a purely descriptive status; it ought to arise only from the independent work of phenomenological reflection, without drawing from the well of ontology." For Heidegger, however, "Husserl's commitment to ontological neutrality does not escape ontology but rather harbors within itself a concealed ontology of the Being of consciousness."[53] This ontology, which is supposed to be displaced by the Dasein analytic, is fundamentally Cartesian. What Heidegger's analysis will ultimately reveal is that knowledge of being cannot begin without presuppositions, that certainty cannot be guaranteed by any reduction, and that any interrogation of being must depart from a "factical understanding" that is historically situated and necessarily replete with unshakable assumptions and epistemological distortion. Caputo concludes: "There is no field of 'pure epistemology' for Heidegger but only an ontology of knowing or understanding. Hermeneutics cannot be understood in ontologically neutral terms."[54] As fundamental as intentionality is for Heidegger, the so-called hermeneutic circle is even more so.

Heidegger's hermeneutic adaptation of Husserl is in part motivated by a desire to establish that reality can only be interpreted through the embodied phenomena of facticity and being in the world. These are ontologically basic ways in which both everyday understanding and philosophical reflection are born out of Dasein's experience of being at every moment of existence, suspended between two inaccessible events, birth and death, or history and the future. Fundamental to his analysis of Dasein is the fact that birth and death absolutely resist phenomenological analysis. There is no possible phenomenology of birth, just as there is no phenomenology of death, only a phenomenology of being toward death. And yet, the "whence and whither" of existence gesture toward two realities that are not reducible to the horizon of Dasein's understanding of the world. If they were, they would not be the realities they are. To be sure, however, his analysis of Dasein requires us to see that our understanding of the world always comes through Dasein's perspective. It is Dasein who understands the meaning and uncovers the truth of being. It is in this sense that Heidegger's ontology in *Being and Time* is phenomenological, which is to say, strong-correlationist.[55]

The question of what is real is intimately linked with Heidegger's exposition of worldhood, which hinges on the distinction he draws between presence-at-hand (objective presence) and readiness-to-hand (instrumental presence). As Merleau-Ponty and Sartre emphasize after him, Heidegger clearly states that when we understand the world as an objective presence (as a material or physical presence, for example), Dasein can only be regarded as arriving on the scene *after* the birth of the world, after being. This is the realist position on the external world, solidified in the modern period by Descartes.[56] From the perspective of how the world is disclosed to Dasein, what Heidegger calls "being in the world," the existence of the world and the existence of Dasein are contemporaneous events, synchronized with one another and structurally interdependent. From this perspective there is no problem of knowing the external world because the world and Dasein are not external to one another, but rather two aspects of a single correlation, what Merleau-Ponty will call the subject-object dialogue.[57] This correlation is analyzed in the analytic of Dasein (Part 1 of *Being and Time*) and forms the condition of possibility of any study of external reality, just as for Kant the limits of our cognition of the external world can only be determined by first critiquing the limits of human reason. "The Real," writes Heidegger, "is essentially accessible only as entities within-the-world. All access to such entities is founded ontologically upon the basic state of Dasein, Being-in-the-world; and this in turn has care as its even more primordial state of Being."[58] Since Dasein always already finds itself in the world, that is, among entities and concerned with its future and its projects (this is the condition of facticity), the a priori existence of entities always remains foreclosed to Dasein's understanding. The world and its objects are always first encountered as *there*, just as Dasein always finds itself there, surrounded by other objects and hemmed in by its past and future. As Heidegger says in *History of the Concept of Time*, "the peculiar thing is just that the world is 'there' *before* all belief."[59] Any attempt to *prove* the existence of the external world and every resolution to simply *believe* in or *assert* its existence are fundamental failures, in Heidegger's view, to understand the internal relationship between Dasein and the world.[60] Both realism and idealism exhibit this failure, although idealism always retains an advantage over realism insofar as it "emphasizes that Being and Reality are only 'in the consciousness'" and that "Being cannot be explained through entities," but only through Dasein.[61] And this is true even if "inherent in the being of the world is that its existence *needs no guarantee in regard to a subject*."[62] How is it that he comes to add this last part?

Following Dilthey and Scheler, Heidegger admits that the reality of the world can be apprehended directly through the phenomenon of resistance, the way in which the brute materiality of things pushes back against our will. But he also qualifies this admission by reaffirming that resistance can only be met, interpreted, and understood on the basis of a more basic (transcendental) disclosure of the world. In short, the phenomenon of resistance does not evince the independent existence of entities as much as it sheds light on the fact that any phenomenological encounter with a "transcendent reality" presupposes Dasein's being in the world as the condition of possibility of this reality.[63] As Heidegger puts it, "only as long as Dasein is (that is, only as long as an understanding of Being is ontically possible), 'is there' Being. When Dasein does not exist, 'independence' 'is' not either, nor 'is' the 'in-itself'."[64] In Braver's words, "the world is Dasein-dependent all the way down."[65]

While Heidegger will at times assert the independent existence of entities (Being and Time, 228), his phenomenology, like Husserl's, cannot support his assertion with evidence. More often Heidegger, like Nietzsche and Hegel, abandons the noumena and the realism that depends on their autonomous existence in favor of an ontology that echoes Hegel's objective idealism. When Heidegger writes as though he is a realist, this is his way of describing phenomenologically how objects in the world present themselves as if they existed independent of their manifestation to Dasein.[66] Their absolute existence remains suspect.

Merleau-Ponty

Merleau-Ponty, too, cites the resistance of things as evidence of their transcendence. Not only do things resist the grasp of perception – the object "tears itself away" [67] – by only permitting us to apprehend one of their profiles at a time, they resist perception by dictating to us the proper manner in which to apprehend their singular identities. As he writes in the Phenomenology of Perception: "For each object, as for each picture in an art gallery, there is an optimum distance from which it requires to be seen."[68] In short, fundamental to Merleau-Ponty's philosophy is the idea that everywhere we turn the world is exceeding perception while at the same time instructing us on how appropriately to access its reality. Merleau-Ponty's lesson at the end of the day is that the world we perceive is always more than what we perceive, and it is perception that discloses this to us. This is why he concludes, with a decisiveness that has influenced many who follow him – notably, the philosophers of alterity and givenness, Levinas and Marion – that the lesson of the phenomenological reduction is that it cannot be completed, the world tenaciously and insistently resists reduction.[69] But what does this resistance imply, and what may the phenomenologist justifiably conclude from it? That there is a world beyond appearances? That there is more to reality than meets the eye? With his signature ambiguity, Merleau-Ponty answers both affirmatively and negatively. The result is an interpretation of phenomenological method that avoids alliance with both transcendental idealism and empirical realism while bequeathing an image of phenomenology that is arguably more influential today than Husserl's own. The sheer breadth of work that is called phenomenological today, and the informality that pervades so much of it, is evidence that phenomenology is more often taken to be a *style* of philosophy (or qualitative research) than a strict method.

The preface to the *Phenomenology of Perception*, a text often referenced for its straightforward and concise presentation of what phenomenology is and is not, begins by asking the question that we are still asking today, nearly 70 years later: "What is phenomenology? It may seem strange that this question has still to be asked half a century after the first works of Husserl."[70] Merleau-Ponty's answer is as decisive as it is ambivalent. It sets the stage for the future reception and practice of phenomenology, particularly in the French context, while it avoids hitching phenomenology explicitly to any explicit method or metaphysics. It is both idealist and realist. It is a method and it is not. He makes clear, following Husserl and Heidegger, that phenomenology is defined by its constant return to the question, What is phenomenology?, which is to say, it is defined by its perpetual need to return to the problem of its origin and direction. Through his equivocal presentation of phenomenology, and despite himself, he confirms something that speaks directly to our present concern: phenomenology, whether interpreted as a method or a style, no matter how you slice it, is essentially correlationist.

Merleau-Ponty is exemplary in his anxiety, felt by many would-be Husserlians, over the apparent idealism of the founder's method. Their desire to philosophize about the concrete reality of cocktails, carpets, and cabarets seems to be obstructed by the very method that is meant to exhibit this reality, at least at a theoretical level. This is why Merleau-Ponty spends a substantial portion of his methodological introduction to the *Phenomenology* tackling the question of whether or not phenomenology is a form of transcendental idealism. He argues that it is not. If it is a transcendental philosophy, it finds the conditions of experience in experience itself. The transcendental is immanent to the empirical. It begins from facticity and derives the essential features of existence from existence itself, not from abstract a priori reflection. Its transcendental aspect is provided by the *epoché*:

> It is a transcendental philosophy which places in abeyance the assertions arising out of the natural attitude, the better to understand them; but it is also a philosophy for which the world is always "already there" before reflection begins – as an inalienable presence; and all its efforts are concentrated upon re-achieving a *direct and primitive contact* with the world, and endowing that contact with philosophical status.[71]

A number of things are signaled here. First, that phenomenology is transcendental insofar as it brackets our naïve faith in the existence of the world and carries out its studies at the level of phenomena, which Merleau-Ponty identifies as the transcendental field. Second, phenomenology does not assume a detached perspective on this field, but lives and investigates it from inside. This is what it means to be embodied. This "concrete" investigation yields a "direct" encounter with the world. In other words, phenomenology does not merely result in knowledge of the world itself as it is mediated by phenomena (as in Kant). The phenomenal world just is the world itself (as in Hegel and Heidegger). Third, Merleau-Ponty marks a certain distance from idealism by asserting that the world is there before we arrive on the scene. We are, in Heidegger's words, "thrown" into it. It is not our invention or fantasy. But, fourth, he marks a certain distance from realism by placing scare quotes around "already there," indicating that he is not making a metaphysical claim, but rather noting that the world *appears to us* to have existed prior to our consciousness of it. His double avoidance of idealism and realism is palpable in his quotation marks.

The *Phenomenology*'s preface reinforces phenomenology's distance from transcendental idealism at several other points. As is typical in the phenomenological corpus, it does not, however, set up a symmetrical distance from, or worry that phenomenology might be mistaken for a brand of, realism. While post-Husserlian phenomenologists are keen on breaking equally from the realist tradition as from the idealist, they do not signal their distance from realism as vehemently as they do their distance from idealism. This is because there is a marked desire for the real that runs throughout the phenomenological tradition. The exigency of this realism is heightened when the phenomenological lens is focused on God or the divine, for what would it mean to say that God exists only *for us*? Phenomenology's asymmetrical safeguarding against idealism, along with the rhetorical strategies it uses to render materially tangible its descriptions, betrays a desire to embody something like a new realism while at the same time assuming a posture vis-à-vis the things themselves that replicates key features of German (and Berkeleyan) idealism. As Tom Rockmore has argued,

> [Merleau-Ponty] is especially close in various ways to Berkeley and Hegel. He explicitly accepts Berkeley's view that in the last analysis things, which are not in themselves, are inseparable from a perceiver. This thesis is reflected in the further claim that any statement about the world as in some way independent of human beings presupposes prescientific experience of it. He is also close to Hegel's view of knowledge as intrinsically historical, hence limited.[72]

The legacy of Berkeleyan idealism is evident in Merleau-Ponty's "primacy of perception" thesis, which states that the phenomenology of perception is prior to, and thus founds, our knowledge of the world. His Hegelianism, as signaled by Rockmore, is evident in his insistence on the finitude of human knowing, which is a feature of the primacy of perception thesis. This finitude is detectable in the account of the reduction he gives in the *Phenomenology*'s preface and stands as a rebuttal of the theses of figures like Plato and Descartes who argue that knowledge transcends experience and somehow accesses a subject-independent real. The rejection of this view, as any reader of phenomenology knows, is fundamental to the phenomenological perspective.

On the one hand, Merleau-Ponty says that phenomenology is "accessible only through a phenomenological method."[73] Central to this method is the phenomenological reduction, which asks us to suspend our faith in the existence of the world and to describe only what is directly experienced as it gives itself to perception. When exposing the meaning of the phenomenological reduction Merleau-Ponty fully realizes how simple it is to mistake it for the idealist maneuver that reduces the noumenal to the phenomenal. But to undercut this mistake, he says, the reduction to immanence "is absolutely distinct from the idealist return to consciousness."[74] Unlike the idealist, for Merleau-Ponty, the conscious subject is not detached from its world like the Cartesian or Kantian ego, but fully embedded within it and amongst (not set over against) the things themselves. Perception testifies to this immanence. Immanence entails that the objects of perception present themselves as transcendent, opaque, and therefore resistant to our attempts to represent them completely. Take any perspective on an object and its back side will remain unperceived. This is the nature of perspective and, consequently, embodied perception. Everywhere we turn our finitude, and the limitations of the idealist position, are revealed to us. Nevertheless, Merleau-Ponty maintains the (idealist) thesis that "the world is what we perceive."[75]

If idealism were true, then perception would lack the opacity intrinsic to it and the objects of perception would not elude perception's grasp. "A logically consistent transcendental idealism rids the world of its opacity and its transcendence," says Merleau-Ponty.[76] His argument is effectively Nietzschean in that it holds that all knowledge is perspectival, historical, and therefore limited. This limitation is precisely what reveals the world as more than us, more than our representations, even though this "more" remains inaccessible to us. There is no view from nowhere that would enable us to articulate a comprehensive representation of the world's content. There is no disembodied knowledge. Our representations are always reflections, at least to some extent, of our being in the world. This, oddly, is Merleau-Ponty's case *for* realism, not against it. I call it odd because it supports the constructivist interpretation of phenomenology, which holds that the given of experience is, in Rockmore's words, "a mere construction, since so-called pure givenness is no more than a myth. Or, to put the same point differently, we never go directly to experience, but always do so on the basis of our prior experience."[77]

If this is true, then we should be suspicious of any claims, including Merleau-Ponty's, that the world is there before our analysis of it. He compounds his evidence of the world's subject-independence with the assertion that "the world is there before any possible analysis of mine" and it is "'real'."[78] The real is not posited or deduced, as it is for Kant, but "'lived' as ready-made or already there."[79] The conclusion of this oblique argument against idealism arrives when Merleau-Ponty announces that "the most important lesson which the reduction teaches us is the impossibility of a complete reduction."[80]

If the reduction is essential to the phenomenological method, but the reduction is impossible to complete, then we must ask if phenomenology is itself impossible. Merleau-Ponty affirms that yes, phenomenology is impossible, in two senses. First, it is impossible because it must infinitely return to and reflect on its beginning, which means that it can never actually begin.[81] Second, and more important for our analysis, it is impossible to carry out *as a method* because its central methodological step, the reduction, is a step that cannot be taken.[82] This, I think, is why Merleau-Ponty decides to characterize phenomenology as a "style" of thinking and not as a philosophical method, even while also maintaining that phenomenology is "only accessible through a phenomenological method." If the reduction is indeed impossible, then the viability of the phenomenological method itself is undermined. It is not surprising that Merleau-Ponty redefines the nature of phenomenology, since it would seem that it has no other option but to recast itself as a style of philosophy. This seems to be what Merleau-Ponty not only anticipates, but also establishes, quite decisively, in his preface to the *Phenomenology*. He marks, in his own way and perhaps contrary to his own desire, the end of phenomenology. He may not make a thorough break with phenomenology, but he does announce the inevitability of its descent into methodological instability. No matter how rich and evocative Merleau-Ponty's descriptions of the world are, if these descriptions do not issue from within the reduction, then they remain, as Eugen Fink argued, mundane and nonphenomenological. They do not, moreover, demonstrate the ability of phenomenology to adduce the subject-independence of the real.[83]

Despite his break with the phenomenology that came before him, Merleau-Ponty continues in his early writings to identify his work as continuous with the phenomenological project. He presents his results as the results of phenomenological investigations which are, he would have us believe, little more than amendments of Husserl's own.[84] Whether or not we concede that the *Phenomenology of Perception* is in fact a work of phenomenology, it is clear that Merleau-Ponty remains committed to the primacy of the subject/object correlation and the authority of what is given immanently in perception. This is clear when he asserts that the evidence of perception demonstrates to us that the world itself and our consciousness of it (that is, the intentional relation) are born at the same moment. Contrary to any causal theory of perception, he rejects the idea that the natural world is the source of what appears, while the observer is the recipient of appearances.[85] The world just is its appearance and consciousness just is part of this appearance. In this important respect Merleau-Ponty is very close to Hegel and quite removed, as he believes, from Kant.[86] Even when in *The Visible and the Invisible* he acknowledges that the *Phenomenology of Perception* upheld a fundamental dualism that should have been abolished,[87] he nevertheless reaffirms the primacy of the subject/object correlation by asserting the internal relation between seer and seen, visible and invisible. This is his celebrated ontological doctrine of "the flesh," which moves Merleau-Ponty even further away from Husserlian and closer to Hegelian phenomenology.[88]

Like so many phenomenologists after Husserl, Merleau-Ponty is compelled to reassure his readers that, despite appearances, there is a world that exists beyond the world of perception. It is there before any analysis of it. And yet, at the same time, he contends that it is not possible to experience either subject or object as distinct from each other. The "objective world" is nothing other than the "world of perception." By the time we get to *The Visible and the Invisible,* he is arguing that subject and object are, ontologically speaking, inseparable from each other: they *are* the same thing, flesh. Merleau-Ponty's correlationism is as evident in his phenomenology as it is in his ontology. In his early texts it is a version of Husserlian phenomenology, while in his later texts his correlationism moves closer to the objective idealism of Hegelian phenomenology. To avoid the unsavory antirealism associated with both of these philosophical positions, as we have seen, he makes a concerted effort to signal his belief in the subject-independent real, even if this belief cannot be justified by his chosen method. His positing of the subject-independent real, I contend, must be seen as distinctly nonphenomenological even when it is made by a quintessential phenomenologist such as Merleau-Ponty.

Whether we are talking about Husserl, Heidegger, or Merleau-Ponty, phenomenology simply cannot get us to the real unless we are willing to concede that the real is nothing other than what appears *as real* to human consciousness.

Phenomenology ≠ Phenomenologist

At this point I want to solidify a distinction that sounds obvious, but whose obviousness does not have an adequate presence in discussions of phenomenological method. This is the distinction between phenomenology (or phenomenological method) and phenomenologists (or those who identify as such). It is assumed that philosophers like Husserl, Heidegger, Marion, Levinas, and the rest of the usual suspects are phenomenologists because they voluntarily identify their work as phenomenology. This has the unfortunate effect of encouraging readers to interpret everything they write as phenomenological statements, or encouraging readers to hunt for the phenomenology in their writings even when there is none to be found. Moreover, when we overlook the distinction between phenomenology and phenomenologist, or when we identify phenomenology with its practitioners rather than regard it as a method of philosophical investigation, then we run the risk of misunderstanding the limits of phenomenology. In other words, we assume that phenomenology is capable of establishing, legitimating, and supporting metaphysical commitments, like realism, that it cannot.

When the phenomenologist steps outside the reduction to say something about what does and does not actually exist independently of human experience, these statements must be flagged as what they are: *claims made without the support of a method.* Or, in Fink's view, mundane reportage of subjective experience. The phenomenologist who actually affirms or denies the transcendent existence of what is immanently given to him is philosophically unequipped to legitimate his affirmation or denial, precisely because affirmation and denial are what phenomenological method prohibits at the moment it introduces the phenomenological reduction. So, for example, when Levinas insists on radical otherness that cannot be thought, experienced, represented, or intuitively fulfilled, or when Heidegger asserts the existence of the real beyond phenomenal appearance, the significance of the distinction between phenomenology and phenomenologist comes into stark relief and we must demand evidence for these realist commitments.

Apart from the reduction, whose possibility, and therefore necessity, is rendered suspect by Merleau-Ponty, or intentionality, whose necessity is compromised by Heidegger, there is no agreed upon methodological criterion for phenomenology amongst phenomenologists. In this sense, phenomenology as a clear method of philosophical investigation has come to an end. If it is conceded that the reduction or intentionality, or even the reduction *to* intentionality, is the *sine qua non* of phenomenology, it would still be the case that phenomenology cannot yield metaphysical realism. This means that any phenomenology which claims to practice a phenomenological method – and I have argued that this is the only meaningful sense of what phenomenology is – must be a form of correlationism. A phenomenology without a method can only remain a style of philosophy, and – insofar as it lacks the methodological tools necessary to establish realism – one ill-equipped to deliver the real on its own terms. Phenomenology, as such, ends in correlationism, if not idealism or antirealism. The latter two labels refer to a position that nearly every phenomenologist after Husserl explicitly disavows. And this disavowal, as we have seen with Heidegger and Merleau-Ponty, is usually accompanied by a transgression of Husserl's method.

This is Not the Realism You Are Looking For

The devolution of the phenomenological method after Merleau-Ponty has been interpreted in many ways – as excess, betrayal, liberation, orthodoxy, heterodoxy. The current landscape is fraught with tensions and little agreement about exactly who are the legitimate heirs of phenomenology. Is the naturalization of consciousness the destiny of phenomenology, or does phenomenology end in mysticism, mystery, and negative theology? Is the so-called theological turn simply the newest instantiation of phenomenology or is it a form of postmodern apologetics, and therefore a dogmatism that is intolerable from the phenomenological viewpoint?[89] All of these positions have defenders. As François-David Sebbah summarizes the current state of things, "[Husserl's] progeny seem to have no possibility of communication between them," and this is because "their fundamental differences result from a chiasmic connection to their common source."[90] Indeed, even the relation between phenomenology and phenomenologist is correlationist! The question now, I think – and here I agree with Sebbah – is whether the diversity of phenomenology is a sign of its fecundity or a symptom of its fragility.[91] Is phenomenology after Merleau-Ponty marked by an absence of rigor and, if so, does this spell the end of phenomenology? I will continue to argue that it is and it does.

In order to set up my discussion of how speculative realism appropriates the "realism" of phenomenology, it is worth turning briefly to two of the ways that phenomenology's diversification is currently assessed. These we might call the conservative view (adopted by Dominique Janicaud) and the progressive view (espoused by Lee Braver). Both views regard the evolution of phenomenology as a form of transgression, although they interpret this transgression in negative and positive terms, respectively. I interpret it not only as a weakening of phenomenology, but as the end of phenomenology, a metamorphosis into something other than what it claims to be. In this respect, I am more sympathetic to Janicaud's position and agree with Lawlor when he says that any phenomenology that crosses the threshold of what appears – to reveal the existence of God, for instance – is a questionable phenomenology.[92] On the other hand, I think Braver uncovers something important for the future of continental philosophy: a middle path between antirealism and realism, but one that does not bear the name of phenomenology.

The Conservative View: Transgressive Phenomenology as Theology

The last decades of the twentieth century witnessed the appearance of a number of works which wedded phenomenology with a theological sensibility, if not theology itself. Meillassoux will speak of this in *After Finitude* as the complicity of strong correlationism and fideism (see Chapter 3 below). For now it is enough to note that the theological turn in French phenomenology includes prominent figures like Levinas, Marion, Henry, Ricoeur, Derrida, and some lesser figures, Jean-François Courtine and Jean-Louis Chrétien. Today the theological turn has been rebranded as the "new phenomenology," but this, I think, is a misnomer that results when we ignore the distinction, already articulated by Janicaud, between phenomenology and those who identify their work as phenomenological.

Janicaud's critique of the theological turn is often read as a reactionary defense of phenomenological orthodoxy, the writings of a disgruntled purist. What Janicaud seems most concerned with, however, is trying to understand why some philosophers insist on identifying as phenomenologists when it would be more advantageous for their objectives to escape the confines of phenomenological method. Or, in Janicaud's words: "Why keep playing along at phenomenology when the game is fixed? Why claim to overcome intentionality, only to reintroduce an 'intention' of sense or an intentionality of transcendence?"[93] In asking this question, Janicaud effectively affirms the validity of the distinction between phenomenology and phenomenologist. Consequently, he calls into question the metaphysical statements about the reality of the divine made by "phenomenologists" like Levinas, Henry, and Marion. If they simply discarded the cloak of phenomenology, there would be no controversy. Speaking of Henry, Janicaud writes: "There would be no reason to object to [Henry's] mutation [of phenomenological method] if it presented itself as what it is, a conversion or leap toward an experience more secret than that of any phenomenology."[94]

At stake, of course, is the reality of the divine. The theological phenomenologist is keen to adduce evidence of God and he believes that phenomenology provides the (only?) means to get there. But if phenomenological analysis is restricted to the evidence of immanence, it is simply contradictory to claim that intentionality can reach the transcendent. This is, roughly, Janicaud's thesis. Or, as Sebbah characterizes it, Janicaud's complaint is that French phenomenology (including Sartre and Merleau-Ponty) "betrays the requirements of philosophical rigor in its tendency to bring together an originary outside, beyond consciousness."[95] While suspicious of the rigor of Janicaud's own criticism, Sebbah does find in Janicaud the impetus for opening his own Kantian critique of French phenomenology, one which "trace[s] the limits of the phenomenological field beyond which the radical nature of the quest for the originary suddenly and excessively reverses."[96] This critique, which fills the pages of *Testing the Limit*, is more valuable, argues Sebbah, than focusing on whether or not French phenomenology preserves the "orthodoxy" or "purity" of phenomenological inquiry. This, I would contend, is not what Janicaud is all about. His is not an unsubtle, naïve polemic against phenomenological heretics. It is, rather, the suggestion that if you want transcendence, absolute otherness, and God, then phenomenology is not for you. And when you claim that phenomenology can disclose transcendence, absolute otherness, and God, then you are either mistaken about the limits of phenomenology or using phenomenology in a loose sense that renders it nearly meaningless.

Sebbah is not the only one to push back against Janicaud's critique of the theological turn. A recent collection of essays offers a "companion" or counterpoint to Janicaud. Bruce Ellis Benson recalls in the introduction to *Words of Life* that the so-called French debate is a matter of phenomenological orthodoxy that hinges on the following question: Can phenomenology disclose transcendence in immanence or has the theological turn injected "transcendence in its fullest form" into the phenomena.[97] Janicaud affirms the second half of the disjunction, to which Benson replies: "contrary to Janicaud's contention that phenomenology has been taken hostage by theology, might it not be more accurate to say that the very conception of phenomenology has been radically transformed?"[98] This is a false choice. Benson here presents us with a disjunction which is actually an identity. That is, the radical transformation of phenomenology *is nothing other than* its abduction (in this case, by theology). Contrary to Benson's suggestion, this is not phenomenology finally being true to the things themselves, but rather a neglect of the authority of the things themselves. To settle this point it is not necessary to show that the theological phenomenologists are actually being hyperloyal to the principles of phenomenological method, which is of course their own self-understanding. Instead, it is only necessary to establish that the God of the biblical tradition is simply not intuited phenomenally. Or, if he is, his existence must be posited as something that exceeds the phenomenal realm, a fact that would oblige the phenomenologist to *speculate* on his excess and make some metaphysical decision about its content. But this is problematic if we agree that metaphysical commitments, and speculation, of this sort are prohibited by Husserl's method.

If we accept that at a minimum phenomenology must practice the reduction and adhere to the authority of immanence, then it is difficult to see how God or the Giver of the given or the wholly Other – in short, absolute transcendence or pure givenness – can be the object of phenomenological inquiry. Note that this point does not require strict adherence to orthodoxy or the scientific version of phenomenology, but only to two simple principles that seem impossible for the phenomenologist to discard. If phenomenology is to mean anything, I contend that this meaning entails a commitment, at least, to: 1) minimizing presuppositions; 2) the absolute authority of the phenomena, or the immanent content of consciousness (the "principle of principles"). This does not mean that there cannot be a phenomenology of religious life, including a phenomenology of, for example, hope, faith, prayer, hospitality, and so forth.[99] It does mean, however, that there cannot be a phenomenology of God, if by "God" we mean a transcendent entity that cannot, without contradiction, appear immanently to consciousness. As Husserl says in *The Idea of Phenomenology*: "transcendence is in principle not experienceable."[100]

The French phenomenologists critiqued by Janicaud and defended by Sebbah, Benson, and others reach for and claim to deliver, by phenomenological means, the existence of the divine. But even if phenomenology could deliver evidence of the divine, phenomenology is prohibited from committing itself to the metaphysical reality (or unreality) of the divine. This does not mean that Levinas, Marion, and Henry cannot commit themselves to the reality of the divine – indeed, they all do. It means that they cannot make these commitments *as phenomenologists*. Commitments such as these remain a matter of faith or metaphysical argument, neither of which belong to phenomenology.

The Progressive View: Transgressive Phenomenology as Realism

As a complement to the magnificent history of continental antirealism he provides in *A Thing of This World* – a landmark reference work for speculative realism – Lee Braver, while not a speculative realist himself, has outlined an underground current of "transgressive realism" (his term) in the continental tradition. Transgressive realism is found in figures like Kierkegaard, Heidegger, and Levinas, all of whom acknowledge the potential for experience to "surprise" us with unforeseeable events and insights that we are incapable of anticipating or fully comprehending. As Braver puts it, "These aporetic experiences enter our awareness not through pathways prepared by our Active Minds but in spite of them, short-circuiting our anticipatory thought processes and violating the recollective model of learning that has haunted philosophy since Meno's slave learned a little math."[101] The recollective model holds that every new piece of knowledge we gain is nothing other than the retrieval of what we already know in advance. It is the model introduced by Plato and radically transformed by Kant and Hegel, the model that has been handed down through the continental tradition and which continues to dominate today. It is the model against which speculative realism rebels. Usually we just call it transcendental or objective idealism, or, more simply, idealism.

Even before speculative realism, Braver contends, we can discern in the history of continental philosophy a strain of transgressive realism whose force comes from its rejection of idealism and the recollective model of learning. Transgressive realism is particularly salient in Kierkegaard and certain members of the phenomenological community, especially Levinas. It is arguably a position that Merleau-Ponty is sympathetic to, but does not explicitly endorse. When Levinas rails against Husserlian idealism by saying that "we find in Husserl a privilege of presence, of the present, and of representation," he is positioning the transgressive realist cause against the transcendental philosophy of Husserl.[102] The transgressive realist is a realist in the sense that he or she affirms that genuine otherness, actual learning, and surprise are all possible. We are not the omniscient master of our own experience.

While Braver includes Heidegger in the line of transgressors, it is Levinas who stands as the "poster child" for transgressive realism. In Levinas we find a "heterodox form of phenomenology" whose defining trait is its break with the idealism of orthodox Husserlian transcendentalism. In Janicaud's view, what Braver calls Levinas's transgression is denounced as a "biased utilization"[103] of phenomenological concepts. Levinas, in Janicaud's assessment, has left phenomenology behind; his is not a heterodox phenomenology, it is no phenomenology at all. It is apostasy. "Levinas imposes his schema," argues Janicaud, "only at the price of considerable distortions of his phenomenological referents." The cost of his imposition "is the abandonment of the phenomenological *method*, a farewell to the Husserlian ambition of rigor."[104] Braver's view, of course, is more generous than Janicaud's. What Levinas delivers like no other is an account of the trauma of a direct encounter with the real, with "a reality unformed by human concepts" and "a true beyond [that] touches us, sending shivers through our conceptual schemes, shaking us out of any complacent feeling-at-home."[105] This is not the feeling of anxiety or dread that accompanies our experience of the uncanny, but the shocking encounter with the absolutely other who makes contact with us.

As Braver describes it, phenomenological intentionality is about expectation. When we intend an object that is not present before us, we call that intention empty. We can pursue experiences that will present the object to us, as we intend it in its absence. If the object presents itself as we expect it to, our originally empty intention is fulfilled. If it does not, the intention remains unfulfilled; but this is also when surprise occurs. Surprises are, on Braver's view, when reality "confounds my tacit expectations." The confounding of expectation is what Levinas analyzes better than anyone else, and in such a way that surprise takes on an ontological aspect in his work. It is much more than a psychological phenomenon: surprise entails a rupture of the immanent world which reveals the transcendent beyond. This rupture is the work of the transcendent, not the result of a faulty or failed phenomenological seeing. Genuine surprise involves the absolutely unanticipated and unfathomable appearance of a transcendent reality, which Levinas identifies as divine, sometimes calls God, and metaphorizes in the figure of "the face" of the Other. This kind of radical transcendence, in Levinas's view, is impossible in Husserl's idealist version of phenomenology.[106] In Braver's words: "Nothing in the world could be absolutely foreign to the [Husserlian] subject. Phenomenological consciousness inherited Kant's allergy to radical alterity."[107]

Using Husserlian ideas Levinas finds radical alterity at the heart of consciousness itself, in "experiences that violate our concepts and expectations."[108] What is more, this radical alterity is uncovered by supposedly phenomenological means by Levinas. "We only find these trans-phenomena," says Braver, "by adhering fastidiously to phenomenology's own method."[109] The paradigmatic transphenomenon that short-circuits our intentionality and expectations is the face of the Other, which presents us with "an experience that exceeds and overloads expectations, one that cannot be anticipated or contained within the boundaries of a concept."[110] The experience of the Other, then, is the experience of a reality that no idealism can anticipate or comprehend. This is what makes the Other *other*. His affirmation of the Other's transcendence is what makes Levinas a realist, and it is the fact that this transcendence is revealed within experience that makes him, in Braver's view, a phenomenologist, albeit heterodox in method.

Now, while it may be the case that another person (the Other) can never be known as well as one knows oneself and is, by this definition, incomprehensible, I am skeptical that our experience of the Other is an experience of absolute transcendence. And even if the Other did harbor an absolute transcendence, this would not mean that our experience could reveal its absoluteness. Indeed, this is Levinas's view. The absolute transcendence of the Other introduces us to the idea of infinity in such a way that we can think the idea of infinity but cannot comprehend it. As Levinas writes, "The idea of the infinite consists precisely and paradoxically in thinking more than what I thought while nevertheless conserving it in its excessive relation to thought. The idea of the infinite consists in grasping the ungraspable while nevertheless guaranteeing its status as ungraspable."[111] For Levinas, as for other phenomenologists, transcendence reveals itself in immanence. It is therefore a relative transcendence. But is this not just another way of saying that some things *seem* to transcend our conscious grasp of them? This is what phenomenological analysis reveals, as Husserl shows.

What makes Levinas different from Husserl with respect to the reality of transcendence, however, is that Levinas characterizes surprises as *in principle* beyond our capacity to anticipate them. They are impossible expectations. A phenomenologist like Husserl could easily reply that surprises are not ontological events, but are instead functions of the phenomenological horizons we project. A surprise is just a failure of our anticipations, not ontologically impossible to predict or epistemologically impossible to comprehend. The transcendence of the Other, or alterity more generally, would then be relative to and determined by consciousness and its finite limitations. In short, there is reason to be skeptical that phenomenology, if it is committed to describing the evidence of experience as it is given immanently to consciousness, provides evidence of the real understood as what absolutely transcends and disrupts experience. And yet, Levinas is no doubt committed to this kind of realism. But is this what Braver calls transgressive realism?

I do not think that Levinas gives us a realism justifiable with phenomenology, although he is committed to a metaphysical realism with respect to the Other, God, and the Good. What he provides at the phenomenological level, perhaps better than anyone else (even Heidegger or Freud), is an account of what it is like or what it means to be, in Braver's words, "unsettled"[112] by reality. Levinas's phenomenological account does not, however, provide us with the necessary metaphysical evidence to establish the existence of an absolutely transcendent Other. This is why I think Stella Sandford is right when she says:

> Levinas's philosophical method therefore consists in a series of metaphysical declarations apparently extrapolated from and further supported by phenomenological evidences. Metaphysical truths are revealed through phenomenology, both in the sense that phenomenology allows one to encounter them and that it functions verificationally after the event of disclosure. In this way, the strong claim for the intelligibility of transcendence is apparently based on, revealed through or justified by the appeal to the phenomenology of the ethics of affect.[113]

We must be careful here. I do not think we should read this passage as an endorsement of phenomenology's ability to verify metaphysical claims, but to emphasize that Levinas's "metaphysical declarations" are *"apparently extrapolated"* from phenomenology. While absolute transcendence may in fact be intelligible, this tells us nothing about whether it is verifiable through phenomenological means. Intellectualism and rationalism, as Merleau-Ponty teaches, are quite problematic from the phenomenological standpoint. It is not at all clear that the conceptual intelligibility of transcendence entails that absolute transcendence is phenomenologically accessible. Indeed, it seems that the whole force of Levinas's philosophy implies the contrary.

Just because something surprises us does not necessarily indicate an ontological rupture in immanence. It could just as well indicate a failure of our imagination about what will arrive in the future. This does not provide us with evidence of the existence of the infinite, but it does provide us with evidence of our finitude.

Braver's concept of transgressive realism as it appears in Heidegger and Levinas assumes that phenomenology and realism are compatible, that a phenomenology can be realist. This assumption mitigates the crucial distinction, defended above, between phenomenology and phenomenologist. Braver takes Levinas at his word when Levinas claims to find, by phenomenological means, absolute alterity revealed in experience. This leads him to identify Levinas's transgressive realism as a "heterodox phenomenology," rather than calling it a break with phenomenology itself. I concede that Levinas provides us with a transgressive realism. But this realism must be counted among Levinas's many nonphenomenological, or metaphysical, commitments. It is not the result of any phenomenological analysis, and this is precisely for reasons identified by Braver himself when he recalls that Heidegger recognized that "phenomenology's implicit ontology" is equivalent to Hegelian objective idealism in that both restrict "reality to what we can encounter, which means the kinds of beings that fit our pre-ontological understanding of being." Phenomenology, despite its love for the things themselves, is "among the enemies of noumena."[114] This is why Braver is wrong to characterize Levinas as a phenomenologist, heterodox or otherwise. If phenomenology is at bottom antirealism, then a philosopher who practices phenomenology implicitly endorses an idealist ontology. They must begin from the premise that "Phenomena are what are; the way we experience the world is the way it is." If Levinas transgresses the limits of idealism, then he transgresses the limits of phenomenology too. His realism must be regarded as something that exceeds phenomenology, as Janicaud argues. If the *epoché* entails a suspension of ontological realism, then any phenomenology that takes the *epoché* seriously cannot subscribe to ontological realism without covertly importing a metaphysics into the heart of a metaphysically neutral methodology. "Levinas was clearer and more convincing," writes Janicaud, "when he spoke frankly of 'overflowing' phenomenology."[115] Indeed, at times, Levinas's own statements support this conclusion.[116]

Transgressive realism offers a fascinating and promising middle path between speculative realism and the antirealism which remains a formidable force in continental and analytic philosophy. But transgressive realism is not consistent with phenomenological method if that method is in the last analysis consonant with idealism and the recollective model of learning which prohibit us from "appealing to a reality lying behind our comprehension *in principle*," as Braver puts it.[117] But this is exactly what Levinas appeals to when he says that the Other is *in principle* ungraspable. This appeal, rather than confirming Levinas's transgressive realist credentials, should be what revokes them.

In Braver's view the advantage enjoyed by transgressive realism over speculative realism is that the latter includes too many discussions of a reality that is impossible to make contact with. Speculative realism talks at length about how "inanimate objects 'experience' or 'encounter' each other in the dark after we've all gone to bed," but Braver thinks that this is nothing more than "mere speculation."[118] Braver, with Graham Harman's object-oriented philosophy obviously in mind, prefers his realism derived from phenomenology because it is motivated by the testimony of experience; it is anchored in the concrete, not free-floating musings. But if what I have said about the relation between realism and phenomenology is true, and if Levinas's realism is only nominally phenomenological, then phenomenology cannot deliver realism of any kind, transgressive realism included, precisely because phenomenology prohibits both *mere speculation* about the real (criticized by Braver) as well as *motivated speculation* about the real (endorsed by Braver).

For the phenomenologist the limits of ontology, of what is real, are aligned with the limits of human experience. Whatever, if anything, lies beyond the limit of human experience is epistemologically off limits for phenomenology, just as it is for the critical philosophy of Kant. If it is true that human understanding is finite, and that the real lies beyond the limits of human experience, then a motivated speculation about the real becomes essential to any realism that is discontent with the view that what appears as real for human consciousness simply is the totality of the real. Given the fact of human finitude, there is no other road to the real. The question for speculative realism then becomes: *of what does speculation consist?* The answers to this are as diverse as the field of speculative realism itself. What they have in common, however, is a desire to break with the recollective model of knowledge as well as the authority of phenomena, and to engage problems that are, roughly speaking, metaphysical in nature. Starting from the evidence of phenomena, Graham Harman resists phenomenological conclusions by calling into question the accessibility of real objects and the possibility of direct causation. Quentin Meillassoux dissects the incompatibility of phenomenological philosophy and realist scientific statements made about the "past which has never been present" – a favorite expression of Bergson, Merleau-Ponty, and Levinas. Ray Brassier and Iain Hamilton Grant, using divergent premises and sources of argumentation, each contest the primacy of perception in order to dig into the ground of existence and interrogate its coherence, reason, and value.

All four of the original Goldsmiths speculative realists – along with those who have been drawn into their orbit – are committed to the view that there is a reality that exceeds the bounds of perception and phenomenological intuition; that human thought is capable of transgressing the limits of phenomenological evidence; and that being is not identical to knowing. In short: speculation, they maintain, is theoretically capable of disengaging objects from subjects in nonarbitrary ways, some of which approximate science fiction but none of which are, in the last analysis, fictitious. After all, even if it is true that all consciousness is consciousness-of something (this is the basic thesis of phenomenology), this does not entail that every something is the object of consciousness. Consciousness may indeed be empty without content, but there is little reason to outlaw the claim that content can get along in the world just fine without humans tending it. And once this content is released from the bondage of perception, almost anything (within reason) is possible.

Notes

1. For a positive assessment of phenomenology as the rigorous retrieval of all we take for granted in everyday experience, or the evasion of sedimented ways of thinking, see John Sallis, *Phenomenology and the Return to Beginnings* (Pittsburgh: Duquesne University Press, 2003).

2. Zahavi, *Husserl's Phenomenology*, 52. It seems odd to lump meaning and truth (both of which are obviously human-dependent) with reality (whose human-dependence is controversial). Why does the fact that the world's *appearance* requires subjectivity entail that it cannot *be* without subjectivity?

3. Edmund Husserl, *The Idea of Phenomenology*, trans. William P. Alston and George Nakhnikian (The Hague: Martinus Nijhoff, 1964), 1.

4. Husserl, *The Idea of Phenomenology*, 1, 25.

5. Husserl, *The Idea of Phenomenology*, 3–4.

6. Husserl, *The Idea of Phenomenology*, 4.

7. Husserl, *The Idea of Phenomenology*, 5. The pure phenomenon, achieved through the phenomenological reduction, is not external to consciousness, but absolutely given within it (33–4).

8. Husserl, *The Idea of Phenomenology*, 6. He elaborates at 24ff.

9. Husserl, *The Idea of Phenomenology*, 7ff. "Seeing" roughly means immanent intuition, that which is given purely to consciousness; it implies the "absolute givenness" of what is seen.

10. Husserl, *The Idea of Phenomenology*, 7.

11. Husserl, *The Idea of Phenomenology*, 26, 33.

12. Husserl, *The Idea of Phenomenology*, 42–3.

13. Husserl, *The Idea of Phenomenology*, 71.

14. Merleau-Ponty, *Phenomenology of Perception*, xiii.

15. See, for instance, Husserl, *Ideas*, §41.

16. Husserl, *Cartesian Meditations*, 84.

17. Heidegger, *History of the Concept of Time*, 71.

18. Zahavi, *Husserl's Phenomenology*, 73.

19. Rockmore, *Kant and Phenomenology*, 125.

20. Rockmore, *Kant and Phenomenology*, 126–7.

21. Rockmore, *Kant and Phenomenology*, 127–8.

22. Karl Ameriks, "Husserl's Realism," *The Philosophical Review* 86, no. 4 (October 1977), 504. See also Edmund Husserl, *Formal and Transcendental Logic*, trans. Dorion Cairns (The Hague: Martinus Nijhoff, 1969), 165.

23. Ameriks, "Husserl's Realism," 504.

24. Tautologies like this are taken almost as first principles in discussions of phenomenology, deconstruction, and the like. Challenging them, it is assumed, entails a performative contradiction. Another common tautology runs like this: "You cannot think a thing without turning that thing into a thought." Asserting the absolute truth of this proposition is one of the key strategies employed by correlationism to ensure that anyone who claims to think a mind-independent thing gets caught in a perilous contradiction. As I show in Chapters 3 to 5, there is reason to reject this.

25. Merleau-Ponty, *Phenomenology of Perception*, 302.

26. Ameriks, "Husserl's Realism," 505, 506. Ameriks holds that the thing in itself is discarded by Husserl and Hegel because it is an "absurd" postulate in that it lacks sense from the phenomenological standpoint. With the thing in itself out of the picture, the

apparent world becomes the only true world, which means that Husserl's epistemological idealism is equivalent to metaphysical realism insofar as it is capable of providing a coherent and "fully harmonious experience of something transcendent." That is, while it "does not entail the existence of things ... it does make absurd the denial of their [transcendent] being" (507).

27. Ameriks, "Husserl's Realism," 509.
28. Meillassoux, *After Finitude*, 46.
29. Meillassoux, *After Finitude*, 47.
30. Meillassoux, *After Finitude*, 46, emphasis omitted.
31. Quoted in Zahavi, *Husserl's Phenomenology*, 73.
32. On the varieties of correlationism, see what Graham Harman calls "Meillassoux's Spectrum," in *Quentin Meillassoux: Philosophy in the Making* (Edinburgh: Edinburgh University Press, 2011), 14.
33. Husserl, *Cartesian Meditations*, 33.
34. Husserl, *Ideas*, §41.
35. Rockmore, *Kant and Phenomenology*, 128.
36. Martin Heidegger, *Being and Time*, trans. John Macquarrie and Edward Robinson (San Francisco: Harper & Row, 1962), 62. This method does contain three distinct components – reduction, construction, and destruction – but it must be emphasized that this is the method of Heidegger's *ontology*, only the first part of which (reduction) is explicitly linked to Husserlian phenomenology. It is difficult to see how the other two parts, especially destruction (which is a historico-critical practice), can be carried out phenomenologically. See *The Basic Problems of Phenomenology*, 19–23.
37. Heidegger, *Being and Time*, 58.
38. Heidegger, *History of the Concept of Time*, 79.
39. Heidegger, *The Basic Problems of Phenomenology*, 21.
40. Heidegger, *Being and Time*, 60.
41. Heidegger, *The Basic Problems of Phenomenology*, 21.
42. Heidegger, *Being and Time*, 61.
43. Heidegger, *Being and Time*, 62.
44. Heidegger, *The Basic Problems of Phenomenology*, 21; see also Heidegger, *Being and Time*, 191–5, on the forestructure of understanding.
45. Heidegger, *Being and Time*, 228.
46. Lee Braver, "On Not Settling the Issue of Realism," *Speculations* IV (2013), 11; Heidegger, *History of the Concept of Time*, 72.

47. James Risser, ed., *Heidegger Toward the Turn: Essays on the Work of the 1930s* (Albany: SUNY Press, 1999), 2.

48. Risser, "Introduction," *Heidegger Toward the Turn*, 2.

49. Heidegger, *Being and Time*, 50.

50. In *The Basic Problems of Phenomenology*, 17, Heidegger calls the ontological difference "the basic presupposition needed to set about the problems of ontology regarded as the science of being."

51. Heidegger's minute attention to words, particularly the etymology of words, plays an integral role in his philosophy, but it is not always clear what relationship these etymologies bear to his phenomenology. See his discussion of "is," for example, in Martin Heidegger, *Basic Concepts*, trans. Gary Aylesworth (Bloomington: Indiana University Press, 1993).

52. When Gadamer, in "Heidegger and the Language of Metaphysics," writes that "the transcendental-phenomenological conception of *Being and Time* is already essentially different from Husserl's conception of it," he has in mind the way in which his analysis of Dasein is primarily an analysis of the "absolute historicity that forms the transcendental ground of all objectivities," that is, the need to hermeneutically ground phenomenology. See Hans-Georg Gadamer, *Philosophical Hermeneutics*, trans. and ed. David E. Linge (Berkeley: University of California Press, 1976), 233.

53. John Caputo, *Radical Hermeneutics: Repetition, Deconstruction, and the Hermeneutic Project* (Bloomington: Indiana University Press, 1987), 54.

54. Caputo, *Radical Hermeneutics*, 61.

55. On the problem that mortality and death pose for the phenomenologist, Heidegger included, see Meillassoux, *After Finitude*, 56–7.

56. As Braver puts it in *A Thing of This World*, 165: "Realism is singled out [by Heidegger] by its exclusive focus on presence-at-hand as the sole mode of Being. It interprets all experience in terms of this one mode, which profoundly distorts our daily lives." For Descartes's realism, see 167.

57. See Merleau-Ponty, *Phenomenology of Perception*, 132.

58. See Heidegger, *Being and Time*, 246–7.

59. Heidegger, *History of the Concept of Time*, 215–16.

60. Heidegger, *Being and Time*, 249.

61. Heidegger, *Being and Time*, 251–2.

62. Heidegger, *History of the Concept of Time*, 216.

63. Heidegger, *Being and Time*, 253–4. For other aspects of realism in Heidegger, see Braver, *A Thing of This World*, 164–71.

64. Heidegger, *Being and Time*, 255.

65. Braver, *A Thing of This World*, 185.

66. Braver, *A Thing of This World*, 181, 182, 191, 193.

67. Maurice Merleau-Ponty, "The Primacy of Perception," in *The Primacy of Perception and Other Essays*, ed. James M. Edie (Evanston: Northwestern University Press, 1964), 18.

68. Merleau-Ponty, *Phenomenology of Perception*, 302.

69. Merleau-Ponty, *Phenomenology of Perception*, xiv.

70. Merleau-Ponty, *Phenomenology of Perception*, vii.

71. Merleau-Ponty, *Phenomenology of Perception*, vii, emphasis added.

72. Rockmore, *Kant and Phenomenology*, 194. See Merleau-Ponty, "The Primacy of Perception," 16.

73. Merleau-Ponty, *Phenomenology of Perception*, viii.

74. Merleau-Ponty, *Phenomenology of Perception*, ix.

75. Merleau-Ponty, *Phenomenology of Perception*, xvi.

76. Merleau-Ponty, *Phenomenology of Perception*, xi–xii.

77. Rockmore, *Kant and Phenomenology*, 193.

78. Merleau-Ponty, *Phenomenology of Perception*, x, xvi.

79. Merleau-Ponty, *Phenomenology of Perception*, xvii.

80. Merleau-Ponty, *Phenomenology of Perception*, xiv.

81. These themes are explored in books like Maurice Natanson's *Edmund Husserl: Philosopher of Infinite Tasks* (Evanston: Northwestern University Press, 1974) and Sallis's *Phenomenology and the Return to Beginnings*.

82. This creates a problem for the concept of intentionality, also central to the phenomenological view. If intentionality is revealed through the reduction, then the impossibility of the reduction implies that intentionality cannot be completely revealed. Indeed, Merleau-Ponty notes and exploits the basic ambiguity of intentionality to buttress his view of the world as inescapably opaque to perception. See, for example, the discussion of operative intentionality in *Phenomenology of Perception*, xvii–xviii.

83. See Lawlor, *Thinking Through French Philosophy*, 149. Rockmore puts the point in more abrasive terms in *Kant and Phenomenology*, 128.

84. This "strange game of sacralizing the reference to Husserl" (Janicaud et al., *Phenomenology and the "Theological Turn,"* 21) is not only practiced by Merleau-Ponty, but also by many who come after him as a way of authenticating their phenom-

enological claims at the very moment they push phenomenology to (or beyond) its limits.

85. The story he tells is a little different in his courses on nature.

86. Rockmore, *Kant and Phenomenology*, 197, 204.

87. Maurice Merleau-Ponty, *The Visible and the Invisible*, trans. Alphonso Lingis (Evanston: Northwestern University Press, 1969), 200.

88. On the relation between Hegelian metaphysics and the doctrine of the flesh, see David Storey, "Spirit and/or Flesh: Merleau-Ponty's Encounter with Hegel," *Phaenex* 4, no. 1 (2009), 59–83.

89. See Christina M. Gschwandtner, *Postmodern Apologetics? Arguments for God in Contemporary Philosophy* (New York: Fordham University Press, 2013).

90. Sebbah, *Testing the Limit*, 18.

91. Sebbah, *Testing the Limit*, 18.

92. Lawlor, *Thinking Through French Philosophy*, 150.

93. Janicaud et al., *Phenomenology and the "Theological Turn,"* 42.

94. Janicaud et al., *Phenomenology and the "Theological Turn,"* 81.

95. Sebbah, *Testing the Limit*, 28.

96. Sebbah, *Testing the Limit*, 30.

97. Bruce Ellis Benson and Norman Wirzba, eds., *Words of Life: New Theological Turns in French Phenomenology* (New York: Fordham University Press, 2010), 3.

98. Benson and Wirzba, *Words of Life*, 3.

99. See Martin Heidegger, *Phenomenology of Religious Life*, trans. Matthias Fritsch and Jennifer Anna Gosetti-Ferencei (Bloomington: Indiana University Press, 2004).

100. Edmund Husserl, *The Idea of Phenomenology*, trans. Lee Hardy (Dordrecht: Kluwer, 1999), 59.

101. Lee Braver, "A Brief History of Continental Realism," *Continental Philosophy Review* 45, no. 2 (2012), 261–89. "Active Mind" is Braver's term for what we otherwise refer to as "constructivism." Notably, Active Mind tames the world of experience by accounting a priori for any possible experience. It thereby renders surprises impossible and the extramental world unknowable.

102. Emmanuel Levinas, "Nonintentional Consciousness," in *Entre Nous*, trans. Michael B. Smith and Barbara Harshav (New York: Columbia University Press, 2000), 125.

103. Janicaud et al., *Phenomenology and the "Theological Turn,"* 27.

104. Janicaud et al., *Phenomenology and the "Theological Turn,"* 39.

105. Braver, "On Not Settling the Issue of Realism," 12.

106. See, for example, Emmanuel Levinas, *The Theory of Intuition in Husserl's Phenomenology*, second edition, trans. André Orianne

(Evanston: Northwestern University Press, 1995) and Levinas, "Nonintentional Consciousness."

107. Braver, "A Brief History of Continental Realism," 281.
108. Braver, "A Brief History of Continental Realism," 281.
109. Braver, "A Brief History of Continental Realism," 282.
110. Braver, "A Brief History of Continental Realism," 282.
111. Quoted in Braver, "A Brief History of Continental Realism," 283.
112. Braver, "On Not Settling the Issue of Realism," 13.
113. Stella Sandford, "Levinas in the Realm of the Senses: Transcendence and Intelligibility," *Angelaki* 4, no. 3 (1999), 69–70.
114. Braver, "A Brief History of Continental Realism," 273.
115. Janicaud et al., *Phenomenology and the "Theological Turn,"* 48.
116. See Emmanuel Levinas, *Totality and Infinity*, trans. Alphonso Lingis (Pittsburgh: Duquesne University Press, 1969), 27.
117. Braver, "A Brief History of Continental Realism," 284, emphasis added.
118. Braver, "On Not Settling the Issue of Realism," 12. Meillassoux, as we will see, distinguishes between mere speculation (dogmatic, metaphysical) and speculation proper (nonmetaphysical) in *After Finitude*. The criticism here is clearly directed at Harman's OOP, and by extension the OOO of Bryant, Morton, and Bogost.

2

The Rhetoric of Realism in Phenomenology

It is evident that Husserl's followers acutely saw the parallel between phenomenology and idealism and, in an attempt to preempt the charge of idealism, devised strategies to clearly signal the realism at the root of their phenomenological practice. These strategies are meant not to demonstrate realism, but to reinforce the philosophical and argumentative modes of phenomenology. One of the most effective is what I call the *rhetoric of concreteness*. This rhetorical strategy operates as a realist supplement to the method of phenomenology, which Levinas once identified as a "new mode of concreteness." The rhetoric of this new mode should be familiar to readers of Husserl's *The Crisis of European Sciences and Transcendental Phenomenology*, Heidegger's *Being and Time*, Merleau-Ponty's *Phenomenology of Perception*, Sartre's *Being and Nothingness*, Levinas's *Totality and Infinity*, Henry's *Material Phenomenology*, and countless other texts in the canon. It is the rhetorical adjunct to the phenomenologist's commitment to the "real," taken in a qualified sense to mean, roughly, phenomenally evident and experientially tangible.

The rhetoric of concreteness is mobilized by those intent on carrying on Husserl's endeavor, but discontent with his residual transcendental idealism and anxious to place philosophy right in the middle of everyday experience. While it is certainly present in Husserl himself, it is the hallmark of phenomenology's existential turn. It is made up of a constellation of terms intended to denote immediacy and corporeality, including "embodiment," "thrownness," "facticity," "existential," "immanence," "lifeworld," "concrete," "pregiven," "praxis," and the famous slogan "Back to the things themselves!" With the help of this rhetoric, phenomenology provides the solid ground for abstract thought and incorporeal ideas, as Levinas describes: it "encompasses and sustains the naïve abstractions of everyday consciousness, but also those of scientific consciousness, absorbed in the object, bogged down in the object."[1] The attachment to realism is palpable in phenomenology's rhetoric, but is this attachment philosophically justified? In other words, does the language of phenomenology really get us closer to the things themselves?

Take Sartre, for example. He consistently describes the self, others, and objects as "concrete" presences so that readers are reminded that he is talking about things that are right there in front of us, everyday real things, even if it sounds like he is repeating familiar idealist analyses. In the introduction to *Being and Nothingness* he sets up his phenomenological ontology in the same terms used by Berkeley to defend a radical antirealism. Sartre is well aware of this parallel, which is why he tempers his terms by insisting on the need for concrete analyses. He jettisons abstract epistemology, in favor of lived experience, as the foundation of our knowledge of being. But he also affirms that the being of consciousness is not the product of consciousness itself. It arises out of something prior to consciousness. He writes, "the absolute here is not the result of a logical construction on the ground of knowledge but the subject of the most concrete of experiences."[2] Consciousness, he asserts, "is a concrete being *sui generis*, not an abstract, unjustifiable relation of identity."[3] This is not a reiteration of the Kantian point, for with phenomenology, Sartre assures us, "we have escaped idealism."[4] The explicit renunciation of idealism echoes Merleau-Ponty's preface to the *Phenomenology*. Intentionality reveals to us that "consciousness is born *supported by* a being which is not itself."[5] Both the being of the *percipere* and the being of the *percipi* transcend the immanence of the subject/object correlation: they are, in Sartre's words, "transphenomenal,"[6] which means that they exist independently of one other. The evidence for this independence, however, is neither forthcoming nor pursued by Sartre.

The rhetoric of concreteness works to counteract the antirealism that haunts phenomenologists of every stripe. It is the antidote to the correlationist formula that structures so many of their texts and aligns them with Kantianism or Hegelianism. Although there are some who will insist that Husserl is not, or is not completely, an idealist, most commentators see him as a proxy for Descartes or German idealism. Husserl's most famous heirs, beginning with Heidegger, see him as an idealist whose philosophy needs to be injected with a deeper appreciation of the realities of history, language, the unconscious, and similar forces that operate at the margins of phenomenological seeing. At the very least they see him as someone whose phenomenology can serve as the idealist contrast to their own versions, which lean realist. There are many reasons for this, some of which I explored earlier in this text.

Even Husserl himself, in the preface to the English edition of his idealist treatise, *Ideas*, is wary of the antirealist implications of his philosophy. Whereas the body of this text is covered with countless declarations of the prejudices of the natural standpoint and its attendant naïve realism, Husserl feels obliged to assert that "the real world indeed exists," although he is quick to add that its essence "is relative to transcendental subjectivity" and "it can have its meaning as existing (*seiende*) reality only as the intentional meaning-product of transcendental subjectivity."[7] He is, of course, more emphatic about the essence and meaning of the objects of consciousness than he is about the substantial reality of the world independent of consciousness. All of the "arguments" of *Ideas* betray this emphasis, which is prescribed by the *epoché* and transcendental reduction, both of which are meant to neutralize our uncritical attitude toward reality and open up the phenomenological field to nonmetaphysical as well as nonphysical descriptions. Nevertheless, Husserl clearly does not wish to be seen as another Berkeley: "It is ... a fundamental error to suppose that perception ... fails to come into contact with the thing itself."[8] Husserl continues: "If anyone objects, with reference to these discussions of ours, that they transform the whole world into subjective illusion and throw themselves into the arms of an 'idealism such as Berkeley's', we can only make answer that he has not grasped the *meaning* of these discussions."[9]

This is a common rebuttal to criticism of phenomenology. Whenever it is characterized as idealist or conservative or outdated the critic is charged with failing to grasp the meaning of it. If they did, they would clearly see that Husserlian idealism ostensibly subtracts nothing "from the plenitude of the world's Being."[10] But is this not precisely what Berkeley insisted about his own subjective idealism, that it does not take anything away from the world but instead compels us to see that material things are actually immaterial ideas? If Husserl is here distancing himself from Berkeley, then he must regard the world as something *more* than ideal.

Better than anyone else in his tradition, Merleau-Ponty captures in language the tangibility of the things themselves. He does
this by returning to the evidence of perception, which cannot
fail to provide us with the richest, deepest, and densest possible
encounter with objects. Although operating against any form
of reductionism or naturalism, each one of his descriptions is
designed to deliver to our attention the physicality and vibrancy
of material things. His descriptions seem to bring us closer to the
material world because they evoke in us *what it is like* to be an
embodied creature among the things themselves, "incrusted into
[the] flesh" of the things themselves.[11] As he writes in the *Phenomenology of Perception*, "my body is not only an object among
all other objects ... but an object which is *sensitive to* all the rest,
which reverberates to all sounds, vibrates to all colours, and provides words with their primordial significance through the way
in which it receives them."[12] Merleau-Ponty's entire philosophy
insists that our bodies put us in touch with the real; it constantly
refers us to the immediate data of perception in an attempt to
render the objects of perception materially present to our minds.
He often insists that this anti-idealist impulse is already present in
Husserl's mature thinking about object-constitution, which
"becomes increasingly ... the means of unveiling a back side of
things that we have not constituted." On this view, transcendental phenomenology is merely the radicalization of classical idealism "pushed to the limit" beyond which is a world of "beings
beneath our idealizations and objectifications which secretly
nourish them."[13] These beings must be brought into the phenomenological fold. Just how to do this remains an open question,
although certainly the body is somehow involved.

The autonomous reality of perceptual objects is affirmed at a
number of points in Merleau-Ponty's texts. You only need to read
the preface to the *Phenomenology of Perception* or "The Primacy
of Perception" to see this. In the former he famously states that
the phenomenological reduction can never be completely performed, suggesting that the reality of the world cannot possibly
be contained by human consciousness or its machinations. It is
not merely the product of a synthetic act; it announces its priority in perception. This he calls the "lesson" of the reduction, the
condition of our facticity.[14] As he puts it in the *Phenomenology*:
"The world is there *before* any possible analysis of mine, and it
would be artificial to make it the outcome of a series of syntheses

which link, in the first place sensations, then aspects of the object corresponding to different perspectives, when both are nothing but products of analysis, with *no sort of prior reality*."[15] Here again is Sartre making a similar point:

> Even if I wished to reduce this table to a synthesis of subjective impressions, I must at least remark that it reveals itself *qua* table through this synthesis, that it is the transcendent limit of the synthesis, the reason for it and its end. The table is *before* knowledge and can not be identified with the knowledge which we have of it; otherwise it would be consciousness – *i.e.*, pure immanence – and it would disappear as table.[16]

Phenomenology is not meant to analyze or explain this presynthetic world, it is meant to describe it as it is lived through. It should "[make] explicit our primordial knowledge of the 'real', of … our perception of the world as that upon which the idea of truth is forever based," as Merleau-Ponty says.[17] We are capable of doing this because what we perceive is not some representation of the world, but the *world itself*. When I reach out to touch a lamp whose back side is invisible to me, I do not grab an image or an illusion: I grab a real thing.[18] Hence, objects really do exist … *for us*. Otherwise put, the "intentional objects" (Husserl) of perception are the "in-itself-for-us" (Merleau-Ponty). The reality of the in itself is, to be sure, qualified by the phenomenologist's scare quotes. The real, then, is never detached from human consciousness. What the phenomenologist identifies as real is always at most "real." As Harman points out, Merleau-Ponty is a staunch champion of the world as distinct from human perception. And yet, "as usual with all phenomenologists, we also sense pangs of guilt in Merleau-Ponty about pushing this too far and slipping into some sort of naïve version of scientific realism." Despite his sympathies, "Merleau-Ponty remains a philosopher of perception rather than of objects."[19]

There is further evidence of perception's ability to encounter, paradoxically, a world that transcends perception. Following Husserl, Merleau-Ponty maintains that consciousness reveals objects as the "infinite sum of an indefinite series of perspectival views."[20] Recall that Husserl believes we can intuit the essence of an object, despite our inability to gather all of its perspectives together at once. Merleau-Ponty interprets this to mean that each of our viewpoints entails a "deformation" of the object, which is a consequence of the object being "'real'."[21] The implication here is that there is some way for the object to be apart from how it is perceived, but that we are forever barred from accessing this object as it is apart from us. It is, moreover, impossible for me to even imagine this object without deforming it. Objects given to perception always "recede" beyond their immediately given aspects; they are more than any one of their profiles. Yet we see them *as* wholes. This is what is called the "paradox of immanence and transcendence in perception." "Immanence, because the perceived object cannot be foreign to him who perceives; transcendence, because it always contains something more than what is actually given."[22] It is difficult to see how this "more" can be compatible with the given if it is somehow other than the given, and yet the given is all that exists. It should also be emphasized that Merleau-Ponty's view of the "real" object seems to be that it is more than any of its profiles, but nothing more than the "indefinite" sum of those profiles, which is to say, its reality is a product of how it is perceived. Would it not be more appropriate for a realist to say that the reality of a thing is how *the thing* "perceives"?

Instead of accepting this simply as a paradoxical point about perception, Harman takes the recession of objects as a clue to their autonomous withdrawal beyond the finite reach of perception. Prima facie this sounds like a recapitulation of Merleau-Ponty's view. But it is decidedly not. To grasp the methodological difference between phenomenology and Harman's speculative realism it is crucial to recognize that the autonomous reality of objects is something that cannot be affirmed by Merleau-Ponty or any other phenomenologist. Like Husserl, Merleau-Ponty has pledged his faith to intentional objects, the object as it is directly intended in perception. An intentional object is apprehended through innumerable profiles that only partially reveal its unity. They are encrusted with qualities that attract attention and lend the object a "concrete" density which makes the intentional object feel like it is right there before our eyes. This is what Harman calls the "stubborn tenacity of the intentional object, which forever resists the machinations of the ego or absolute knowing."[23] The object's profiles signal beyond themselves to a nonphenomenal world of hands-free interobjectivity, the world into which *real* objects "withdraw" from the intentional relations that "caricature" them.[24] The phenomenologists recognize and often affirm the duality opened up by intentional objects, but unfortunately their method bars us from speculating down the rabbit hole into which objects recede. Harman's "object-oriented" perspective, by contrast, "begins by providing us with a world of ghostly realities that never come into contact with each other, a universe packed full of elusive substances stuffed into mutually exclusive vacuums."[25] Harman delivers us real objects because he is free to speculate. No degree of drenching in sensuousness – not even the "baroque world"[26] of Husserl – can do such a thing. We will return to Harman at greater length in Chapter 4.

If we attribute sufficient importance to the role that methodology plays in philosophy, then I think we must always remain on guard when a phenomenologist begins to talk about prereflective, prepersonal, preperceptual, and, above all, transcendent things. And this for the same reason that we might, for instance, find indecorous Kant's attachment to the noumenal realm. Why can we not see adumbrations as a series of asignifying images (Bergson) or mere ideas (Berkeley), rather than as a series of necessarily linked profiles which refer us to an autonomous object that resides beyond any and all of its profiles? Is not Hegel's lesson that we do not need a thing in itself to explain why phenomena differ from themselves and elude conceptual closure? Reiterating Hegel's point, Lyotard notes that Husserl's prepredicative *Lebenswelt* occupies the same position as the noumenon in Kant: "Insofar as this originary lifeworld is prepredicative, all predication and discourse certainly implies it, but equally lacks it, and cannot properly say anything about it. Here again ... *Glauben* replaces *Wissen*, and the silence of faith puts an end to all of man's dialogue concerning Being."[27] These questions must be asked.

Let me just suggest here that if phenomenological method requires anything, it requires a commitment to phenomena, that is, to what is presented immanently to consciousness. If phenomena appear to signify beyond themselves, this signification is meaningful only within consciousness and whatever excess it points to must always be understood as an excess relative to the finite limits of cognition. *If* it gives arguments, phenomenology argues on these grounds. Accordingly, it is obliged to withhold any assertions that reach beyond immanence, for this would entail a relapse into metaphysics. And yet it often speaks

of objects that recede from the consciousnesses that deform
them. Such language seems to indicate a desire for the comfort
of metaphysical commitments.

The phenomenological attachment to the real requires, yet
lacks, metaphysical justification, for such a thing is prohibited
by the authority of the phenomena. The lack of justification is
therefore filled by the constellation of concepts that includes
"immanence," "worldhood," "field," "facticity," "givenness,"
"*il y a*," "wholly other," "*Lebenswelt*," "pregiven," "wild" or
"brute" being, and so forth. Each of these terms in its own way
is meant to suggest that the human subject is not the source of its
world, that reality is not entirely constructed or conditioned by
human perception, but *given* by something other than ourselves.
The post-Husserlian commitment to the real is, perhaps, captured
in a single term around which crystallizes the phenomenologist's
rhetoric of realism: *concrete*. This is the term often chosen to
denote the here-and-now of phenomenological investigation, as
opposed to the abstract or merely historical or conceptual matters of classical philosophy. In the discussion portion following
the presentation of "The Primacy of Perception," a certain M.
Lenoir commends Merleau-Ponty for his "resolutely realistic
attitude." When asked about his relation to the realist tradition,
the phenomenologist boldly dismisses the realist label as a hin-
drance to philosophical progress, asserting that he "would prefer
to answer a *concrete* question rather than a question bearing on
the interrelations of historical doctrines."[28] Phenomenology, we
are to understand, does not negotiate with established doctrines:
it solves philosophical problems by interrogating things on the
ground, that is, the concrete world.

Writing under the influence of Heidegger the later Husserl
deploys the rhetoric of concreteness to characterize the presence
of the lifeworld. He writes the following in *The Crisis*:

> Though the peculiar accomplishment of our modern objective sci-
> ence may still not be understood, nothing changes the fact that it is
> a validity for the life-world, arising out of particular activities, and
> that it belongs itself to the concreteness of the life-world. Thus in
> any case, for the sake of clarifying this and all other acquisitions of
> human activity, the concrete life-world must first be taken into con-
> sideration; and it must be considered in terms of the truly concrete
> universality ...[29]

Reading this passage, one gets the impression that its author is attempting to bring the materiality of the lifeworld into existence by incantation. As if repetition of the magic word could solidify the density of the lifeworld as it is described. Say the name three times into the mirror of nature and Nature itself will appear in its absolute materiality.

Merleau-Ponty sees the task of his *Phenomenology* as "determining and expressing in concrete form" the *Lebenswelt* of Husserl and the *Umwelt* of Heidegger, and his readers are left to wonder whether he felt that this could only be achieved through a strategic conjuration of our immersion in the sensuous folds of perception.[30] His later, unfinished ontology insists on the tangibility of being: "We must not think the flesh starting from substances, from body and spirit ... we must think it ... as an element, as the concrete emblem of a general manner of being."[31]

The pervasive rhetoric of concreteness – to be sure it spans the entire corpus of phenomenology and its commentary – is mobilized to assure the reader that when phenomenology delivers the things themselves, these things are certifiably real things. The effect aimed at, however, falls short for the same reason that nature writing, or what Timothy Morton calls "ecomimesis," fails to deliver nature uncontaminated by the poetic devices of the nature writing genre. As Morton argues, ecomimesis attempts to transcend its literary and discursive frame through a "vivid evocation of atmosphere"[32] meant to offer up experience, not merely as it is lived immediately, but as it exists materially. Ecomimesis employs a "situatedness" rhetoric meant to evoke "where I am." Morton cites Thoreau's *Walden* to illustrate: "When I wrote the following pages ... I lived alone, in the woods, a mile from any neighbor, in a house which I had built myself, on the shore of Walden Pond, in Concord, Massachusetts, and earned my living by the labor of my hands only."[33] In his scene-setting it is as if Thoreau, by zeroing in on the precise coordinates of Walden, were trying to transubstantiate this place into words – only to discover that the finer his descriptions get, the more the actual Walden vanishes into the linguistic figures he chooses to describe it. The same fate awaits the phenomenologist, who can never get close enough to the things themselves.

As a species of ecomimesis, the rhetoric of concreteness works as what Morton calls "an authenticating device."[34] It says: *I have seen this mailbox, this lamp, this carpet. They are real things, not mere fabrications of my mind. Even more, I have lived among these things!* These things are in part real because they belong to a surrounding milieu which can never be circumscribed by a subject because of the finite perspective of the subject. To exhibit this milieu ecomimesis conscripts what Morton calls a "poetics of ambience:" "Ambience denotes a sense of a circumambient, or surrounding, *world*. It suggests something material and physical, though somewhat intangible, as if space itself had a material aspect."[35] The opening lines of Merleau-Ponty's chapter on "The Cogito" in *Phenomenology of Perception* deftly apply the ambient poetic strategy. This enables Merleau-Ponty to set the tone of his upcoming analysis while simultaneously performing the very displacement of the cogito, from the mental into the corporeal, that he traces in his yet-to-be-carried-out analysis. He writes: "I am thinking of the Cartesian *cogito*, wanting to finish this work, feeling the coolness of the paper under my hand, and perceiving the trees of the boulevard through the window. My life is constantly thrown headlong into transcendent things, and passes wholly outside me."[36] This device is also exploited by Levinas – against Husserl and Heidegger – to capture the affective or elemental dimension of earthly dwelling. He writes about how human being

> gets a foothold in the elemental by a side already appropriated: a field cultivated by me, the sea in which I fish and moor my boats, the forest in which I cut wood; and all these acts, all this labor, refer to the domicile ... Man plunges into the elemental from the domicile ... He is *within* what he possesses, such that we shall be able to say that the domicile, condition for all property, renders the inner life possible. The I is thus at home with itself. Through the home our relation with space as distance and extension is substituted for the simple "bathing in the element."[37]

As Harman has explored in *Guerrilla Metaphysics*, Levinas's entire account of dwelling attempts to communicate how we "depend on a surplus of reality that comes from beyond the sphere of intelligible meaning." The elemental names the qualitative medium that surrounds my body and upon which my sensibility nourishes itself. Its concreteness is evinced in the feeling of existence that overflows any possible representation.[38] Levinas writes: "One does not know, one lives sensible qualities: the green of these leaves, the red of this sunset."[39] Perhaps more than any other of his cohort, Levinas demonstrates what it *feels* like to be alive. He is at pains to convey the concrete conditions of a subjectivity that would otherwise be mistakenly regarded as the originator of the world it lives from.

Like ecomimesis, the rhetoric of concreteness gestures outside the field in which it writes. It represents an attempt, on the one hand, to position the writing subject within the thicket of its object, whether the natural environment, the equipmental field, or the elemental atmosphere. On the other hand, it is an attempt to extricate the object from the very correlation which renders it as a phenomenon present to human consciousness. The concreteness trope is meant to accomplish the extrication of the object, the winning of its material presence. Methodologically abstaining from the game of metaphysical speculation, the phenomenologist with a taste for realism substitutes a rhetoric of realism for the arguments of his predecessors. After Kant's critical project this does seem to be a legitimate mode of access to the world beyond my horizon. But does it truly get us outside the subject/object correlation? Kant's project circumscribed the limit of reason (the negative aspect of the critique), thus invalidating truth claims about the real beyond the norms of intersubjective cognition. But if you ask a phenomenologist if objects exist when no one is around to cognize them, they will most likely say they do. Or, perhaps, they will say that such a question relies on the senseless disjunctions of classical metaphysics, now long discarded by phenomenological method. At best one must be agnostic about the mind-independent real.

No doubt phenomenology invokes and evokes an intersubjective field, a world unconstituted by thought – a nature and a material universe which cannot be reduced to an *ego cogito*. It does not, however, establish their material existence. That would require something foundational like Descartes's God. "But," argues Morton, "in many ways [phenomenology] offers a sense of what Cartesianism 'feels like'," without actually getting outside of Cartesianism.[40] By cutting itself off from metaphysical speculation, phenomenology confines itself methodologically to life within the subject/object correlation. It cannot transgress the limits of the correlation, and so remains bound to conjure the real rhetorically while being careful not to commit to anything more than what it accesses phenomenally. It is, as a friend once put it, a rhetoric in search of an ontology.[41] Ambient poetics names this rhetoric and provides the most useful tool for thinking about what realism means in phenomenology. It helps us make sense of the apprehensive way in which phenomenologists avail themselves of the "real" without appearing naïve or dogmatic. But why, if phenomenology is supposed to get us beyond the idealism/realism debate, continue to invoke the reality of the things themselves?

It is, I think, impossible to enter the phenomenological standpoint without engaging its poetics. The rhetoric of phenomenology forms an essential dimension of its style of philosophizing. Gaston Bachelard is simply the most striking example of this style.[42]

Whatever its precise form, the initiation into phenomenology effects a suspension of metaphysics. And yet the evidence of phenomenology is complicit with the antirealist streak of post-Kantian philosophy. The closest it will get to the real is the "in itself for us," although it often invokes or conjures the reality of the nonhuman. Phenomenology, therefore, can only be a kind of antirealism, for it is a loyal adherent to what Harman calls the "philosophy of access" and an exemplary form of correlationism.[43] As such, when a phenomenologist offers us statements about extraphenomenal, transphenomenal, or nonphenomenal entities we should be quick to point out that such statements represent a breach of the phenomenological contract and cannot be made from within the phenomenological standpoint. This explains why someone like Harman can construct a metaphysics of objects from Heidegger's broken hammer, but Heidegger himself *qua phenomenologist*, could not do such a thing. Their methodological and metaphysical commitments are not only different, but in many respects opposed. This is also why we should be cautious about the phenomenologist who finds evidence for God or absolute otherness in the things themselves, while at the same time recognizing that it is a correlationist logic that enables such findings to qualify as legitimate beliefs.

Correlationism insists on the primacy of the correlation between thinking and being. Neither thinking nor being can be accessed independently of one another. Considered apart, they are meaningless. For the correlationist any philosophy that is not dogmatically realist – including those that suspend the "naturalistic attitude" or "perceptual faith" – instantiates correlationism. In Meillassoux's words:

> Correlationism consists in disqualifying the claim that it is possible to consider the realms of subjectivity and objectivity independently of one another. Not only does it become necessary to insist that we never grasp the "in itself," in isolation from its relation to the subject, but it also becomes necessary to maintain that we can never grasp a subject that would not always-already be related to an object.[44]

Whenever the phenomenologist – whether Merleau-Ponty or Husserl or Hegel – claims that we only grasp the in itself for us, he affirms the "unsurpassable character of the correlation."[45] Consequently, whenever thought or language reach out beyond the horizon of the world, attempting to transcend the immanence of consciousness, this transcendence can only be relative to the correlation. It is, indeed, the "transcendence in immanence" of the phenomenologist. In Meillassoux's view this is no transcendence at all, since it is not an entry into another world so much as an exploration of "the two faces of what remains a face to face – like a coin which only knows its own obverse."[46]

As we have seen, Husserl, Heidegger, and Merleau-Ponty are each committed to the view that phenomenology is a method, a "how," of getting at the things themselves. Their commitments vary considerably, but there is a common thread between them. Meillassoux names that thread: correlationism. He specifies that in each of these thinkers, especially the latter two, what we find is a "strong" version of correlationism that prohibits the thought of the in itself. Phenomenology restricts the thinkable to what is *given* within the correlation, that is, given to us or intended. Givenness is equiprimordial with being; being just *is* however it manifests itself to whomever thinks it.[47] It is absurd to believe, after Kant, that it can be otherwise.[48]

As Ray Brassier makes clear, correlationism need not entail a privileging of the transcendental ego over being – "it can just as easily replace it with 'being-in-the-world', 'perception', 'sensibility', 'intuition', 'affect', or even 'flesh'. Indeed, all of these terms have featured in the specifically phenomenological varieties of correlationism."[49] He adds: the "increasing 'corporealization' of the transcendental" in phenomenology does nothing to threaten the strength of correlation-ist truth.[50] Any knowledge of how things stand with being outside the correlation is constantly threatened by skeptical criticism. Hence correlationism's complicity with fideism and the theological turn in phenomenology.[51]

Theological phenomenology, like fideism, makes religion out of reason by undermining the legitimacy of metaphysics and, disturb-ingly, opening philosophy up to mysticism and fanaticism.[52] These remain live options because both schools absolutize facticity and, as a result, they can exploit the limits of reason to make all sorts of claims about what lies outside the correlation. Meillassoux rec-ognizes that to rein in fideist fanaticism, it is the contingency of facticity that must be absolutized. If this can be demonstrated, then the contingency of the correlationist circle will be exposed as a necessary presupposition of correlationism. Meillassoux's specula-tive materialism carries out this demonstration, thereby displacing the necessity of the for us and establishing the necessity of the in itself.[53] Metaphysics is, as a result, placed back on the table.

If the realist pronouncements of phenomenology are invalidated by its fidelity to correlationism, then perhaps its only hope for sur-vival is an enthusiastic embrace of radical antirealism. This would necessarily entail, I suppose, not a return to Husserl, but the exalta-tion of Hegel as the true master of phenomenology.[54] Or, perhaps more curiously, a rigorous retooling of Berkeleyan idealism. Either figure would permit phenomenologists to keep their methodologi-cal commitments. Many of them would see this as an absurd proj-ect or a slanderous portrayal of Husserlian phenomenology, but why see it as such? Why not regard the world as an (inter)subjec-tive representation, as Kant does? Some will reply that the world resists such a reduction. To which we might reply that a phenom-enal contestation is no proof of the noumenal. If it is argued that *any* viable philosophy must necessarily be a form of correlationism, and consequently all of this talk about the mind-independent real is without ground, then it becomes incumbent upon the advocate of correlationism to demonstrate why Husserl does not ultimately recapitulate Hegelian phenomenology.

The downside of the antirealist prospect, however, is that if phenomenology does choose to raise the antirealist flag, then it will have to sacrifice its theological faction, which presumably could not tolerate a God whose only necessity is his contingency. That is, a God who only *might* exist one day in the future.[55]

Notes

1. Levinas, "Nonintentional Consciousness," 124.
2. Jean-Paul Sartre, *Being and Nothingness: A Phenomenological Essay on Ontology*, trans. Hazel E. Barnes (New York: Citadel Press, 1956), lvi.
3. Sartre, *Being and Nothingness*, 215.
4. Sartre, *Being and Nothingness*, lvii.
5. Sartre, *Being and Nothingness*, lxi.
6. Sartre, *Being and Nothingness*, li.
7. Husserl, *Ideas*, 14.
8. Husserl, *Ideas*, §43.
9. Husserl, *Ideas*, §55.
10. Husserl, *Ideas*, §55.
11. Maurice Merleau-Ponty, "Eye and Mind," in *The Primacy of Perception*, 163.
12. Merleau-Ponty, *Phenomenology of Perception*, 236.
13. Maurice Merleau-Ponty, "The Philosopher and His Shadow," in *Signs*, trans. Richard C. McCleary (Evanston: Northwestern University Press, 1964), 180.
14. Merleau-Ponty, *Phenomenology of Perception*, xiv, xvii.
15. Merleau-Ponty, *Phenomenology of Perception*, x, added emphasis.
16. Sartre, *Being and Nothingness*, lvii, added emphasis.
17. Merleau-Ponty, *Phenomenology of Perception*, xvi.
18. Maurice Merleau-Ponty, "The Primacy of Perception," in *The Primacy of Perception*, 13–14.
19. Graham Harman, *Guerrilla Metaphysics* (Chicago: Open Court, 2005), 50.
20. Merleau-Ponty, "Primacy of Perception," 15.
21. Merleau-Ponty, "Primacy of Perception," 16.
22. Merleau-Ponty, "Primacy of Perception," 16.
23. Graham Harman, *Towards Speculative Realism* (Winchester: Zero Books, 2010), 152.
24. "Withdrawal" and "caricature" are technical terms in Harman's philosophy. Heidegger's broken hammer is the emblematic signal of the netherworld of objects as well as what induced Harman to develop his own metaphysics.
25. Harman, *Guerrilla Metaphysics*, 75–6.
26. Merleau-Ponty, "The Philosopher and His Shadow," 181.
27. Jean-François Lyotard, *Phenomenology*, trans. Brian Beakley (Albany: SUNY Press, 1991), 67.

28. Merleau-Ponty, "Primacy of Perception," 31–2.

29. Edmund Husserl, *The Crisis of European Sciences and Transcendental Phenomenology*, trans. David Carr (Evanston: Northwestern University Press, 1970), 133. Jean-Luc Marion employs a rhetoric of *givenness* that, in its attempt to evoke a certain realism in phenomenology, parallels the rhetoric of concreteness.

30. Merleau-Ponty, *Phenomenology of Perception*, viii.

31. Merleau-Ponty, *The Visible and the Invisible*, 147.

32. Timothy Morton, *Ecology without Nature: Rethinking Environmental Aesthetics* (Cambridge, MA: Harvard University Press, 2007), 31.

33. Morton, *Ecology without Nature*, 31, 32.

34. Morton, *Ecology without Nature*, 33.

35. Morton, *Ecology without Nature*, 33.

36. Merleau-Ponty, *Phenomenology of Perception*, 369.

37. Levinas, *Totality and Infinity*, 131–2.

38. Harman, *Guerrilla Metaphysics*, 36–8.

39. Levinas, *Totality and Infinity*, 135.

40. Morton, *Ecology without Nature*, 135. Merleau-Ponty describes the cogito as a thought "which *feels* itself rather than *sees* itself, which searches after clarity rather than possesses it, which creates truth rather than finds it" ("Primacy of Perception," 22).

41. Here I must extend my gratitude to Adam Hutchinson.

42. See, for instance, Gaston Bachelard, *The Poetics of Space*, trans. Maria Jolas (Boston: Beacon, 1994) and *The Poetics of Reverie*, trans. Daniel Russell (Boston: Beacon, 1969). Dylan Trigg takes up as well as anyone the spirit of Bachelard in *The Memory of Place: A Phenomenology of the Uncanny* (Athens, OH: Ohio University Press, 2012).

43. See Chapter 4 below. For another compelling defense of this thesis, see Rockmore, *Kant and Phenomenology*. On antirealism in continental philosophy, see Braver, *A Thing of This World*.

44. Meillassoux, *After Finitude*, 5.

45. Meillassoux, *After Finitude*, 5.

46. Meillassoux, *After Finitude*, 7.

47. Someone like Marion, however, might argue that the given precedes being (if not temporally, at least ontologically), whereas Hegel would see the objectivity of being as isomorphic with its givenness to subjectivity.

48. For a list of realist absurdities, see Meillassoux, *After Finitude*, 14.

49. Ray Brassier, "The Enigma of Realism," *Collapse* II (2007), 19.

50. Brassier, "The Enigma of Realism," 29.

51. Meillassoux, *After Finitude*, 41, 48.

52. See Meillassoux, *After Finitude*, 46–9. This is not to say that there cannot be a phenomenology of mystical experience or religious life or prayer, for example, but that a transcendent God cannot be constituted in immanence. On the link between phenomenology and mysticism, see Anthony Steinbock, *Phenomenology and Mysticism* (Bloomington: Indiana University Press, 2009).

53. Meillassoux, *After Finitude*, 54; Brassier, "The Enigma of Realism," 38.

54. On phenomenology (Heidegger, Merleau-Ponty) as a variant of Hegelian objective idealism, see Braver, *A Thing of This* World, 185.

55. This is the thesis of Meillassoux's much-anticipated, yet still unpublished, *The Divine Inexistence*.

3

Phenomenology as Strong Correlationism

Many phenomenologists will fight tooth and nail against the claim that phenomenology necessarily ends, or should end, in idealism. They will argue that this claim completely misses the radical program of phenomenology, or they will assert that phenomenology operates outside the idealism/realism schema and, consequently, cannot be idealism. However the phenomenologist resists the charge of idealism, their resistance will be premised on the claim that phenomenology does not recognize the subject/object dualism as fundamental, but rather subject and object always come as an inseparable pair. Their respective independence is a secondary abstraction from the phenomenological experience from which philosophy must depart. As we have seen, Quentin Meillassoux has a name for the philosopher who insists on the irreducible dependency of subject and object, thinking and being: *the correlationist*. Correlationism, once again, is "the idea according to which we only ever have access to the correlation between thinking and being, and never either term considered apart from the other."[1] Correlationism claims that subjectivity and objectivity cannot be analyzed apart from one another because both terms are always already intertwined or internally related. Phenomenologists should not be scandalized by the characterization of their basic standpoint as correlationist.[2]

Correlationism has been the default attitude – or what Ray Brassier dubs "the reigning *doxa* of post-metaphysical philosophy,"[3] by which he means philosophy after Heidegger and Wittgenstein – of most continental, as well as some analytic, philosophy since Kant. It is perhaps because Meillassoux has given it a name that his *After Finitude* has proven so attractive, not only for young academics but even for established veterans. Correlationism comes in several different forms, some of which are idealist, and each of which privileges some species of the correlate. In earlier chapters we noted that Meillassoux regards phenomenology as "strong" correlationism. The purpose of this chapter is to unpack what this means for phenomenology's realist aspirations. As we will see, for Meillassoux, phenomenology's metaphysical agnosticism effectively aligns it with idealism, even if it is not idealism itself, as I argued in earlier chapters. Its correlationism also aligns phenomenology with a fideist irrationalism. To see how these allegiances are forged we will focus here on three primary concepts analyzed by Meillassoux: correlationism, fideism, and factiality. While his discussion of these concepts in *After Finitude* and elsewhere is not always framed with exclusive reference to phenomenology, phenomenology is always one of Meillassoux's opponents, whether named or unnamed.

The Promise of the "Great Outdoors"

In the spring of 2012 I met a phenomenologist colleague at a café in the small, conservative town of Grove City, Pennsylvania. It was our second meeting to discuss Meillassoux's *After Finitude*. Given the political and religious composition of our meeting place, there was an air of subversion to our discussion and I was reminded of what attracted me to philosophy in the first place. I suspect that many readers of Meillassoux's little book are similarly reminded, and this in part explains its rapid success. Clearly impatient with Meillassoux's project, my phenomenologist friend asked how we could know anything that lies beyond the scope of what we can know and, moreover, why we would care about such things. What does it have to do with us? My friend is a committed correlationist not so much because he does not believe in the thing in itself – and that to attempt knowledge of it entails a "pragmatic contradiction"[4] – but because he believes the noumenal (or the absolute) has nothing to do with us. This is precisely the anthropocentric conceit of correlationism: whatever is not indexed to human experience, says the correlationist, is either meaningless or not worth knowing. Or, perhaps better said: it is not worth knowing *because* it is apparently meaningless.

The problem is that this supposition reduces the real to the meaningful, as if our finite capacity to make sense of the universe encompassed the totality of what the universe is. In Meillassoux's view, the correlationist's allegiance to finitude is mistaken in two

important ways: 1) it fails to see that human knowledge is capable
of accessing the primary qualities of the absolute, and 2) it fails
to account for the possibility of scientific knowledge about what
he calls "the ancestral." In order to demonstrate that we can have
knowledge of the absolute, and how it is possible to legitimate scientific statements about the ancestral, or "ancestral statements,"
it is necessary to see how Meillassoux radicalizes correlationism
into a position that he identifies as *speculative materialism*.

A common opinion about speculative realism is that it unilater-
ally opposes correlationism in all its forms. While it may be true
of the other three Goldsmiths speculative realists, this is not quite
true of Meillassoux. What Meillassoux attempts is not a rejection
of correlationism, but an isolation of its most formidable species,
not so that he can destroy it, but so he can push it to the point at
which its methodology opens thought to what he calls "the great
outdoors." This phrase must not be associated with Husserl's
slogan "back to the things themselves"[5] any more than it should
be confused with a similar trope discussed by Meillassoux, "the
Rich Elsewhere."[6] The latter is a rhetorical maneuver deployed by
those who reject the correlationist argument on the grounds that it
reduces the boundless beauty and complexity of the world's experiences to the narrow view of human experience portrayed in so
many books of philosophy. It proceeds by describing or evoking
this complexity, as if this were enough to silence the correlationist.
This maneuver is reminiscent of what I called in the last chapter the
"rhetoric of concreteness" and it is just as prevalent in phenomenology. As Meillassoux points out, however, the rhetoric of the
Rich Elsewhere does nothing to refute the truth of correlationism;
it merely dismisses and overwhelms it. Meillassoux, by contrast,
takes on correlationism directly and at its strongest. This is the
only rational road to the great outdoors.

Of the several species of correlationism that fall along
"Meillassoux's Spectrum," we need only focus here on two: weak
correlationism and strong correlationism. The weak form of correlationism is derived from Kant. It holds that, while the in itself
is unknowable, it is nevertheless *thinkable*. For Meillassoux, following Kant's first *Critique*, this means that thinking the in itself
does not entail a contradiction. Meillassoux writes, "Although
we cannot apply categorical cognition to the thing in itself, the
latter remains subject to the logical condition that is the prereq-
uisite for all thought."[7] This entails, for Kant, that the in itself
is noncontradictory and that the in itself exists, because without

it we would be left with appearances (phenomena) but nothing that appears, which is contradictory. Weak correlationism, then, allows thinking and the absolute to make contact, but "proscribes any knowledge of the thing in itself (any application of the categories to the supersensible)."[8] Meillassoux remains skeptical about the legitimacy of this Kantian move, which "miraculously" steps beyond the realm of the phenomenal in order to say something determinate about the noumenal. In this respect Meillassoux is sympathetic to the Hegelian critique of Kant.[9]

Meillassoux finds the strong model of correlationism to be a much more tenacious opponent, as well as a potential ally in his own fight. It is the model he associates with phenomenology in both its transcendental and existential forms, and insofar as he uses it as a means to his own speculative materialism he can be said to bear a certain debt to phenomenology. This debt is two-fold: Meillassoux finds that phenomenology not only rigorously sticks to the evidence of the phenomenal world, more so than Kant, it also endorses a kind of intellectual intuition (at least in its Husserlian variant) that Meillassoux will find necessary for guaranteeing knowledge of the absolute.

The basic formulation of strong correlationism holds that not only is the absolute (in itself) unknowable, it is also *unthinkable*. Or, in Meillassoux's words, "the strong model of correlationism maintains not only that it is illegitimate to claim that we can *know* the in-itself, but *also* that it is illegitimate to claim that we can at least *think* it."[10] This entails that thinking the in itself is precisely contradictory, and therefore impossible. The nature of this contradiction is familiar to those of us who are habituated to believe that as soon as you think the in itself you convert the in itself into a thought. This is one of Merleau-Ponty's chief lessons: when it comes to perception, the very ground of all knowledge, it is possible to perceive the in itself, but this in itself is always only the in itself *for us*. Or, as he puts it in "The Primacy of Perception:" "I cannot even for an instant imagine an object in itself."[11] Any attempt to represent the in itself in its pure form leads us into a performative contradiction of the following, Fichtean type, given by Meillassoux at Goldsmiths:

No X without givenness of X, and no theory about X without a pos- iting of X. If you speak about something, you speak about something that is given to you, and posited by you. Consequently, the sentence: "X is", means: "X is the correlate of thinking" in a Cartesian sense.

That is: X is the correlate of an affection, or a perception, or a conception, or of any subjective act. To be is to be a correlate, a term of a correlation. And in particular, when you claim to think any X, you must posit this X, which cannot then be separated from this special act of positing, of conception. That is why it is impossible to conceive an absolute X, *i.e.*, an X which would be essentially separate from a subject. We can't know what the reality of the object in itself is because we can't distinguish between properties which are supposed to belong to the object and properties belonging to the subjective access to the object.[12]

Thinking the absolute effectively renders the absolute relative to thought, and therefore undermines its absoluteness. Whenever the realist philosopher claims to have attained knowledge of the subject-independent in itself, what he or she does is engage in a viciously circular pragmatic contradiction that effectively converts the thing in itself into a concept of the thing in itself.[13] Meillassoux calls this the "correlationist circle." He sees it as not only a simple argument, but an exceptionally powerful one as well.[14]

For the strong correlationist, then, we are necessarily condemned to understand the world only as it presents itself from within the correlation. This is what Heidegger refers to as our facticity. In *Being and Time* he writes that "the 'factuality' of the fact of one's own Dasein is at bottom quite different ontologically from the factual occurrence of some kind of mineral, for example. Whenever Dasein is, it is a Fact; and the factuality of such a Fact is what we shall call Dasein's '*facticity*'."[15] Dasein's factical way of encountering the world is ordered by a collection of what Heidegger calls "*existentiales*," or "*existentialia*," which are unpacked in the analytic of Dasein. *Existentialia* are analogous to the Kantian categories of the understanding in the sense that they are responsible for the specific invariant way in which Dasein experiences and "copes" with the world, as Dreyfus puts it. Heidegger continues: "The concept of 'facticity' implies that an entity 'within-the-world' has Being-in-the-world in such a way that it can understand itself as bound up in its 'destiny' with the Being of those entities which it encounters within its own world."[16] For Meillassoux, what is significant to note about the Kantian categories and Heidegger's *existentialia* is that they can only be described, they cannot be grounded. Just like Wittgenstein says about the logical form of the world, it is something that can be specified, but whence it came is a matter that must be passed over in silence.[17]

Epistemologically speaking, the correlationist circle's inescapability is cited as the reason phenomenological method restricts its scope to what is given within the correlation, which includes the principle of intentionality that sutures subject and object together. It is our embodied, embedded, historical condition. It is the condition of finitude. The assertion of the correlation's primacy is what Meillassoux calls the "first decision" of all correlationism. "This decision alone," he writes, "suffices to disqualify every absolute of the *realist* or *materialist* variety."[18] Against the correlationist both of these positions assert that there is an in itself that exists apart from human thought or subjectivity, and that it is possible to think this in itself. Before examining how Meillassoux demonstrates this possibility it is necessary see how strong correlationism avoids absolute idealism of the Hegelian brand.

What Meillassoux calls the "second decision" of strong correlationism is the rejection of the metaphysical strategy that absolutizes the correlation. This is Hegel's strategy against Kant. Since the Kantian in itself is unknowable, and its thinkability – according to the strong correlationist – entails a performative contradiction, it seems that it would be better to simply discard the in itself altogether. When this is done the only thing left is to hypostatize the subject/object correlation in one of its common forms. This results in a metaphysics of spirit (Hegel), nature (Schelling), will (Schopenhauer, Nietzsche), perception (Bergson, Merleau-Ponty), consciousness (Husserl), life (Deleuze), and so forth.[19] Unlike Kant, Hegel maintains that the structure of the correlate (whichever one we choose) is not only describable, but deducible from within the correlate. So, while he maintains that the in itself is meaningless and unthinkable, he simultaneously holds that the absolute is thinkable as the factical conditions of the correlate. Only the correlate absolutely exists. As Brassier explains, however, Hegel uses the norms of knowledge to ground knowledge, a gesture Meillassoux sees as illegitimate because these norms only pertain to the phenomenal. As soon as the strong correlationist rejects the absolutization of the correlation (as a necessary entity), he has no other choice but to affirm the contingency of correlation.[20]

Meillassoux answers this line of reasoning by pointing out to the absolute idealist and strong correlationist that the unthinkability of the in itself does not entail that only the correlate exists. Instead, what it implies is that "it is unthinkable that the unthinkable should be impossible."[21] It is true that from within the correlation we have no knowledge of why the correlation exists. But we also have no knowledge of what is possible outside the correlation or what can happen *to* the correlation. Its whence and whither is without reason. We only know *that* it exists. This tells us nothing about whether or not it has to be as it is, or whether or not anything lies outside it. A fortiori, it is not necessary to absolutize the correlate. It is, on the contrary, necessary to absolutize facticity itself. This means that Meillassoux must show how, from a perspective internal to the correlate, the correlate is *necessarily contingent*. This is the absolute he seeks to deduce.

Whereas Hegel regards the correlate as absolute, the phenomenologist replies that in fact the opposite is true. It is not possible to establish the absolute necessity of the correlate because it is not possible to think the absolute from within the relative perspective afforded us within the correlate. To claim otherwise is to engage in a dogmatic metaphysics that is not supported by phenomenological evidence. Here Meillassoux takes sides with the phenomenologist: all that we have at our disposal is the contingency of the correlate (facticity). As Brassier summarizes it, "strong correlationism, as exemplified by figures such as Heidegger and Foucault, insists – contra Hegel – that the contingency of correlation cannot be rationalized or grounded in reason."[22] Against the phenomenologist, however, Meillassoux holds that we can in fact ground facticity. It is possible to know the conditions of givenness, to establish these absolutely, and to know that the correlate could be completely different than it is.

Meillassoux, then, is not as enamored of finitude as are so many postmetaphysical philosophers. What interests him most is the possibility of showing that "being and thinking must be thought as capable of being wholly other."[23] This is the unacknowledged "fundamental postulate" of strong correlationism, and therefore phenomenology. It is implied in the very concept of facticity. What is not implied, and what must be deduced, is the necessity of this postulate. This is not something that phenomenology can accomplish, for it requires a rational *deduction* of the absolute conditions of thinking and a properly speculative discourse (not "mere speculation") on the existence of what precedes all thought and all facts. As Meillassoux puts it, "if you

want to speak about what exists you can only *describe*, as phenomenology does – phenomenology is a description ... And what
I try to do is to show that if you can describe it, it's not for a
contingent reason. It's because what exists is just *a fact*."[24] The
aim of Meillassoux's project is not to describe these facts, but to
demonstrate that the facticity of these facts is not just another
fact. At the end of the day Meillassoux's method is rationalistic in
the Cartesian sense.

There is a sense in which phenomenology appears to transcend the
correlate on its own. But this kind of transcendence is only apparent;
it does nothing to open the correlational circle onto what lies outside it. Heidegger speaks of this as an *"ekstasis,"* while Sartre calls
it an "exploding" toward the world. Merleau-Ponty simply calls it
the "movement of transcendence." None of this, however, gets us
to realism because it all takes place from within the "transparent
cage" of consciousness and language. This is the phenomenologist's
own correlationist credo. "Consciousness and its language certainly
transcend towards the world," concedes Meillassoux,

> but there is a world only insofar as a consciousness transcends itself
> towards it. Consequently, this space of exteriority is merely the
> space of what faces us, of what exists only as a correlate of our own
> existence. This is why, in actuality, we do not transcend ourselves
> very much by plunging into such a world, for all we are doing is
> exploring the two faces of what remains a face to face – like a coin
> which only knows its own obverse.[25]

At best the most evocative and poetic descriptions of the movement of transcendence get us to "rediscover the richness of the
concrete world," and this through what Morton calls ambient
poetics/ecomimesis. Meillassoux calls it the rhetoric of the Rich
Elsewhere, whose slogan reads: "'Let's stop discussing, and let's
open the windows: let's inhale things and feel the breeze'."[26] This
"realist" enjoinder is effectively performed when Samuel Johnson
kicks a stone to "refute" Berkeley. As every correlationist knows,
however, no amount of touching or cataloguing or kicking the
facts of the world can determine the uncorrelated reality of those
facts. Realism does not call for a more faithful or comprehensive description of what exists, but for a demonstration that what
exists can exist without the thought that represents it or the foot
that boots it down the sidewalk.

From Facticity to Factiality (*Factualité*)

Phenomenology is in the business of describing facticity. It takes what is given as it is given (the "principle of principles") and does its best to tease out the invariant structures of the given, whether perceptual, cognitive, logical, or intentional. Whatever these invariants turn out to be, the phenomenologist will insist that their reason is inaccessible to consciousness. Their existence constitutes a fact about the given, but this fact is precisely not an absolute because it cannot be grounded in reason or shown to be necessary according to strong correlationist logic. Facticity, then, is a negative form of knowledge. It is a not-knowing why the world is given in such and such a way or with this or that set of fixed laws.[27] As Levinas might put it, *there is* a world. Full stop. Or, in Beckett's laconic words from *Endgame*: "Time passes. That is all." Meillassoux, by contrast, is not content to take the world as it is given. He does not restrict himself to cataloguing the invariant facts or transcendental conditions of the given – Kant's twelve categories or Heidegger's *existentialia* – but instead opens an inquiry into the absolute status of givenness itself. His objective: to deduce the necessary contingency of facticity, or what he terms the *principle of factiality* (*factualité*). In order to do this he must show, contra the correlationist, that it is possible to know the in itself not as it is for us, but as it is in itself.

On the face of it facticity seems to find us dropped right into the middle of objective reality. And indeed this is what existential or embodied phenomenology emphasizes against the transcendental phenomenologist who sets the philosophical stage after the manner of Descartes, with the subject and object locked face to face in an interrogation room, with neither coming out until the object yields its eidetic secrets. In contradistinction to the Cartesian/early Husserlian scene of phenomenological investigation, the embodied phenomenologist reminds us that we do not begin first and foremost from a perspective that takes things as present-at-hand or objectively present. We always already begin our inquiries situated among objects in the lifeworld, employing them for our everyday existence. They are ready-to-hand; we are engaged in, embedded in, and reliant on reality, not detached and indifferent spectators of it. Ironically, despite our location within the heart of being, our location does not enable us to gain privileged access to reality. What facticity represents, as Meillassoux says, is instead

> the unsurpassable limits of objectivity confronted with the fact *that there is* a world; a world that is describable and perceptible, and structured by determinate invariants. It is the sheer fact of the world's logicality, of its givenness in a representation, which evades the structures of logical and representational reason.[28]

Our position within the world forbids our knowledge of the world as it stands without us. For the strong correlationist this fact is nearly enough to decide on the inexistence of any possible world without us. Nearly.

Facticity does not dictate that there cannot be a world outside the correlationist circle. This is what absolute idealism does. Instead, facticity compels us to consider the "possibility" (and here, Meillassoux is clear: the scare quotes are indispensable) that structural invariants of the world could be *wholly otherwise* than they are. Crucially, for the correlationist, this possibility is not known to be a real possibility, but it signals for us the *impossibility of establishing any impossibility*. This negative determination of the possibility of the facts of the given becoming wholly other than they are is the closest we can come, from our factical position, to knowledge of the in itself. Facticity marks us as finite beings, incapable of grounding our condition in reason or specifying the foundation of our world.[29]

Finitude compels us to adopt a certain *agnosticism* about reality outside the correlate. It effectively prohibits us from making any positive philosophical claims about the existence or inexistence of entities in themselves, lest we burden ourselves with metaphysical dogmatism or unmotivated speculation. The contemporary emphasis on our finitude, which sometimes verges on fetishism, has at least two important results, one negative and one positive. The first is that it disqualifies the absolute truth of the principle of sufficient reason. Meillassoux writes that

> facticity fringes both knowledge and the world with an absence of foundation whose converse is that nothing can be said to be absolutely impossible, not even the unthinkable. In other words, facticity pushes the critique of the principle of sufficient reason to its ultimate extreme, by pointing out not only that the ontological argument is

illegitimate, but also that the principle of non-contradiction itself is without reason, and that consequently *it can only be the norm for what is thinkable by us, rather than for what is possible in an absolute sense.*[30]

The disqualification of the principle of sufficient reason beyond its application within the thinking/being correlate is behind all of the ontological talk, familiar to readers of Heidegger as well as existential phenomenology and its literary offspring, of groundlessness, the abyss, absurdity, *Abgrund*, and nothingness. As Meillassoux writes, "Facticity is the 'un-reason' (the absence of reason) of the given as well as its invariants."[31] Rather than see this as a horrific state of affairs, the absence of reason is often celebrated as the condition of possibility of the end of metaphysics and its evils, and the fertile soil for antifoundationalist philosophy and the interminable criticism of ontotheology.

Second, the disqualification of the principle of sufficient reason has the positive consequence of authorizing, not an explosion of treatises on the validity of nihilism, but an indefinite series of mystical, theological, or even irrational discourses on the absolute. Once the necessity of the law of noncontradiction is eliminated, by showing that its necessity only applies to what is given within the correlationist circle – or, in other words, that the impossibility of contradiction is only a fact, not a necessary law – a "specific and rather remarkable consequence" follows:

> it becomes rationally illegitimate to disqualify *irrational* discourses about the absolute on the pretext of their irrationality. From the perspective of the strong model [of correlationism], in effect, religious belief has every right to maintain that the world was created out of nothingness from an act of love, or that God's omnipotence allows him to dissolve the apparent contradiction between his complete identity and His difference with his Son.[32]

Despite the mythical and unscientific nature of these beliefs, they nevertheless must enjoy legitimacy in our current milieu according to the limitation on reason drawn by the strong correlationist's concept of facticity. It is no wonder that phenomenology has recently produced a plethora of theological discourses despite its overt methodological commitment to confining its research to the phenomenal world.

It is worthwhile to emphasize that Meillassoux says that any *belief*, even irrational beliefs, cannot be disqualified by reason according to the strong correlationist model. Beliefs, unlike knowledge claims and judgments, do not need to be rationally justified. They may be given support in some other way, but if they do not call upon reason to back them up, they are just as "permissible" as beliefs backed by argument. In this respect they hang somewhere between arbitrary assertions and rationally grounded judgments. Since only the latter are subject to the strictures of reason, beliefs enjoy a right that rational judgments do not. They are a form of nonknowledge that reaps some of the benefits of knowledge, but without the responsibility demanded of knowledge. The delegitimation of any rational critique of even irrational discourses safeguards beliefs – and here we are speaking specifically about beliefs pertaining to the absolute – from the charge that they are unthinkable and as such untenable. This is why Meillassoux says that criticizing Levinas's concept of the "wholly other" (*tout autre*) as logically incoherent would totally miss the point of Levinas's discourse.[33] This is not to imply that Levinas's philosophy trades fundamentally in mere belief, but that his conceptual apparatus operates according to a logic that permits even contradictions to exist in principle outside the correlationist circle. According to correlationist logic, the unthinkability of the absolute does not entail that there are no absolutes, just that correlationists are not permitted any positive commitment to a specific absolute. Only dogmatic metaphysicians are given this permission. As Meillassoux says,

> this trajectory culminates in the disappearance of the pretension to *think* any absolutes, *but not in the disappearance of absolutes*; since in discovering itself to be marked by an irremediable limitation, correlational reason thereby legitimates *all* those discourses that claim to access an absolute, *the only proviso being that nothing in these discourses resembles a rational justification of their validity*.[34]

The contemporary end of metaphysics is underwritten by precisely this line of thinking.

Correlationist reason bears in its heart a skeptical posture toward the absolute. This skepticism is responsible for the "exacerbated return of the religious"[35] in contemporary philosophy and politics. It is the correlationist's skepticism which effectively quarantines faith and reason in two separate logical orders, which allows him to chastise any attempt to justify or disqualify any claims about the absolute. Meillassoux's name for this posture is *fideism*: "Fideism invariably consists in a sceptical argument directed against the pretension of metaphysics, and of reason more generally, to be able to access an absolute truth capable of shoring up (or *a fortiori*, of denigrating) the value of faith."[36] At the basis of the contemporary end of metaphysics lies this kind of fideist argument. Contemporary fideism, unlike historical fideism, is not aligned with a particular religion. Its scope is much wider, to the extent that it encompasses a "defence of religiosity in general."[37]

The idea that the end of metaphysics is necessarily skeptical in form is contested by Husserl and many of his followers, who argue that despite phenomenology's rejection of representationalist epistemology and the thing in itself, along with the apparently subjective nature of the "as structure" of perception, it retains the resources to establish truth. This truth is modeled on the intersubjective truth necessitated by the Kantian critique of reason. But phenomenology can only deny its skeptical stance if it affirms that knowledge of the "in itself for us" just is knowledge *tout court*. If, in reply, we insist that the correlationist logic at work in the phenomenological reduction and its attendant replacement of the world with the *Lebenswelt* nevertheless tells us nothing positive about the uncorrelated world, for fear of being charged with illicit metaphysical commitments, then we should insist that phenomenology is complicit with the fideist skepticism that results in what Meillassoux calls a "religionizing of reason." After all, as Meillassoux concludes, fideism is just another name for strong correlationism.[38]

In order to diminish the force of the skeptico-fideist argument, and thereby undercut its long-uncontested obviousness, Meillassoux proposes a subtle modification of the strong correlationist view. His own speculative materialism emerges from this internal critique. Since the correlationist is committed to facticity, he must recognize that facticity can only be facticity if the possibilities for the correlate to be wholly other (because of death or extinction, for example) are not just possibilities for us; if they are genuinely unthinkable they must be possibilities that exceed thought, or absolute possibilities.[39] This places the correlationist in a double bind. If the correlationist denies that these possibilities are absolute, then he must admit that the correlate is necessary and that absolute idealism is true. If the correlationist affirms the possibility that the correlate could be wholly other than it is (absolutely contingent), then he must admit that we can know that facticity is necessary, which is a violation of his own epistemological principles. Correlationism, in Brassier's words,

> cannot de-absolutize facticity without absolutizing the correlation; yet it cannot de-absolutize the correlation without absolutizing facticity. But to absolutize facticity is to assert the unconditional necessity of its contingency, and hence to assert that it is possible to think something that exists independently of thought's relation to it: contingency as such.[40]

The correlationist must therefore admit that he has mistakenly attributed to our finite relation with things something positive about the in itself: its necessary contingency. "Thus," concludes Brassier, "when facticity is absolutized, it is the contingency or groundlessness of the for-us (the correlation) which becomes in-itself or necessary precisely insofar as its contingency is not something which is merely for-us."[41] This is what Meillassoux calls the *principle of factiality*. It is the hallmark of his book's title, *After Finitude*.

The principle of factiality (also called the principle of unreason) states: "There is no reason for anything to be or to remain the way it is; everything must, without reason, be able to be and/or be able to be other than it is."[42] He demonstrates its truth in the following way. In order to escape the correlationist circle, it is necessary to absolutize the principle that disqualifies the thought of an absolute on the grounds that such a thought enacts a performative contradiction. In other words, we must absolutize facticity itself. This we can only do from within facticity itself, which presents itself to us as the fact of a finite thinking. Strong correlationism, phenomenology in particular, experiences this fact as an "intrinsic limit" on our capacity to think. Meillassoux counters that what we experience in facticity is not the limit of thought, but the unlimited means of accessing the absolute.[43] This absolute, however, is not an absolute entity. It is the absolute unreason of everything that exists, including the laws of nature.

This absolute, contends Meillassoux, is already presupposed by the correlationist who inevitably draws a distinction between the "in itself" (which harbors unthinkable and even irrational possibilities) and the "for us" whose laws are conditioned by the factual invariants of factical existence. The absolute is simply the skeptico-fideist claim that it is possible – because not thinkable as impossible – for the world to be wholly other than it is. This capacity-to-be-other of the world, however, is not a feature of human ignorance or unknowing, but "the *knowledge* of the very real possibility of [any] eventualities" whatsoever.[44] It is knowledge because, as the correlationist agnostic maintains, it is possible for us to conceive ourselves as not being. But, whereas the correlationist will stop at the (noncontradictory) thinkability of our annihilation, it is necessary to go one step further and insist that the capacity-to-be-other must be a *real* possibility, a possibility that is more than a correlate of thought. Without this further step it is still possible for the speculative idealist to insist that the thinkability of our annihilation is actually just an annihilation for us, a relative annihilation. The absurd consequence of this thesis is that death becomes merely an ideal and none of us would ever actually pass away but instead, as Meillassoux says, "agonize indefinitely." In order to avoid this consequence, the correlationist is forced to conclude that the capacity-to-be-other (facticity) entails the real possibility of our actual mortality and extinction as a species. He must therefore commit to knowledge of an "absolute whose reality is thinkable as that of the in-itself as such in its indifference to thought; an indifference which confers upon it the power to destroy me."[45] At this point the correlationist has transgressed the correlationist circle and installed the principle of factiality at the center of facticity.

If it is objected that no reason can be given for the real possibility that the world could be completely other than how it is – Meillassoux's nondogmatic, speculative thesis – Meillassoux will respond that, even if we can narrow this possibility by postulating a necessary entity responsible for creating the world – the dogmatist's metaphysical thesis – this postulate can only be entertained on the condition that the speculative thesis is already true. There is no reason for why the world is the way it is, and this is absolutely true because it is impossible that there is a necessary being that could provide such a ground.[46] "From this perspective, the failure of the principle of reason follows, quite simply, from the *falsity* (and even the absolute falsity) of such a principle – for the truth is that there is no reason for anything to be or to remain thus and so rather than otherwise."[47] Accordingly, the principle of factiality is alternatively formulated in the following way: "it is because the principle of reason is absolutely false that the principle of non-contradiction is absolutely true."[48]

So, what makes the principle of reason absolutely false? The fideist logic exemplified by strong correlationism, despite its commitment to the possibility that the world could be wholly other than it is, remains problematically committed to the principle of sufficient reason. This is evident in the fact that it legitimates religious discourse and, consequently, leaves "open the possibility that there might be a hidden reason, an unfathomable purpose underlying the origin of our world."[49] Because this reason is unthinkable, we must respect that it might exist. Strong correlationism continues to believe in an ultimate reason, or *arché*, even as it remains agnostic about its actuality. Meillassoux has shown that, on the contrary, no such ultimate reason exists. "There is nothing beneath or beyond the manifest gratuitousness of the given – nothing but the limitless and lawless power of its destruction, emergence, or persistence."[50] Only contingency is necessary, which means that the principle of sufficient reason is not.

Whereas the strong correlationist maintains that we can only *believe* in an uncorrelated absolute, Meillassoux counters that in fact we can *know* that an absolute is possible.[51] He suggests that if we can establish a "modicum of absoluteness" in thought, then it becomes possible to trade in strong correlationism and the straitjacket of the correlationist circle for a speculative materialism that opens the aperture of philosophical thinking. This knowledge is derived not from a description of facticity, which makes no judgment about the necessity of facticity, but from a deduction of the necessity of facticity.[52]

Factiality is the name given by Meillassoux to the "speculative essence of facticity."[53] It says that facticity itself must be more than the fact that the given displays invariant structures. This "more" is not the excess of New Phenomenologists like Jean-Luc Marion (whether this excess takes the form of God, the inapparent, the impossible, or the invisible – the so-called conditions of phenomenality itself), which operates according to the agnostic logic of the fideist.[54] It is an extension of the reach of reason into what phenomenology believes to be untouchable: the uncorrelated in itself. "Meillassoux's rationalist critique of the critique of reason," writes Brassier, "aims to rehabilitate reason's claim to be able to access reality as it is in itself by purging rationalism of its metaphysical accoutrements."[55] By the same token, it proceeds by disabusing phenomenology of its belief that the finitude of human thought determines the limits of the real. This is crucial to recognizing how strong correlationism's epistemological claims about finitude and human ignorance are converted by Meillassoux into a materialist ontological thesis.[56]

The Ancestral Challenge

As I argued in earlier chapters, it is not uncommon for phenomenologists to assert their allegiance to the autonomous reality of the world, or to claim that their descriptions of phenomenal things actually get us in touch with the things themselves or God. When they pledge their allegiance to the subject-independent real, I argued, we must take this as a nonphenomenological assertion, not a conclusion that is drawn from phenomenological evidence. In her assertion of the autonomous reality of the world, the phenomenologist ceases to be a phenomenologist and turns into a naïve realist for fear of being mistaken for an idealist. But can we call this naïveté irrational? Meillassoux's concept of fideism shows us that we cannot. The consequence is that the phenomenologist can only believe in the uncorrelated real, she cannot lay claim to a philosophical justification for her belief.

Contemporary fideism of the sort we find in phenomenology's theological turn or in continental philosophy of religion descends from the pietistic and mystical aspects of figures like Heidegger and Wittgenstein, often cited as the two most responsible for the postmetaphysical landscape of twentieth-century philosophy in both its continental and analytic forms.[57] Heidegger and Wittgenstein are not single-handedly responsible for the prevalence of fideism today, of course. They simply stand as the most luminous transformations of the critique of reason initiated by Kant. It is necessary to recall that Kant's critical philosophy was not aimed at disqualifying irrational discourses on the absolute or chastening religious thinking. It was instead directed at limiting the reach of rational, scientific discourse in order to make room for faith. In other words, the critique of pure reason has the express objective of circumscribing a zone of thinking wherein religious discourse can enjoy an immunity to the strictures of reason. This does not require an endorsement of the legitimacy of religious discourse of any variety, nor does it authorize the legitimacy of atheism (quite the contrary), but it does impose a certain agnostic imperative with respect to the truth of these discourses.

This places the post-Kantian philosopher in an uncomfortable situation with respect to science. As we have seen, Kantian transcendentalism, Hegelian speculative idealism, and phenomenology refuse all knowledge claims about the in itself. It is true that Hegel attempts to absolutize the correlation, and therefore claims to know that the correlation is necessary in itself. But we also saw how Meillassoux rescinds this claim by insisting that Hegel's own principles forbid such knowledge. The problem facing the post-Kantian philosopher, whether correlationist or idealist, is how to make sense of science's claim to positive knowledge of what precedes human thought. In other words, how do we take *literally* the scientific statements made about the in itself which predates the for us – what Meillassoux calls the ancestral? The post-Kantian correlationists cannot have their cake and eat it too: either correlationism is inescapable, which means that we cannot take scientific statements about the ancestral at face value, or it is escapable, in which case we can endorse science's statements in their literality, but at the expense of the soundness of correlationist reason. If the correlationist wishes to defend his position's capacity to deal with ancestral statements, he must "stop 'compromising' with science and stop believing that he can reconcile [the correlationist and realist senses of scientific statements] without undermining the content of the scientific statement which he claims to be dealing with."[58] Let us see what forces the correlationist into this decision.

An ancestral statement is one that makes a truth claim about "any reality anterior to the emergence of the human species."[59] Meillassoux cites the dates of the origin of the universe, the accretion of earth, the origin of life on earth, and the origin of *Homo habilis* as examples.[60] These statements are prompted by the evidence of the "arche-fossil," which is any "materials indicating the existence of an ancestral reality or event; one that is anterior to terrestrial life."[61] This evidence does not furnish a direct proof of realism; the situation is much thornier than that. For, the arche-fossil refers us to a reality that precedes human consciousness and therefore the conditions of givenness laid out by the critical philosophy: space, time, the categories of the understanding, and so forth. It thus raises the question of how a committed correlationist will make sense of what science says about the arche-fossil, for the former cannot take the latter literally. The ancestral poses, as Harman puts it, an "aporia" for postcritical philosophy.[62] The aporia is ramified by the series of commitments made by the correlationist to avoid dogmatism. They include "the correlationist circle and two-step; the replacement of adequation by intersubjectivity in the redefinition of scientific objectivity; the maintaining of the correlation even in the critique of representation; the cloistered outside."[63] In the end, Meillassoux aims to break free of these commitments to vouchsafe knowledge of the primary – mathematical – qualities of ancestral materials. He will do so with intellectual intuition, but in what precise way we do not yet know at the close of his book.[64]

It is imperative for Meillassoux that we take ancestral statements literally. This is what fidelity to science requires. They are not merely true for us, for they do not merely refer to a reality that is the product of the subject/object dialogue or any other correlationist trope – they refer to a reality absolutely untethered from thought. For the Kantian, by contrast, it is absurd to ask what the world was like without humans. It is absurd not because there would be no world, but because that world cannot be known and therefore cannot make any sense to us.[65] Meillassoux is convinced that ancestral statements not only make sense, but that their literal sense is their deepest sense.

The problem is this: how are we supposed to establish the real existence of the ancestral? We have already seen that Meillassoux has found a way out of the correlationist circle, so he has the means of justifying the literal interpretation of ancestral statements. This is what his speculative materialism, with its principle of factiality, does. Nevertheless, the correlationist will resist Meillassoux and the scientific realist. But on what grounds?

The correlationist line of resistance to realism is already familiar to us, so we need not rehash again. There are two additional dimensions to it, however, that we have not yet discussed. The first is rhetorical, while the second is philosophical. First, the correlationist is apt to claim that his philosophical work has no direct bearing on the legitimacy of the scientist's research, but then he will qualify this reassurance by specifying that at the most fundamental level (the ontological) there really is a discrepancy between the realism of science and the results of transcendental criticism. The latter possesses a "specific type of knowledge which imposes a correction upon science's ancestral statements" and the naïve realism that underlies them.[66] More often than not, however, the correlationist will "compromise" with science and drop the issue.

The correlationist has a second, more philosophical, reason for resisting the literal interpretation of ancestral statements. If being and thinking are coextensive, then the manifestation of being cannot occur without thinking (or consciousness). Ancestral statements refer us to a time when thinking did not exist, so they refer us to a time when being could not have manifested itself. In other words, they refer us to a contradiction: the "givenness of a being anterior to givenness."[67] We have already suggested that this is not a genuine contradiction, but an aporia. There must be a way through it then. The correlationist works it out in the following way. Since givenness enjoys a priority over existence insofar as givenness furnishes the spatiotemporal conditions of manifestation, we can make sense of ancestral statements by saying that the arche-fossil of which she speaks is given to the scientist *as though it were anterior* to givenness. In this formulation the givenness of the arche-fossil does not precede in time the conditions of givenness (conscious life). When considered from the standpoint of the present, the evidence of the arche-fossil "is not something that is anterior to givenness, but merely something that is given in the present but gives itself *as* anterior to givenness."[68] The ancestral past only seems to precede givenness, says the correlationist, when in fact it is co-present with the community of scientists who study it. In the final analysis, correlationism, in order to make sense of ancestral statements without succumbing to naïve realism must insist on the priority of the present over the past, and the priority of human consciousness over an uncorrelated existence in itself. It is in this respect that "every variety of idealism converges and becomes equally extraordinary – every variety of correlationism is exposed as an extreme idealism, one that is incapable of admitting that what science tells us about these occurrences of matter independent of humanity effectively occurred as described by science."[69]

Despite its extraordinary nature, correlationism will continue its resistance of realism by holding that *if* consciousness was present during the ancestral period, then it would be perceived in accordance with the conditions of givenness familiar to any student of postcritical philosophy. Because the ancestral was so far in the past, the correlationist will continue, it seems like it poses a unique challenge to correlationism.[70] But, in fact, it does not. Meillassoux's rejoinder to this is simple and direct: the ancestral does not represent a time in the super-distant past, but a time that is ontologically out of step with the time of givenness, that is, a *diachronic* time. "The ancestral does not designate an absence *in* the given, and *for* givenness, but rather an absence *of* givenness as such" and "*in its entirety*." Meillassoux summarizes: "the time at issue here is the time wherein *consciousness* as well as *conscious time* have *themselves emerged in time*. For the problem of the arche-fossil is not the empirical problem of the birth of living organisms, but the ontological problem of the coming into being of givenness as such."[71] The question of the emergence of the given/transcendental conditions of experience is precisely one that phenomenology, as correlationism, cannot investigate because it pertains to a time prior to the very possibility of phenomenological description. Only a speculative or metaphysical program can address it.

Keeping with this line of criticism, Brassier reminds us that phenomenology explicitly rejects the idea of a nature (Husserl) or time (Heidegger) before human being.[72] Nature and time are, in Heidegger's words, equiprimordial with Dasein's existence. For Husserl, phenomenology shows that nature is not and cannot be the condition of consciousness, but the reverse is true: consciousness is the condition of nature. Consequently, since ancestral statements are about a natural temporality that precedes human consciousness, phenomenology simply cannot accept ancestral statements literally, nor can it account for the real existence of the phenomena to which these statements refer. Phenomenology is what comes before scientific realism and naturalism, and thus what comes before – ontologically speaking – nature and time. If phenomenology wishes to be the ground of science, then it must reject the literal truth of ancestral statements. This is the point of Husserl's "Phenomenology as Rigorous Science."

Some will correct Meillassoux's characterization of phenomenology by pointing out that correlationism is not an ontological thesis, but an epistemological one. Husserl and Heidegger are not claiming that nature and time get their existence from human consciousness; they get their *meaning* from it. It is in this sense that science is grounded in phenomenology. As Peter Hallward contends, "correlationism as Meillassoux defines it is in reality an epistemological theory, one that is perfectly compatible with the insights of Darwin, Marx or Einstein. There's nothing to prevent a correlationist from thinking ancestral objects or worlds that are older than the thought that thinks them, or indeed older than thought itself."[73] This, I think, underestimates the aspiration of phenomenology, if not transcendental philosophy more generally. Any correlationist is certainly capable of thinking the ancestral *as* older than thought, but the strong correlationist cannot commit to anything more than the purely logical possibility of its prehuman existence without contradicting the logic of strong correlationism. That is, strong correlationism is committed to an ontological thesis about the conditions of givenness, not a thesis about the conditions of knowledge.[74] Or, perhaps, we must understand correlationism as an epistemological thesis with ontological aspirations, which is what seems to have happened after Kant and what seems to be correlationism's mark of distinction. Even if Hallward is right about the weaker Kantian version of correlationism, it is necessary to take the strong form espoused by phenomenology as an ontological thesis.[75] After all, if *Being and Time, Being and Nothingness,* and *The Visible and the Invisible* are phenomenological texts, then it is clear that phenomenology takes itself to be advancing an ontological program, for each of these texts presents a fundamental ontology, phenomenological ontology, and ontology of the flesh, respectively.

Meillassoux's interest in establishing the autonomy of things in themselves is not primarily philosophical, but stems from a pronounced desire to legitimate the literal truth of science and to force transcendental philosophies, whether Kantian, Husserlian, or Heideggerian, to admit that their ontological views are fundamentally incompatible with natural science's realist interpretation of ancestral statements. This poses a serious challenge for the Husserlian program of grounding natural science in the science of phenomenology. Nevertheless, phenomenology retains a formidable army of defenders who continue to declaim its fundamental nature. It has also, in Meillassoux's view, "established a mechanism of intimidation and of elaborate sophistry that aims at making [questions about the emergence of life in the world] appear naïve."[76] Meillassoux's characterization is certainly sharp, but not untrue in essence. For a long time now questions about the genesis of the transcendental conditions of knowledge, the emergence of consciousness, and the features of the world apart from human access have been regarded as out of bounds for continental philosophy. Anyone who asks them is accused not so much of metaphysical hubris as of a critical faux pas. And yet these questions persist, whether they are regarded as serious or boorish or unsophisticated. Phenomenology, as Meillassoux frames it, remains "a formidable *descriptive* enterprise of the complexities of the given,"[77] but has yet to look the ontological problems of genesis and emergence squarely in the face, despite the turn to "genetic" phenomenology.

After Phenomenology

The reception of *After Finitude* in the English-speaking world has been mostly favorable, and at times positively enthusiastic. There is something quite refreshing about its theses and what they promise – an escape from the philosophical milieu which accepts correlationism's supremacy as a *fait accompli* – and many have flocked to it for leverage or inspiration. The style of Meillassoux's argumentation is equally refreshing, as it presents itself in a methodical step-by-step reminiscent of either Scholasticism or analytic philosophy – it is difficult to tell which. Critical discussion of Meillassoux often exhibits a degree of skepticism toward the legitimacy of his refutation of correlationism, on the one hand, and toward the validity of his argument, on the other. A certain degree of suspicion has been cast over his text as well. Perhaps *After Finitude* is little more than subtle sophistry? Lucky for Meillassoux, suspicion is not something a philosopher has to worry about, unless, of course, that philosopher is Socrates. Even if the argument of *After Finitude* does come off as suspicious, this has nothing to do with its validity. The same could be said about an argument's rejuvenating quality. We do not accept or reject an argument because it strikes us as shady or because it motivates its reader to ponder new ideas. Although, maybe sometimes we should.

However it is judged, Meillassoux's program for the future is clear. It no doubt follows a trajectory inspired by his teacher, Badiou, and the set theoretical mathematics of Cantor. It harkens back to the days when philosophers mobilized the language of primary and secondary qualities, and it is markedly Cartesian in spirit if not in method. Meillassoux summarizes it like this:

Thus our question becomes: how is mathematical discourse able to describe a world where humanity is absent; a world crammed with things and events that are not the correlates of any manifestation; a world that is not the correlate of a relation to the world? This is the enigma which we must confront: *mathematics' ability to discourse about the great outdoors; to discourse about a past where both humanity and life are absent.* Or to say the same thing in the form of a paradox (which we will call 'the paradox of the arche-fossil'): how can a being manifest being's anteriority to manifestation?[78]

This chapter has provided a glimpse into how Meillassoux resolves the paradox of the arche-fossil, although it remains to be seen how intellectual intuition will open the window to the great outdoors.

Although Meillassoux maintains that we can access the absolute, he is not what Harman calls a "philosopher of access" because an intellectual intuition of the mathematizable properties of the arche-fossil does not result in mathematical knowledge *for us*. It is simply uncorrelated, unqualified knowledge of mind-independent properties. Here Meillassoux is more ambitious than Harman with respect to finitude. Where Meillassoux aspires toward a philosophical position that has left finitude behind, Harman, as we will see in the next chapter, argues that human finitude is unsurpassable.[79] But while Harman's object-oriented perspective derives from phenomenology, he does not believe that talk about objects must remain within a phenomenological horizon. Just as Meillassoux radicalizes strong correlationism to generate his speculative materialism, Harman radicalizes phenomenology to generate his own speculative realism.

Notes

1. Meillassoux, *After Finitude*, 5.
2. This chapter does not provide an exhaustive summary of correlationism, for these already exist. Instead, it draws upon these summaries and recommends them to the reader. See, for instance, Harman, *Quentin Meillassoux*; Ray Brassier, *Nihil Unbound: Enlightenment and Extinction* (Basingstoke: Palgrave, 2007), Chapter 3; Ennis, *Continental Realism*.
3. Brassier, *Nihil Unbound*, 50.

4. Ray Brassier et al., "Speculative Realism," *Collapse* III (2007), 411.

5. As Meillassoux notes in an interview, Husserl's slogan "in no way corresponds to my idea of philosophy: as it only consists, by this call, in returning to the things as correlates of consciousness, Dasein, phenomenon, being, or Being." Meillassoux's return, by contrast, is "to the in-itself seen as indifferent to what is given to us, because indifferent to our opening-[onto]-the-world." See Rick Dolphijn and Iris van der Tuin, eds., *New Materialism: Interviews & Cartographies* (Ann Arbor: Open Humanities Press, 2012), 76.

6. See Brassier et al., "Speculative Realism," 423.

7. Meillassoux, *After Finitude*, 31.

8. Meillassoux, *After Finitude*, 35.

9. In Hegel we find the "absolute idealist" form of correlationism, which characteristically absolutizes the correlation and identifies thinking and being, substance and subject, reality and rationality.

10. Meillassoux, *After Finitude*, 35.

11. Merleau-Ponty, "Primacy of Perception," 16.

12. Brassier et al., "Speculative Realism," 409, 411. For more on Fichte's relevance for phenomenology, see Jeremy Dunham et al., *Idealism: The History of a Philosophy* (Montreal and Kingston: McGill-Queen's University Press, 2011), 126–8.

13. Brassier et al., "Speculative Realism," 412.

14. Brassier, by contrast, believes it possible to demonstrate, following David Stove, the logical fallaciousness of this Fichtean argument. Consequently, and in the last analysis, the formidability of strong correlationism comes down to whether or not this is in fact a good or bad argument. See Ray Brassier, "Concepts and Objects," in *The Speculative Turn*, 59–60.

15. Heidegger, *Being and Time*, 82.

16. Heidegger, *Being and Time*, 82.

17. Meillassoux, *After Finitude*, 41. See Wittgenstein, *Tractatus Logico-Philosophicus*, prop. 6.522.

18. Meillassoux, *After Finitude*, 36.

19. Meillassoux, *After Finitude*, 37.

20. Meillassoux, *After Finitude*, 38. See Ray Brassier, *Nihil Unbound*, 66–7.

21. Meillassoux, *After Finitude*, 41, emphasis omitted.

22. Brassier, *Nihil Unbound*, 65; see Meillassoux, *After Finitude*, 36. See also Martin Heidegger, *The Principle of Reason*, trans. Reginald Lilly (Bloomington: Indiana University Press, 1996), 113, where

Heidegger discusses the principle of sufficient reason as a principle of being. Following Heraclitus's image of a child that plays for no other reason than that it plays, he concludes that being is without ground and therefore without reason.

23. Meillassoux, *After Finitude*, 44, emphasis omitted.

24. Brassier et al., "Speculative Realism," 391–2.

25. Meillassoux, *After Finitude*, 7.

26. Brassier et al., "Speculative Realism," 423.

27. Meillassoux, *After Finitude*, 39. For a series of perspectives on facticity, see François Raffoul and Eric Sean Nelson, eds., *Rethinking Facticity* (Albany: SUNY Press, 2008).

28. Meillassoux, *After Finitude*, 40.

29. Meillassoux, *After Finitude*, 40.

30. Meillassoux, *After Finitude*, 40–1, emphasis added.

31. Meillassoux, *After Finitude*, 41.

32. Meillassoux, *After Finitude*, 41.

33. Meillassoux, *After Finitude*, 43–4.

34. Meillassoux, *After Finitude*, 44–5.

35. Meillassoux, *After Finitude*, 45, emphasis omitted.

36. Meillassoux, *After Finitude*, 46.

37. Meillassoux, *After Finitude*, 46. Theological phenomenology, or what Simmons and Benson call the "new phenomenology," enjoys its philosophical status in part because of the installation of fideism in contemporary philosophy.

38. Meillassoux, *After Finitude*, 47–8. The religionizing of reason is an ironic twist to the critique of dogmatism initiated by Kant, since it was Kant's weak correlationism that rebuffed dogmatic metaphysics, but it is phenomenology's strong correlationism that makes "philosophy ... incapable of fundamentally distinguishing itself from fanaticism" (49).

39. Harman, *Quentin Meillassoux*, 27.

40. Brassier, *Nihil Unbound*, 66–7.

41. Brassier, *Nihil Unbound*, 67.

42. Meillassoux, *After Finitude*, 60.

43. Meillassoux, *After Finitude*, 52.

44. Meillassoux, *After Finitude*, 56.

45. Meillassoux, *After Finitude*, 57.

46. Meillassoux, *After Finitude*, 60. On the impossibility of a necessary entity, see *After Finitude* 65–7 and Harman, *Quentin Meillassoux*, 35.

47. Meillassoux, *After Finitude*, 53.

48. Meillassoux, *After Finitude*, 71.

49. Meillassoux, *After Finitude*, 63.

50. Meillassoux, *After Finitude*, 63.

51. Harman, *Quentin Meillassoux*, 26.

52. Meillassoux, *After Finitude*, 76.

53. Meillassoux, *After Finitude*, 79; Harman, *Quentin Meillassoux*, 30.

54. Simmons and Benson, *The New Phenomenology*, Introduction.

55. Brassier, *Nihil Unbound*, 69.

56. Meillassoux, *After Finitude*, 53; Harman, *Quentin Meillassoux*, 26.

57. See, for instance, Richard Rorty, "Wittgenstein, Heidegger, and the Reification of Language," in *Essays on Heidegger and Others* (Cambridge: Cambridge University Press, 1991).

58. Meillassoux, *After Finitude*, 17.

59. Meillassoux, *After Finitude*, 10.

60. 13.5 billion, 4.56 billion, 3.5 billion, and 2 million years ago, respectively. Meillassoux, *After Finitude*, 9.

61. Meillassoux, *After Finitude*, 10. For a detailed discussion of the science of the arche-fossil, see the interview with Oxford scientist Roberto Trotta, "Dark Matter: Probing the Arche-Fossil," in *Collapse* II, 83–169.

62. Harman, *Quentin Meillassoux*, 11.

63. Meillassoux, *After Finitude*, 8.

64. Brassier suggests that Meillassoux is close to Husserl in his Cartesian faith in the strength of intellectual intuition. See "Speculative Realism," 320. On intellectual intuition, see Meillassoux, *After Finitude*, 82ff.

65. Brassier et al., "Speculative Realism," 329.

66. Meillassoux, *After Finitude*, 13.

67. Meillassoux, *After Finitude*, 14, emphasis removed.

68. Meillassoux, *After Finitude*, 16.

69. Meillassoux, *After Finitude*, 18.

70. This is what Meillassoux calls the "lacunary nature of the given," which "has never been a problem for correlationism" (*After Finitude*, 19).

71. Meillassoux, *After Finitude*, 21; for more on diachronicity, discussed in the context of the annihilation of the species, see Chapter 5. For a rebuttal of the second rejoinder to the ancestral, wherein Meillassoux shows that he has not confused the empirical and transcendental levels of the problem, see 22–7.

72. See Brassier, *Nihil Unbound*, 244–5, n.4, where he cites "paradigmatic expressions" of the correlationist credo from Husserl's *Crisis* and *Ideas*, and Heidegger's *Being and Time*.

73. Peter Hallward, "Anything is Possible: A Reading of Quentin Meillassoux's *After Finitude*," in *The Speculative Turn*, 137.
74. Here I side with Nathan Brown, "The Speculative and the Specific: On Hallward and Meillassoux," in *The Speculative Turn*, 152–3.
75. It is, of course, possible to give a coherent ontological reading of Kant's critical philosophy, as Heidegger demonstrates in *Kant and the Problem of Metaphysics*, fifth edition, enlarged, trans. Richard Taft (Bloomington: Indiana University Press, 1997). I take this as an indication of Heidegger's desire to demonstrate the ontological depth of transcendental phenomenology.
76. Harman, "Interview with Quentin Meillassoux," in *Quentin Meillassoux*, 170.
77. Harman, "Interview with Quentin Meillassoux," 170.
78. Meillassoux, *After Finitude*, 26.
79. Harman marks this difference clearly in Graham Harman, "The Well-Wrought Broken Hammer: Object-Oriented Literary Criticism," *New Literary History* 43 (2012), 185.

4

Phenomenology: A Philosophy of Access

Among the philosophers associated with speculative realism, the richest and most extensive engagement with phenomenology is found in the work of Graham Harman. He is also the only member of the original four who continues explicitly to work under the speculative realism label, and it is his object-oriented philosophy (OOP) or object-oriented ontology (OOO) that has generated a ripple of speculative realism in thinkers like Levi Bryant, Timothy Morton, and Ian Bogost. No speculative realist carries out a more detailed reading of a phenomenological figure or theme than Harman provides in his first book, *Tool-Being* (2002), and the introductory *Heidegger Explained*. These texts offer a heterodox interpretation of Heidegger's theory of equipment which serves as the foundation of Harman's own object-oriented philosophy. Harman also draws liberally from Husserl's discussions of intentionality and perception, as well as from the "carnal phenomenologists," the collective name given to Merleau-Ponty, Levinas, and Lingis in Harman's second book, *Guerrilla Metaphysics*. In both *Tool-Being* and *Guerrilla Metaphysics* – as well as many subsequent essays and chapters – phenomenology is shown to prepare, sometimes despite itself, singular metaphysical insights that Harman retains in his own philosophy. But phenomenology is, in Harman's eyes, metaphysically limited because it effectively holds that the totality of what exists is identical to the totality of what appears to human consciousness. Phenomenology's realism can only ever be a tentative realism of the phenomenon.

If it is the things *themselves* we want, then phenomenology must be discarded for a fully committed realist metaphysics that is object-oriented instead of human-oriented. This chapter gives an account of how Harman uses Husserl, Heidegger, and the carnal phenomenologists to construct his own metaphysics of objects. It does not discuss the intricacies of his OOP, but simply follows his phenomenological path in order to unearth the basic duality at the center of Harman's view. It closes with an explanation of why getting back to the things themselves does not mean delivering ourselves over to either a Kantian two-world theory or any kind of materialism.

It should be reiterated up front that phenomenology, for Harman, is an exemplary "philosophy of access." This is Harman's name for what Meillassoux calls correlationism, and it refers to any philosophy which says that human experience includes the totality of legitimate philosophical content. These two terms – correlationism and philosophy of access – are synonymous insofar as they name the philosophical presupposition which says that reality must be approached exclusively through the human lens, whether perceptual, cognitive, or practical. Speculative realism in all variants is united against this tendency which has dominated continental philosophy at least since Kant, and which obliges any discourse on reality to "first perform a series of sophisticated critical and self-reflexive maneuvers so as to ensure that we are *only* talking about objects *as they manifest themselves to us*, not about objects in their own inner life."[1] Anyone trained in continental philosophy is familiar with this tacit obligation, which may now be finally withering away. After all, we are in the midst of a speculative turn.[2] But how can we approach reality otherwise? Are we now supposed to value *un*critical inquiry? Not at all. Harman's entire project demonstrates, beginning from phenomenological insights, that reality can be articulated on its own terms without converting it into thought.[3] While he admits that it is not possible to know what it is like to be a nonhuman thing, whether creature or inanimate object, it is possible to gather metaphysical knowledge about them without accessing them directly.[4] This is the task of Harman's object-oriented philosophy, which traces its roots to phenomenology and, "from the basic insights of Husserl and Heidegger, a strange but refreshing geography of objects begins to emerge, leading to results that can barely be guessed."[5]

Harman's method consists in reading phenomenology for unexpected clues to the hidden lives of objects, sometimes against the phenomenologists themselves. His method is ultimately speculative, however, insofar as he proposes to deduce the primary qualities of objects from the phenomenal. This is not without its complications and attendant metaphysical puzzles.

Husserl's Intentional Objects

Husserl is sometimes derided for his Platonism, other times for his Cartesianism or Kantianism. Sometimes the criticism is more informal: he is too verbose or too indecisive. Recall from Chapter 1 the examiner on my comprehensive exam committee who asked me in a snide tone if I could "see essences" like Husserl. This was his way of asking me to make sense of what he saw as a ridiculous doctrine. And surely this was not an isolated incident. Harman has no patience for curt dismissals of Husserl. Unlike many of his critics Harman never delivers his disagreements with Husserl mockingly. Far from dismissing the founder of phenomenology as merely another idealist, Harman finds a number of things useful for the realist cause in Husserl's account of object perception. Among these are his elaboration of Franz Brentano's concept of intentionality and, especially, Husserl's phenomenological description of "intentional objects," which Harman returns to again and again.

Substantial discussions of Husserl can be found in *Guerrilla Metaphysics* (Chapter 2) and "On the Horror of Phenomenology" from *Collapse* IV, and in abbreviated form in *Towards Speculative Realism* (Chapter 8), *The Quadruple Object* (Chapter 2), and other texts. Harman doubles down on Husserl on what seems like a mundane point, but one which bears considerable critical weight in Husserl's articulation and considerable metaphysical weight for Harman: when we look out at the world we perceive objects, not bundles of qualities that require human synthesis to become unified objects, as the British empiricists maintained. Wherever there is quality it is attached to a particular thing which is composed of a singular set of features. Likewise for the substance of an object: it is never a "bare featureless 'this'," but always teeming with specific qualities.[6] The real enemy of Husserl in the first half of *Logical Investigations* is not psychologism, as is often believed, but empiricism. As Harman summarizes it in 2007 at Goldsmiths: "Somehow the objects are not given for British empiricism. What's given are qualities, and those qualities are fused together by the human subject. That's what the entire phenomenological tradition opposes."[7] What Husserl notices is that intentionality does not aim at qualities; it aims at objects. Even when I investigate an object from a series of angles that yields countless disparate profiles (even drastically disparate, as in the case of a subway system or funhouse), I always take those profiles to be perspectives on *the same* object. My "taking it to be" does not guarantee that the object really is the same, but it is nevertheless the case that I *intend* what seems to be a single substantial object. The fact that there are discernible objects, whatever their structure turns out to be, is the basis of Harman's entire philosophy.[8]

What intentionality aims at throughout any series of profiles is not a real object located in the physical world. It is an "ideal unity" or unifying form that binds all the qualities of the object together. The substantial form of the object, however, is always only immanent to consciousness. It is a product constituted within intentionality. On the one hand, Husserl has a Platonic streak running through his analysis of objects insofar as he says that the object's unity is not the result of synthesis. It eludes and exists independently of every human perspective. This is how he distances himself from empiricism, and Kant for that matter. On the other hand, he refuses to situate the object – largely because of his methodological commitment to bracketing questions of realism – directly in the nonhuman realm. This is, as Harman explains, "for fear of letting naturalism back into philosophy through the side door." The resultant effect is summarized by Harman like this: "Stripped of its objectivity, though obviously more unified than the separate appearances that announce it, the object is trapped in a difficult position. It is irreducible to its series of appearances, yet it exists outside of them only as an ideal principle, not as something truly independent."[9] Husserl's object lacks depth. Intentionality completely exhausts its existence. Every partial profile still delivers the object in its full presence. A profile is not a fragment of an object or an image, but an aspect of the whole object itself, although intentionality does elicit an intriguing tension on the surface of objects that attracts Harman's attention. In order to reanimate the autonomous lives of objects Harman must show that intentionality actually *alludes* to a real object replete with a hidden depth never to be traversed by any immanent encounter. But for this he will need Heidegger.

Intentional objects are intrinsic to the privileged human drama of intentionality. They do not exist outside human consciousness and they are the only objects that phenomenology as phenomenology is capable of talking about. What Harman notices is that intentionality itself can become an intentional object. With this idea he attempts a revival of phenomenology by "expanding the concept of intentionality to the point where it covers the entirety of the things themselves, thereby freeing us from the growing staleness of the philosophy of access."[10] Harman expands the concept of intentionality in his own work so that intentions are not just something enacted by humans. Intentionality comes to figure as the very of structure of an object. Here is how Harman put it at Goldsmiths:

> My intentional relationship with the table for Husserl can be viewed as a unit, the relation itself as a whole. Why? Because I can talk about this relation, I can retroactively think about it, I can have other people analyse it for me ... and none of those analyses ever exhaust the relation, which is enough to make it an object. That's the definition of the object: not a solid, hard thing, but a thing that has a unified reality that is not exhausted by any relation to it, so that the intention as a whole is one thing.[11]

As every reader of Husserl knows, the intentional relation contains two elements or poles: the ego/noesis pole and the object/noema pole. What Husserl emphasizes, however, is that these poles do not indicate two separate entities fused together or internally related. Their relation is entirely contingent and, within the intention, they are dimensions of an ideal unity. They are simply two sides – one phenomenal (the table), one real (the human onlooker) – of a singular fleeting object. There is, then, a fundamental asymmetry in the relation between subject and object in that only one pole is real, while the other is only phenomenal, or "sensual" in Harman's terms. Note that this relation can also be reversed, with the table becoming a real object while the onlooker is reduced to the way it "appears" to the table.[12] This is not a point that Husserl pushes, but it follows from his analysis according to Harman, who follows it quite far.

Intentionality has two separate functions. First, it brings subject and object together to form a cohesive unity capable of being analyzed as such. Harman calls this its "adhesive" function. Second, intentionality is "selective," and in two senses. When intentionality unites subject and object together it does so with a distinct specificity. The angle, attitude, and ambience of any intention determines that the object is always presented in a specific light. We do not encounter flat ideas or general things in our lives, but distinct sensations and one-of-a-kind phenomena. Its commitment to talking about these things, and not merely the conceptual ground beneath them, is what lends "concreteness" to Husserl's phenomenology.[13]

Intentionality is also selective in that it works to draw out objects from the background of the perceptual environment. When I look out my window I do not see swaths of green, white, blue, and brown. I see the leaves of the oak across the street, my neighbor's house, or the bricks on the sidewalk, depending on where my consciousness aims. Consciousness picks out, or objectifies, some object while allowing the others to blend into an indeterminate horizon. At any moment the background can yield a new object to replace the one previously in focus, which is why Harman writes that intentionality "offers a very *specific* presence, a life that varies from moment to moment."[14] Husserl calls this variable focus that brings objects into relief an "objectifying act." His idea is that we first and foremost perceive things, not raw sense data, and these things are objectified by intentionality. This does not entail that consciousness produces objects, or even that it has total access to them (it does not), but that it articulates experience in a way that makes it seem like we live among real objects. But we do not; we live among profiles of objects, in what Harman calls "a strange medium located somewhere between substances and qualities, unable to touch either of them." Or, citing Sartre's more classical formulation: "The essence of an existent is no longer a property sunk in the cavity of this existent; it is the manifest law which presides over the succession of its appearances, it is the principle of the series … The phenomenal being … is nothing but the well connected series of its manifestations."[15] In delivering the object to consciousness, intentionality never delivers an object's objectivity. It simply provides the object with a coherence that its individual appearances lack.

Saying more about intentionality at this point will lead us too far into the details of Harman's philosophy, so it will suffice here to note that Husserl's notion of intentionality serves as the model for Harman's objects, and that intentionality is democratized to include subject/object and object/object interaction. As well, it raises a tricky problem about causation.[16] Moreover, Harman's entire project is by his own admission an attempt to radicalize two paradoxes of intentional existence. First, within an intentional act subject and object are fused together in a single relation while still remaining separate from each other and the other objects in their vicinity. Second, any intentional object bears within it a tension between its unified core and its sensuous surface. Not surprisingly, this "enmity" within individual objects raises an important question about the object's unity.[17]

What intrigues Harman more than intentionality is Husserl's discovery of the enmity between the phenomenal quality and the substance/essence of intentional objects, or what Harman calls *sensual objects*. As he writes, "Husserl's breakthrough in philosophy has not been fully assimilated if we neglect his revolutionary distinction within the sensual realm between unified objects and their shifting multitude of features."[18] He poetically characterizes this distinction as "an active seismic zone where intentional objects grind slowly against their own qualities," thus noting the separation between the identity of an object and its shifting, contingent appearance.[19] Sensual objects may possess necessary, or eidetic, features, but they are not real, as in autonomous; they hide nothing of themselves from the phenomenological descriptions given of them. They are objects as encountered from the outside, whether by a human, animal, or inanimate thing. They are purely immanent, their real existence bracketed by the phenomenologist's reductions. And yet sensual objects resist subsumption by the egos directed at them. This is their most important aspect. As Harman writes, "they are something different from the profiles through which they become manifest; the mailbox is something more, or perhaps something less, than any of its specific incarnations in perception."[20] A sensual object's essence is never revealed to any spectator but might be attained by "*subtracting* [all of its] adumbrations" through the intellectual exercise that Husserl calls "eidetic variation."[21] What you see is what there is: a specific, excessive thing that is, as Harman describes it, "encrusted" with qualities covering it "like cosmetics and jewels."[22]

Indeed, sensual objects possess real, that is, necessary, qualities beyond the contingently sensual – this is what makes a rabbit *this* particular rabbit whether it is hiding from a predator, hopping gaily, or rapidly scratching its ear. Its fur changes hue in the light and with the seasons, but these surface effects have no bearing on the rabbit's identity. Its identity, however, "can only be inferred indirectly rather than witnessed."[23] It is never presented directly in intentionality; it is not something merely sensual, but it is sensual. Its reality is paradoxical because its independence is dependent on the intentional relation. Crucially, Husserl never locates the object's essence outside of the immanent presentations of intentionality; he maintains that there is nothing concealed below or beyond the object as it appears to us.[24] He never calls objects real in the metaphysical sense and cannot admit of their withdrawn status without committing himself to a metaphysics prohibited by his method of choice.[25] Phenomenology can only take him so far into the inner recesses of the object.

What Harman takes away from Husserl's sensual objects is the concept of "allusion." This is how sensual objects, to the phenomenologically sensitive observer, indirectly refer to their real, hidden features. Husserl, in Harman's view, mistakenly believes that the intellect can directly intuit these features, and that this is what makes them real. But the reality of objects is something that is closed off from both the senses and the intuitive intellect. They are not immanent to intentionality or necessarily correlated with human consciousness, which can only cut them down to human size. "Copper wires, bicycles, wolves, and triangles all have real qualities, but these genuine traits will never be exhausted by the feeble sketches of them delivered to our hearts and minds," writes Harman.[26] The best we can do is allude to these traits with a greater or lesser degree of clarity and distinctness.

With sensual objects Husserl reveals the duality, or duel, unfolding within every object's appearance. By the same token he makes clear that sensual objects are not real objects beyond the reach of human access, but are fully present or presentable to human intuition or intellection. This is a point acutely registered by Levinas, who attempts to add a little more materiality to Husserl's sensual objects. Levinas latched onto a certain deficiency in the reality of Husserl's objects, and made this a recurrent theme in his critical studies of phenomenology in books like *Discovering Existence with Husserl*. Before leaving Husserl we should briefly note how Levinas tries to amend Husserl's account of substantial things.

Levinas, along with Merleau-Ponty and Lingis, is one of what Harman calls the carnal phenomenologists. These thinkers have little time for "objectifying acts aimed at abstract intentional unities" because their energies are spent attending to the "translucent mist of qualities and signals in which our lives are stationed."[27] For Levinas, this mist is "the elemental," that formless and nonobjective materiality out of which all things come and to which they eventually return. This vague layer of existence is without substance and can be described as the ungraspable medium of pure quality from which we derive our sensual enjoyment of the world. Because it is prior to and conditions objectifying acts, it is more primordial than Husserl's sensual objects. Another name for it is "sensibility."[28] And it is sensation that makes contact with it.

Harman is of two minds when it comes to Levinas's attempt to establish the elemental layer of existence operating below intentionality. On the one hand, he sides with Husserl in reasserting that we never enjoy pure qualities, but specific things, a point that Levinas himself recognizes. "The sensible quality [always] already clings to a substance," says Levinas.[29] This means that a clear dualism cannot be maintained between the work of the intellect and the work of sensation. The only dualism that can be gleaned from the sensual enjoyment of objects is "a ubiquitous schism between the thing as a unit and the myriad sensual facets by which it appears," which we already find in Husserl.[30] On the other hand, Levinas provides us with a degree of realism unavailable in Husserl because he insists on the strange, impersonal, *otherness* of the world. The world is at all times capable of surprising us in Levinas's view, in a way that Husserl's restriction of the world to immanence cannot. This point was emphasized by Braver's transgressive realism. No matter how intense or detailed our representations, the alterity of the world cannot be exhausted by language, perception, or intellection.[31] This is admittedly a "minimal trace of realism," but nevertheless it adamantly resists the reduction of reality to representation.[32] And yet, Levinas does not grant any specificity to either the elemental or being in general, the *il y a* of *Existence and Existents* and other early texts. As Harman notes, "All concrete features are to be restricted to the zone of things regarded as visible spectacles for humans, and are forbidden amidst the vague ambient wealth of wind and sea – to say nothing of the hidden mythical depth."[33] Apart from the vague, anonymous rumble of the *il y a*, Levinas leaves nothing real in the dark depths of being when no humans are around to hypostatize it. A full-fledged realism must give an account of interobject encounters and causal interaction when no humans are around as witnesses. This we get in neither Husserl nor the carnal phenomenologists, although, as we will see, we get something close to it in Heidegger.

At the end of the day Husserlian phenomenology, especially after the *Logical Investigations*, cannot be anything other than idealism. "Despite being an idealist," writes Harman, Husserl "*feels* like a realist to such a degree that his followers often assume there is no more reality to be had than the kind that Husserl already addresses."[34] The feel of realism in Husserl is no doubt an effect of the rhetoric of concreteness. This rhetoric has generated the promise of realism in phenomenology, but one which is not forthcoming. Husserl's account of objects is always an account of how objects appear to a human onlooker. He is almost never concerned with particular objects or their interactions, but only with their *eidos*, their essence, their noematic core – none of which escapes intentional disclosure. He likewise leaves causality, a central problem for Harman's ontology, for the natural scientists. Even if there is more to the intentional object than meets the eye, the intentional object, for Husserl, remains a phenomenal correlate of human consciousness. In Harman's terms, Husserlian phenomenology is at bottom a philosophy of access,[35] but it is an object-oriented philosophy with some surprises inside. Next we will see how Heidegger modifies phenomenology to uncover a second duel within objects and, in the process, unwittingly gives rise to a new realist metaphysics.

From Heidegger to Metaphysical Realism

The institution of Harman's object-oriented philosophy is traceable to the unorthodox, yet compelling, reading of Heidegger which forms the bulk of *Tool-Being*. This reading finds an abbreviated recapitulation in many other texts, including the early "Phenomenology and the Theory of Equipment" and "A Fresh Look at *Zuhandenheit*" which date from 1997 and 1999, respectively, and appear as chapters in *Towards Speculative Realism*. If *Tool-Being* reads Heidegger in what Deleuze refers to as "slow motion," then these early essays deliver a kind of time-lapse photography of Harman's commentary. Luckily for us Heidegger turns out under Harman's lens to be a monotonous thinker with little more than a "single repetitive dualism" cycling through his collected works.[36] This means that Harman's reading of Heidegger, minus some of the details, can be gleaned from any of the recapitulations given in works other than *Tool-Being*. If you require a complete defense of the coherence and hermeneutic legitimacy of Harman's interpretation, however, it is *Tool-Being* you want.[37]

Part of Harman's strategy for realism entails reading phenomenology almost against itself, looking for moments when the phenomenologist provides a description that gestures toward a radical metaphysical point yet chooses instead to remain on the surface of the phenomenon under description. This is evident in his analysis of Husserl's intentional objects. Perhaps better than any other, his reading of Heidegger exhibits Harman's methodological shift away from phenomenology and toward a metaphysics of objects. If Harman's method involves a radicalization of phenomenology, it is a radicalization of what phenomenology prefers to leave unsaid, namely, what lies beneath the hustle and bustle of the *Lebenswelt*. If it is Heidegger who inaugurates this shift, he does so "accidentally."[38]

Given the title of his book it would be surprising if Harman's major thesis in *Tool-Being* was not that "the key to Heidegger's philosophy is the concept of *Zuhandenheit* or readiness-to-hand," otherwise known simply as "tool-being."[39] Tool-being unlocks Heidegger's familiar theory of equipment just as much as it explains the concept of "withdrawal" that permeates Harman's speculative realism. A brief exposition of *Zuhandenheit* and its dueling partner *Vorhandenheit* (presence-at-hand) will enable us to get to the bottom of tool-being and, by consequence, the withdrawn status of real objects. For the sake of this discussion, we will focus on withdrawal as a defining feature of real objects, rather than on some other feature.

It is real objects that Heidegger offers us in reply to Husserl, even if he fails to take interest in the interactions between specific inanimate objects. It is symptomatic of his sympathy for phenomenology that Heidegger neglects the invisible life of things, and it is to this neglect that Harman's version of speculative realism gathers like a moth to a flame. As Harman writes, "If there is a sense in which Heidegger can be read as a realist corrective to Husserl, even Heidegger does not see the collision of inanimate things as philosophically meaningful."[40] At the end of Harman's reading Heidegger remains a philosopher of access, for his ontology is always mediated by the phenomenological descriptions of the privileged being called Dasein. This is what prevents it from being a "flat" ontology.[41] "Phenomenology," writes Heidegger, "is our way of access to what is to be the theme of ontology, and it is our way of giving it demonstrative precision. *Only as phenomenology, is ontology possible*."[42] His human-orientation notwithstanding, Heidegger's phenomenology calls for something more. It beckons us like a grim ticket-taker at the entrance to an abandoned mineshaft.

Harman's method of reading Heidegger is clear. He does not attempt to reconstruct Heidegger's manifest understanding of the tool-analysis; he does not attempt a hermeneutic retrieval of Heidegger's true doctrine; instead, he provides an "improved understanding, not of *Heidegger*, but of the concept of *tool-being*, which he was the first to identify with such precision."[43] Harman latches onto tool-being as the key to unlocking objects in their being apart from how their being reveals itself to human observers. But, if for Heidegger it is *Vorhandenheit* that stands as the enemy of our understanding of objects, in his battle against it he misses the full significance of *Zuhandenheit* even as he unpacks an intensive and extensive analysis of its meaning.[44] The critical point lies at the moment when *Vorhandenheit* passes over into *Zuhandenheit*, and vice versa. This is where the object glistens with and veils its reality. For Harman, this is occurring at every instant whether humans are around or not. It will never appear to them, however, no matter how focused their attention or minute their descriptions. It must be inferred from the phenomenology of tools.

Everyone is familiar with the basic duality at the heart of *Being and Time*'s analysis of tools: presence-at-hand (*Vorhandenheit*) v. readiness-to-hand (*Zuhandenheit*).[45] Put simply, this is the difference between explicitly noticing an object, say, staring at a hammer, and implicitly noticing that hammer while explicitly focusing on some end for which the hammer is used as a means – nailing a sign on a wall. For the most part the things we deal with every day are ready-to-hand, mostly unnoticed in any detail or in their own right ... until they breakdown and become unusable. When I use a tool it ceases to be a merely present object before my theoretical or intrigued gaze. It recedes into the background of whatever project I am engrossed in while using the tool. It has become ready-to-hand, something used "in order to...," or what Heidegger calls *equipment*. When this equipment malfunctions, as everyone who has broken a tool or heard about Heidegger's broken hammer knows, it once again becomes present-at-hand and, in its uselessness, "obtrusive."[46] In Heidegger's words,

> In dealings [with tools], where something is put to use, our concern subordinates itself to the "in order to" which is constitutive for the equipment we are employing at the time; the less we just stare at the hammer-Thing, and the more we seize hold of it and use it, the

more primordial does our relationship to it become, and the more unveiledly is it encountered as that which it is – as equipment. The hammering itself uncovers the specific "manipulability" ... of the hammer. The kind of Being which equipment possesses – in which it manifests itself in its own right – we call *"readiness-to-hand"* [*Zuhandenheit*].[47]

This idea develops Husserl's description of intentionality to account for the way an objectifying act effectively pulls other objects into its orbit without making them the focus of the act. Ready-to-hand objects are neither the center of an intentional act nor the unthematized background of that act; they are not the object pole of an intentional act, nor are they merely mute or indifferent things lying in wait for their fifteen minutes of fame. They perform in a liminal realm somewhere between the focused and unfocused, present and absent – deployed as covert operatives in Dasein's existential mission.

The usual reading of the tool-analysis extrapolates from Heidegger's text the following phenomenological lesson: practice precedes theory. This entails that the objective reality of things is dependent on, or conditioned by, how humans use them. This is partially true for Heidegger, but it is beside the point for Harman. It is also partially false because, as Harman notes,

at this moment I am relying on countless items of equipment including the floor, sunlight, and bodily organs. These tend to be invisible to me unless they malfunction. But the point is not that I am "using" them: the point is that I can only use them because they are real, because they are capable of inflicting some sort of blow on reality.[48]

The being of a tool is not the result of its actual human use or even of its potential usefulness, it is the result of "its silent performance of its own reality prior to any theoretical *or* practical contact we might have with it."[49] What does this performance entail and how does Harman know about it if it is always hidden?

In Heidegger's view both presence-at-hand and readiness-to-hand are disclosed phenomenologically. As already noted, even if tools in use recede from explicit thematization, their readiness-to-hand is never completely absent from view. In fact, it is precisely our oblique awareness of them as means to completing a certain task that brings *Zuhandenheit* to light. Heidegger warns against mistakenly interpreting this to mean that tool-being is just an aspect of beings. On the contrary, it is *"the way in which entities as they are 'in themselves' are defined ontologico-categorically."*[50] Tool-being enjoys a certain priority over objectively present things. But, Harman contends, this has nothing to do with human comportment, it has everything to do with how objects deploy themselves at all times against all things, animate and inanimate. Any object whatsoever is a tool-being because tool-being is just another name for the way objects *withdraw from any relation*, rendering themselves invisible while they interact with something else. Another way of putting this is to say that tools perpetually waver between presence and absence. What Heidegger misses is that this duality belongs to *every being whatsoever*, not just machinery, utensils, and other implements. "Tool-being," writes Harman, "is the name for a fundamental dualism that rips through the heart of everything that is: not just tools in the limited sense, but also plants, animals, numbers, machines, rocks, and even people."[51] To understand why this is we must see that "equipment" is not just a synonym for "tool," but the name of a total system in which every object is deployed at all times – otherwise called the meaning of being.

A tool never exists apart from other tools. It is defined by an entire network of tools. Equipment is the name of a system or totality, a multiplicity of tools that operate together as a unit. A single tool is not equipment. There is "no such thing as *an* equipment."[52] There is more to this than the lesson that the use of one tool involves an entire network of tools, or that the readiness-to-hand of a single tool is dependent upon its involvement with other tools. It means that the being of tools is swallowed up in the particular system in which they are deployed. But in this way their being is never exhausted. Instead, it is hidden within a context insofar as "at any given moment, every tool is plugged into certain limited systems of machinery while excluded from others."[53] For Harman the lesson here is not just that every object is always determined by its context (which is nevertheless true), nor that reality is constituted by relations (which is also true, in part). It is that every single thing is always already ensnared in a totality of things – the world – that masks its tool-being behind a multiplicity of facades, functions, objectifications, and deployments. *"Zuhandensein* is the action of *beings themselves."*[54] This is not to say that readiness-to-hand is the entirety of the "real" dimension of objects, whereas presence-at-hand is the "apparent." Both dimensions are real, and tool-being spans both sides. Or, put differently, tool-being is the "duplicitous" interplay of both dimensions together. Every object whatsoever is always at the same time a tool in action and a "broken" tool.[55]

There is no nonarbitrary way to limit tool-being to the narrow set of objects we refer to as tools. As Harman argues, "In the strict sense, all objects in the universe refer to one another. If one of them changes, however slightly, the entire interlaced system of meaning has shifted in some minute but undeniable way."[56] This means that all objects are tool-beings, in the sense that all of them at all times harbor an "ontological fissure" that renders them present and absent from the phenomenal realm. And this is not because everything is connected – a thesis Harman rejects[57] – but because at the level of relation objects *never* stop referring to other objects. This, however, is not the substance of their reality. It is only one half of their reality, the way they make themselves present as this or that thing engaged in this or that context. In Harman's terms, every relation results in the *caricature* of the objects involved; never does a relation render present the tool-being of an object. As he writes, "to see something 'as' such-and-such is to reduce its manifold reality to a small set of limited properties, which both illuminates and caricatures whatever it is we talk about."[58] The limited properties encountered in a relation are those of the sensual object, the object as phenomenally given. But caricature is not an exclusively human action, for as we have seen, all objects are capable of intentionality and the reduction to sensual presence entailed therein.

Harman sums up the basic duality at the heart of things:

> A police officer eating a banana reduces this fruit to a present-at-hand profile of its elusive depth, as do a monkey eating the same banana, a parasite infecting it, or a gust of wind blowing it from a tree. Banana-being is a genuine reality in the world, a reality never exhausted by any relation to it by humans or other entities. The basic dualism in the world lies not between spirit and nature, or phenomenon and noumenon, but between things in their intimate reality and things as confronted by other things. With this single conceptual step, metaphysics is freed from its recent pariah status in philosophy – supplanting all phenomenologies, hermeneutic circles, textual disseminations, linguistic turns, and other philosophies of access, and thereby regaining something of its former status as queen of the sciences.[59]

What Heidegger provides for Harman is not a recapitulation of Kant's distinction between things as they appear and things in themselves, since the double life of objects is not essentially an effect of human cognition, even if Heidegger fails to fully appreciate this point. Against both Kant and Husserl, Heidegger manages to deliver real objects to phenomenology. This comes, of course, at the cost of phenomenology, since the full significance of *Zuhandenheit* cannot be gleaned from any phenomenological analysis because no analysis or description can cut into the withdrawn, hidden structure of objects.

The reason Heidegger restricts *Zuhandenheit* to tools seems to be the result of, in a word, haste. Tools are the most obvious objects to get mobilized as a set in order to accomplish a project. They are what humans use to work, and insofar as work occupies much of our lives, they readily present themselves as remarkable to the phenomenologist engaged in an investigation of the everyday. So, it is not arbitrary that Heidegger singles out tools as exemplarily ready-to-hand. By his own understanding, however, equipment has a much wider significance. Most of the things that populate our world withdraw from conscious awareness in the way that his tools do: baseball bats and tractors, spatulas and rocking chairs, technological and urban infrastructure are just some of the most familiar things we rely on as humans.[60] They may not withdraw in *precisely* the same way, phenomenologically speaking, but they nevertheless withdraw into the same "shadowy subterranean realm that supports our conscious activity while seldom erupting into view."[61] *Zuhandenheit* does not indicate the way the use of equipment becomes invisible when used; rather, it names the way that the reality of equipment becomes invisible when in action. This can occur whether it is in use by some tool-wielding agent – human, primate, raven – or not. And yet, this way of putting it misses Harman's critical point against Heidegger: the withdrawal of objects from presence is not the effect of human interaction alone, but is what occurs whenever an object interacts with the phenomenal surface of any other object. Which is always. Nothing can unearth the object's concealed tool-being; it is hopelessly, absolutely invisible. It is also absolutely real. Beyond this, Heidegger has little more to teach us.

On this reading, Heidegger's phenomenological ontology figures as a "hybrid" correlationism, something different from the nascent strong correlationism we find in Husserl and those working in his vein. Insofar as he initiates a radical break from Husserl and phenomenology, he can be called a "correlationist realist," but not in the sense that this moniker could be applied to Meillassoux. Indeed, Meillassoux may accept the label for himself, but reject it for Heidegger. For Meillassoux, Heidegger is the quintessential strong correlationist. As Harman explains, "with this phrase ["correlationist realist"] I do not mean Meillassoux's own project of establishing realism *by way of* correlationism, but an actual simultaneous belief in correlationism and realism. That is to say, Heidegger holds that human and world must always come as a package, but he also holds that being is not fully manifest to humans." [62] As we saw in earlier chapters, this double commitment to correlationism and realism raises difficult ontological questions for the person committed to it. This is why Harman declines to endorse it.

Object-Oriented Philosophy as Antiphenomenology and Weird Realism

As a renewal of substance ontology[63] Harman's radicalization of phenomenology generates a classical problem. If objects are absolutely distinct from one another, vacuum-sealed units whose real properties can never be accessed or touched by another object, then how is it possible for them to interact? How is causation possible? For medieval and early modern philosophers, most conspicuously Malebranche, the answer was "occasionalism" – the view that at any given moment God is intervening in the order of things to enable them to interact. Harman is no classical philosopher, however. He devises an updated version of this solution that makes no claim on God or any other transcendent entity to explain interobject causation. He calls this *vicarious causation*.

Recall two lessons that Harman culls from the pages of Husserl and Heidegger:

1) Any intentional relation yields a new object.
2) Any object is comprised of phenomenal features available to intentionality and real qualities that remain forever inaccessible to intentionality.

Note that these two roughly phenomenological insights generate a specific metaphysical problem that is at least nonphenomenological, although I would say *anti*phenomenological, in nature. The same year of the Goldsmiths colloquium on speculative realism, Harman published in *Collapse* II the article "On Vicarious Causation,"[64] which later came under discussion at Goldsmiths. Here Harman presents his unique take on the medieval Arabic notion of occasional cause and the weird realism that accompanies it. Although vicarious causation is a primary feature of an earlier text, *Guerrilla Metaphysics*, and returns in later texts like *The Quadruple Object*, my brief exposition mainly focuses on the *Collapse* article.[65]

Vicarious causation is a decidedly antiphenomenological problem because it arises *despite all appearances* to the contrary. Whereas the phenomenologist finds causal interaction occurring everywhere, the speculative metaphysician makes causal interaction a problem of philosophy. To the phenomenologist it is perceptually obvious that one object is capable of causing some effect on another. It could be argued that if we look more closely, we actually never witness a cause. This is Hume's famous point, not lost on either Kant or Husserl. But this would be beside the point, since, phenomenologically speaking, there is no evidence that objects exist completely independent from one another. Thus, the problem of their interaction never faces the phenomenologist head-on; for her, objects are interacting, in trivial and dramatic ways, all the time. In fact, she might even say that they never stop interacting because objects are nothing without their relations. From Harman's perspective it is clear that real objects *cannot* make contact, at least not at the level of their tool-being. If objects do make some sort of contact, however, we must account for this possibility instead of merely describing what is apparent to the onlooker watching two billiard balls crash together. As Harman sees it we still have no idea how physical causation is possible.[66] This is partly because causation remains to be explained at the *metaphysical* level where Harman situates his analysis.[67]

Harman's answer is that objects do relate causally, but only at the level of their sensual surface; in other words, only sensual objects genuinely interact. Otherwise put, all causation is aesthetic, neither physical nor natural.[68] Why is this? All real objects, for Harman, are substances. This means they enjoy an autonomous reality that precludes any and all outside disturbance or change. This is what their withdrawn tool-being entails. Given this status, all their interactions can only be a kind of action at a distance, or vicarious action, mediated by the third object (intentionality) in which they relate. As Harman exemplifies it, "my encounter with a pine tree is a unified [intentional] relation; we can speak of the encounter as a whole, and this whole resists exhaustive description. But in another sense, I clearly do not fuse with the tree in a single massive lump; it remains distinct from me in the perception." Both subject and object "inhabit the interior of the total intentional relation."[69] When this Husserlian insight is added to Heidegger's discovery of the withdrawal of real objects, and intentionality is extended to include interobjective relations, the metaphysical problem of causation comes to the fore.[70] This is not just a problem from the perspective of perceptual experience, a problem for us. It is, quite simply, an objective problem.

How is it that real objects "poke through into the phenomenal realm," the only place where causal interaction and intentional relations transpire? For medieval and modern occasionalists, the answer was that God makes it happen. For Harman the answer is not so obvious, nor is it obviously forthcoming. Taking up again the example of the pine tree, Harman admits that the intentional relation between himself and the pine tree does not constitute a new object, but a *tête-à-tête* of two real objects that occurs within the interior of a new object – the intention taken as a unit. This unit can be glimpsed in its own right when Harman takes a moment to reflect on his encounter with the pine tree, thus thematizing the intentional event as a whole. This new object is the result of a vicarious relation whose existence remains unexplained, but whose reality is undeniable.[71] The new object has both phenomenal and metaphysical aspects, neither of which can be ignored by philosophy.

When two objects come to face one another, as they do within intentionality, it becomes possible for them to interact causally. But this can only occur via the sensual properties that float on or encrust their surfaces, "buffering" real objects from direct contact with other real objects. As Harman puts it,

> sensual objects, far from being withdrawn, exist side by side in the same perceptual space from the outset, since we encounter numerous phenomena simultaneously. This presents the contrary problem to vicarious causation: namely, why do all the phenomena not instantly fuse together into a single lump? There must be some unknown principle of blockage between them. If real objects require vicarious causation, sensual objects endure a buffered causation in which their interactions are partly dammed or stunted.[72]

"A real object," continues Harman, "resides in the core of an intention, pressed up against numerous sensual ones. Somehow, it pierces their colored mists and connects with a real object already in the vicinity but buffered from direct contact."[73] Harman dubs this relation *sincerity* and determines that it is only as sincerity that two real objects can join up and affect one another causally. For Husserl it is only human consciousness that allows this to occur. For Harman any object is capable of sincerity. Sincerity is just another name for an object existing as what it is and nothing else, and understanding this "dynamic" is the rather simple key to vicarious causation.

Sensual objects are inevitably attractive, they force us to take note of them to the extent that we almost never encounter the world as a blur of undifferentiated qualities. The world is first and foremost populated with things that beckon, glimmer, sparkle, glisten, and shimmer. This is the basic fact of both phenomenology and object-oriented philosophy. Moreover, these things have "a unified and basically ineffable effect on us, one that cannot be reduced to any list of traits."[74] Another name for this effect is *allure*. Allure, for Harman, names both the "bewitching emotional effect" that things have over us (something fully appreciated by Walter Benjamin) and the way in which the sensual surfaces of objects *allude* to a withdrawn reality beyond their appearance.[75]

It has already been established that the inner life of objects cannot be accessed directly, neither with intuition nor intellection nor description, but the real substance of an object can be engaged by what Harman calls an "intentional agent." An intentional agent is any real object that encounters the sensual surface of a sensual object while at the same time intending the essential unity of that object throughout all of its partial profiles and accidental changes. Subtract all of these surface effects and what is left over, but never met face to face, is the object itself, sincere and self-identical. "I," or any object, "make contact with another object, not through impossible contact with its interior life, but only by brushing its surface in such a manner as to bring its inner life into play." Intentional agents are what enable sensual objects to be contiguous, and "connection between real ones does not occur except by means of a sensual intermediary."[76] Sensual objects are the liaisons or professional negotiators between real objects. They thus play a diplomatic and facilitative role in ontology.

No matter how hard we try to go further, we only ever encounter sensual objects, never the real objects that perpetually lure us into their unfathomable depths. As Harman concludes, "Relations between all real objects, including mindless chunks of dirt, occur only by means of some form of allusion. But insofar as we have identified allure with an aesthetic effect, this means that aesthetics becomes first philosophy."[77] It is the sensual realm, not some underlying brute matter, that makes physical and efficient causal relations possible. It is the site where each layer of reality, including the duplicitous interplay of *Zuhandenheit* and *Vorhandenheit*, find common ground.[78] Without this common ground, Harman would be left holding the kind of two-world ontology he desperately wants to trade in for a shiny new realism, fully loaded with strange unexpected features.

Objects not only succeed in captivating us with their allure, they are capable of propelling our sensorimotor systems with what Alphonso Lingis calls *imperatives*. An imperative is a directive given to us not by our reason, as Kant teaches, but from some object outside us. Lingis's imperative is thus heteronomous; objects command us to do this or that, move this way or that, regard them in this way or that. As Harman writes in an early essay on Lingis, "The object is an imperative, radiating over us like a black sun, holding us in its orbit, demanding our attention, insisting that we reorganize our lives along its shifting axes. The object is a force, and thus our valuation of it is a gift of force, and nothing like a recognition at all."[79] For this to happen objects must be real. Lingis is unequivocally the only carnal phenomenologist that Harman is not willing to relegate to the philosophy of access, which is not surprising given Lingis's commitment to the autonomous being of things.[80] Unlike Levinas, for whom it is humans and humans alone who are charged with chiseling out objects from the anonymous, undifferentiated mass of being, Lingis holds that objects generate their own form quite independently of consciousness or phenomenological constitution. Their form is not an effect of intentionality; it is housed and actualized in the qualities themselves and the sincere way in which objects present their surfaces to us.[81] Whereas Merleau-Ponty regards the matter of perception as "'pregnant' with its form"[82] and therefore only made meaningful by human perception, Lingis regards objects as fully capable of giving birth to their own distinct meaning, which humans do not so much deliver as obey.

Another feature of Lingis's imperative is its flatness. For OOO, flatness is a virtue of any given ontology. It refers to any ontology that, as Harman says of Manuel DeLanda's assemblage theory, "allows countless layers of larger and smaller structures to have equal ontological dignity." Or, in other words: "*all relations are on the same footing.*"[83] Above all else, flat ontology rejects the privileged correlation of human and world along with the notion that this pair exhausts the entirety, or even half, of reality. In Lingis's imperative we glimpse the ethical dimension of speculative realism, which is often criticized for a lack of ethical and political potential. It is not just humans that are capable of laying down imperatives, shouting orders and chastising unseemly behavior, as if ethical relations could be legislated and adjudicated by humans alone. Any object or relation may embody imperatives that direct actions and decisions for the intentional agents involved. This is just as true of a painting that demands to be regarded in a particular way, from a certain angle and distance (see Merleau-Ponty), as it is for the contours of your coffee mug that demands to be picked up in specific ways, depending on whether it is filled with scalding hot liquid or nothing at all.

Lingis parts company with phenomenology most explicitly in his discussion of *levels*, which bear within them an imperative of their own. With levels Lingis launches a simultaneous critique of both holism and the figure-ground model of perception which dominates phenomenology. A level is Lingis's name for the unrevealed depths of an object which are suggested, hinted at, on its surface but never wholly revealed. The levels are what lure us deeper into the object itself; they are the summons of the object's withdrawn reality, part and parcel of their allure. A level is like a Wonderland rabbit hole whose price of admission is strict observance of its imperatives. For Lingis the levels exist somewhere between intelligible form and formless quality, what Levinas calls the elemental. Harman quotes Lingis as saying, "The levels 'emerge from the sensory elements, as directives that summon. By following them, a field unfolds'."[84] This is the field of sensual qualities that enables causal relations to occur. The levels are just as real as the objects that rub up against them, and no more a product of human perception or projection than the objects themselves. They form the aesthetic medium that conditions any intentional and causal relation at all.[85]

At this point we are beginning to see how unpredictable, or *weird*, Harman's brand of speculative realism is. We can also begin to make sense of what Harman means when he writes that "Object-oriented philosophy is not designed as a magic cudgel able to pulverize all possible counterarguments in advance, but more as a kind of Suez or Panama [canal] through which phenomenology is obliged to transit, without knowing all of the consequences in advance."[86] Harman is not interested in providing an account of reality that precisely matches how the world "really is" when humans are not around to experience it, as if realism is just about being "able to state correct propositions about the real world." "Instead," writes Harman in *Weird Realism*, "it means that reality is too real to be translated without remainder into any sentence, perception, practical action, or anything else."[87] Hence the importance he places on metaphor and allusion *as precise metaphysical devices*, and why speculative realism often comes so close to speculative or science fiction, or why poetry might have something important to tell us about ontology. While it may be possible to give bad descriptions or accounts of things – precisely because things sincerely are what they are and nothing other than what they are – Harman's brand of speculative realism is less interested in accuracy than it is committed to drawing out every possible dimension of the real, no matter how far-fetched, absurd, terrifying, obvious, or paradoxical. And he aims to do so without arbitrariness, frivolity, or rhetorical sleight-of-hand, just like any good realist.

In Harman's texts a number of dualisms emerge, some of which we have already noted: presence/absence, *Zuhandenheit/Vorhandenheit*, tool/broken tool, substance/accident, object/relation, sensual object/real object. Despite his background in phenomenology Harman never pretends to have overcome dualism in his own thinking; in fact, he openly embraces it. As the title of one of his books indicates, Harman is quite fond of mapping the fourfold structures in reality, the quadrupling of objects.[88] If one of the hallmark gestures of phenomenology is the overcoming of classical dualisms, especially the idealism/realism and appearance/reality oppositions, then Harman is driven by an antiphenomenological affection for the multiplication of dualisms. In fact, it is possible to show that at the center of his entire philosophy lies a precious dualism around which everything else swirls: caricatured object/withdrawn object.[89]

This dualism receives various names in Harman's texts, but in every instance it is the name for the two *modes* of being enjoyed by every object whatsoever. It is not the name of two *kinds* of beings. If it were, then Harman's realism – which obviously favors the withdrawn object – would fall into the trap of ontotheology, with the withdrawn object cast in the role of God or Being or Substance or Form. As he likes to say, however, flat ontology means that all things are equally things.[90]

Just as he tenaciously avoids ontotheology, and despite his fondness for dualism, Harman adamantly opposes a two-world ontology. This is not in the interest of "flatten[ing] everything onto a single plane of immanence, but because object and relations are not two fixed points on a map."[91] It should never be thought that his cherished dualism indicates the existence of noumenal things in themselves, or the existence of objects that absolutely transcend the human-world correlate. There is not a world of appearances (sensual objects) *and* a world of concealed toolbeings (withdrawn objects). These are just two dimensions of the same world, the world of objects. And we, too, are examples of those objects: "The world is composed of countless layers of withdrawn real things, each with a molten core where one of its real pieces confronts the sensual image of another piece, thereby forming a bridge between one layer of reality and the next."[92] The rift that exists between caricatured objects and withdrawn objects is internal to the objects themselves. It is not imposed on them by Kantian human onlookers who exist in a world apart and who organize the totality of being according to their unique relation to the world. These onlookers are themselves internally split, because they too are objects.[93] Every object has two sides. For every object other than ourselves we only ever experience one of its sides, the sensual. The other must be deduced. And this is something that phenomenology does not do.

Harman holds clear reservations about the adequacy of phenomenology for the realist enterprise. In his view even the carnal phenomenologists, who still believe they have extricated phenomenology from the prison of Husserlian idealism, only get us halfway to realism and object-oriented philosophy. Even Merleau-Ponty, thought by many to be the realist corrective to Husserl, wavers between realism and idealism before ultimately settling on a relational ontology whose "real" objects are, in his paradoxical phrase, "in themselves for us." As Harman puts it, Merleau-Ponty provides us increasingly with a "metaphysics of relations" that regards "the reality of the thing" as "the sum total of perspectives by which other things perceive it."[94] Nothing lies locked away in the belly of the object; it leaves nothing hidden, as Merleau-Ponty says.[95] The possibility never occurs to Merleau-Ponty that the reality of the thing is not the sum total of perspective *on it*, but the perspective on the world taken *by it*, how the thing encounters the world around *it*. Here is Harman's final assessment of phenomenology as such, so unequivocally stated in *The Quadruple Object* that it deserves quoting at length:

> By confining itself to sensual objects and leaving no room for real ones, phenomenology is idealist to the core, and cannot get away with dismissing as a "pseudo-problem" a difficulty that happens to threaten its own views about the world. Many attempts have been made to salvage some hints of reality from this predicament. The problem is that none of these efforts assault the human-world correlate with adequate vigor. For example, some people try to save phenomenology by claiming that the human subject is not an absolute shaper of the universe, but a passive recipient of something that is "given" to it. But this supposed solution misses the point: the main problem with phenomenology was never the constituting role of the ego or its insufficient passivity over against the world. Instead, the problem is that human and world remain the only two poles of this philosophy, both of them participants in every situation of which one can possibly speak.[96]

Just as he eschews phenomenology and its sworn enemy, naturalism, Harman resists the temptation of materialism, not only as a name for his own program, but as a species of philosophical realism about objects. Both classical and contemporary materialism are unacceptable in Harman's view because they do not take objects as the constituent components of reality, but instead reduce them to their smaller atomic or subatomic parts until "what seems at first like an autonomous object is really just a motley aggregate built of smaller pieces."[97] Materialism thus "undermines"[98] the reality of objects by maintaining that only the basic material elements of objects are real. This is just as true of Democritus, Leucippus, and Epicurus as it is of Meillassoux, whose speculative materialism maintains that the only things that are absolutely real, and consequently absolutely knowable, are the mathematizable primary qualities of an object. For Harman, by contrast, nothing of the real object is absolutely knowable. This is a consequence of accepting the finitude of human knowing, an epistemological limit Meillassoux (after Badiou) rejects.[99]

My purpose in this chapter has been to provide neither a critical reading of Harman's philosophy nor a full account of object-oriented philosophy as such. I have neither contested nor defended his interpretations of the phenomenologists. At times I moved too quickly through his arguments and assertions, but only because my primary purpose was to provide an account of how his speculative project starts from, as well as parts with, phenomenology. Furthermore, I sought to anchor this account in a range of his texts. With any luck, this was accomplished. Numerous criticisms of Harman exist, some of them serious and academic, others territorial, dismissive, or juvenile. The four most common objections to his philosophy are outlined and rebutted in the third chapter of *Bells and Whistles*, and a handful of other criticisms are met head-on in *Skirmishes*.[100]

Notes

1. Harman, *Towards Speculative Realism*, 107, emphasis added.
2. Hence the title of Bryant et al., *The Speculative Turn*.
3. For Harman's take on the strength of what Meillassoux calls the Fichtean "performative contradiction," or what Harman dubs the "supposed paradox" of the "Weak Access position," see Graham Harman, *The Quadruple Object* (Winchester: Zero Books, 2011), 65–7.
4. Harman, *The Quadruple Object*, 110. On page 73: "Access to the things themselves can only be indirect."
5. Harman, *The Quadruple Object*, 77. Braver is skeptical of talk about how objects interact with each other when humans are not around. What Braver misses, I think, is the phenomenological motivation behind Harman's speculation, as well as the "deductive" method Harman employs to get at the structure of objects. Harman is not out to describe what happens when objects are left alone, unsupervised by humans, but what objects do "in the dark" *and* in the bright light of our gaze.

6. Harman, *Guerrilla Metaphysics*, 30. Merleau-Ponty is particularly good on this point in *Phenomenology of Perception*.

7. Brassier et al., "Speculative Realism," 376. See also Harman, *Guerrilla Metaphysics*, 27.

8. Graham Harman, *Tool-Being: Heidegger and the Metaphysics of Objects* (Chicago: Open Court, 2002), 44.

9. Harman, *Guerrilla Metaphysics*, 25, 29.

10. Harman, *Guerrilla Metaphysics*, 23. I am not convinced that Harman attempts a "revival" of phenomenology, even though he doubtless bears certain allegiances to the movement and its method. Perhaps Ian Bogost's *Alien Phenomenology; or, What It's Like to Be a Thing* (Minneapolis: University of Minnesota Press, 2012) is closest to a revival.

11. Brassier et al., "Speculative Realism," 377.

12. Harman discusses this reversal as Whiteheadian prehension in *Tool-Being*, §20.

13. Harman, *Guerrilla Metaphysics*, 22–3; *Towards Speculative Realism*, 152. Incidentally, it is Grant's work, discussed in the following chapter, that takes ground as its primary research subject.

14. Harman, *Guerrilla Metaphysics*, 22.

15. Harman, *Guerrilla Metaphysics*, 24, 25.

16. For more on this, see Graham Harman, "On Vicarious Causation," in *Collapse* II, 182, 189, and the discussion below.

17. Harman, *Guerrilla Metaphysics*, 30.

18. Harman, *The Quadruple Object*, 25–6.

19. Harman, *The Quadruple Object*, 26–7.

20. Harman, *Towards Speculative Realism*, 152.

21. Harman, *The Quadruple Object*, 24, 27.

22. Graham Harman, "On the Horror of Phenomenology: Lovecraft and Husserl," *Collapse* IV (2008), 352; *The Quadruple Object*, 29; *Towards Speculative Realism*, 127.

23. Harman, *The Quadruple Object*, 29.

24. Harman, *The Quadruple Object*, 24, 25.

25. Harman, *The Quadruple Object*, 28; *Towards Speculative Realism*, 127.

26. Harman, *The Quadruple Object*, 28.

27. Harman, *Guerrilla Metaphysics*, 34.

28. Harman, *Guerrilla Metaphysics*, 38. On enjoyment, see Section II of Levinas, *Totality and Infinity*.

29. Quoted in Harman, *Guerrilla Metaphysics*, 39.

30. Harman, *Guerrilla Metaphysics*, 39; Graham Harman, "Levinas and the Triple Critique of Heidegger," *Philosophy Today* (Winter 2009), 412.

31. Harman, "Levinas and the Triple Critique of Heidegger," 409, 411.

32. In addition to his essays on Husserl, see Emmanuel Levinas, "The Ruin of Representation," in *Discovering Existence with Husserl*, trans. Richard A. Cohen and Michael B. Smith (Evanston: Northwestern University Press, 1998).

33. Harman, *Guerrilla Metaphysics*, 40.

34. Harman, *The Quadruple Object*, 30–1.

35. Harman calls him a "zoological oddity among philosophers: an *object-oriented* idealist." *The Quadruple Object*, 20.

36. Harman, *Tool-Being*, 3.

37. *Tool-Being* is not only the place to find Harman's first published presentation of object-oriented philosophy, it is also a formidable and unexpected intervention into Heidegger studies. It is the kind of thing that would have a difficult time finding acceptance among established Heidegger scholars. Harman's writing throughout the book is tinged with an acute awareness of this fact, and he never shies away from directly taking on both the accepted readings of Heidegger as well as the luminaries of Anglo-American Heidegger studies. *Tool-Being* refreshingly discards the ceremony and reverence that often accompany these studies, not to mention the text is fun to read because it trades in Heidegger's famous jargon for lively prose replete with humor and evocative examples.

38. Harman, *Tool-Being*, 2.

39. Harman, *Tool-Being*, 4.

40. Harman, *Guerrilla Metaphysics*, 33.

41. Graham Harman, *Prince of Networks: Bruno Latour and Metaphysics* (Melbourne: re.press, 2009), 214–15. Harman derives flat ontology from Bruno Latour, who regards all objects (material, abstract, fictitious) not as equally real, but as all *equally objects*. Harman's sensual objects are objects but lack some of the reality of real objects. In this sense his ontology is not as flat as Bryant's. In Bryant's view all objects are real because all objects, even fictions, exhibit effects. Bryant's view is indebted more to DeLanda than Latour. See Levi Bryant, *The Democracy of Objects* (Ann Arbor: Open Humanities Press, 2011), 245ff.

42. Heidegger, *Being and Time*, 60. Earlier in the same text: "an entity can show itself from itself … in many ways, depending in each case on the kind of access *we* have to it" (51, emphasis added).
43. Harman, *Tool-Being*, 15.
44. Harman, *Tool-Being*, 16.
45. This discussion can be found *Being and Time*, primarily §§16–18.
46. Heidegger, *Being and Time*, 103. Harman, *Tool-Being*, 18.
47. Heidegger, *Being and Time*, 98. When beings are used as tools, they do not become invisible; we are not rendered "blind" to them, but disclose them in their "Thingly character."
48. Harman, *Towards Speculative Realism*, 111.
49. Harman, *Towards Speculative Realism*, 111.
50. Heidegger, *Being and Time*, 101.
51. Harman, *Towards Speculative Realism*, 46.
52. Heidegger, *Being and Time*, 97; Harman, *Tool-Being*, 22.
53. Harman, *Tool-Being*, 23.
54. Harman, *Tool-Being*, 37.
55. Harman, *Tool-Being*, 46.
56. Harman, *Tool-Being*, 33.
57. See Chapter 8 of Harman, *Bells and Whistles*.
58. Harman, *Towards Speculative Realism*, 112. See also Tool-*Being*, 35–6, and the discussion of Heidegger's "as-structure" in Chapter 7.
59. Harman, *Guerrilla Metaphysics*, 74.
60. From a phenomenological perspective, the ready-to-hand does not withdraw only when it is explicitly used, but also when it is implicitly *relied on*. Right now, as I type, I rely on the architecture of my building, the window next to my desk, and the electrical wiring of my apartment just as much as I use my laptop, chair, and desk to write this sentence. On the reliability of things, see Harman, *Tool-Being*, 18ff.
61. Harman, *The Quadruple Object*, 37.
62. Harman, *Prince of Networks*, 179–80.
63. For a short history of substance ontology and how Harman fits into it, see Timothy Morton, *Realist Magic* (Ann Arbor: Open Humanities Press, 2013), Chapter 1.
64. Harman, "On Vicarious Causation," 171–205.
65. The transcript of the Speculative Realism roundtable is printed in *Collapse* III, 307–449.
66. Harman, "On Vicarious Causation," 173.

67. Unlike Meillassoux, Harman does not draw a rigorous distinction between speculation and metaphysics. Metaphysics in the former's view is dogmatic and posits the necessary existence of an entity, whereas speculation avoids both of these. Harman openly avails himself of metaphysics, but when he does it is not the dogmatic kind or "mere speculation" (Braver) denounced by Meillassoux.

68. This is the thesis of Morton's *Realist Magic*, discussed in the following chapter. It is also one of the reasons Harman does not identify his realism with naturalism, like Brassier. For Harman, naturalism entails the illegitimate reduction of vicarious causation to efficient causation.

69. Harman, "On Vicarious Causation," 181.

70. Harman, "On Vicarious Causation," 189.

71. Harman, "On Vicarious Causation," 193.

72. Harman, "On Vicarious Causation," 179.

73. Harman, "On Vicarious Causation," 196.

74. Harman, "On Vicarious Causation," 198–9.

75. Harman, "On Vicarious Causation," 199.

76. Harman, "On Vicarious Causation," 204.

77. Harman, "On Vicarious Causation," 205. For more on allure, see *Guerrilla Metaphysics*, Chapter 9, especially 151–2, and *Towards Speculative Realism*, 137–8. All causation must be *indirect*. Hence the importance of metaphor in his account of causation. Metaphor is the mechanism we use for articulating something about Object X by borrowing some qualities from Object Y. This is possible because sensual qualities can be transferred from one thing to another. Metaphor enables us to *translate* real objects into the sensual objects we meet in intentionality. Harman, *The Quadruple Object*, 73. On metaphor, see *Guerrilla Metaphysics*, Chapter 8, and "On Vicarious Causation," 199–200.

78. Harman, *Guerrilla Metaphysics*, 154; *The Quadruple Object*, 75.

79. Harman, *Towards Speculative Realism*, 20.

80. Harman deeply admires Lingis's essay "A Phenomenology of Substances," *American Catholic Quarterly* 71, no. 4 (1998), 505–22. In my view, there is good reason to question whether or not Lingis is a phenomenologist at all. His original writings are rich, evocative descriptions of his ceaseless globetrotting, with a style that often mimics Merleau-Ponty and a conceptual spirit haunted by Levinas, but this does not entail that he practices the phenomenological method in any technical sense.

81. Harman, *Guerrilla Metaphysics*, 60; *Towards Speculative Realism*, 18.

82. Merleau-Ponty, "Primacy of Perception," 15.

83. Harman, *Towards Speculative Realism*, 180, 202. Different flat ontologies are found in Latour, Bhaskar, DeLanda, Bryant, Harman, and Morton.

84. Harman, *Guerrilla Metaphysics*, 66.

85. Harman, *Guerrilla Metaphysics*, 67.

86. Harman, *Guerrilla Metaphysics*, 90.

87. Graham Harman, *Weird Realism: Lovecraft and Philosophy* (Winchester: Zero Books, 2012), 16.

88. See the helpful figures provided in *The Quadruple Object*, especially figure 8, page 114, which diagrams the "tensions" within the quadruple object.

89. I should qualify this by saying that Harman identifies two primary, intersecting axes in an object: (1) sensual object/sensual quality and (2) real object/real quality. This is what he means by the "quadruple object." With caricature/withdrawal I have identified what I think is the central dualism in Harman's OOP.

90. See, for example, Graham Harman, "Object-Oriented France: The Philosophy of Tristan Garcia," *continent* 5.1 (2012), 7.

91. Harman, *The Quadruple Object*, 111. Harman's ontology is not as flat as Garcia's. As Harman puts it, the fourfold structure of objects entails that his ontology is "bumpy," not completely flat. See Graham Harman, "Graham Harman: Garcia's Jungle," YouTube video, 42:50, posted by pmilat, July 25, 2012, available at <http://www.youtube.com/watch?v=Ef1ERMGsfWY> (accessed October 5, 2013).

92. Harman, *Prince of Networks*, 215.

93. For more on the identity of persons and objects, see Morton, *Realist Magic*.

94. Harman, *Guerrilla Metaphysics*, 51.

95. Merleau-Ponty, *Phenomenology of Perception*, 79. The closest Merleau-Ponty comes to object realism is with his concept of "style," discussed by Harman in *Guerrilla Metaphysics*, 55–8.

96. Harman, *The Quadruple Object*, 139; see also *Guerrilla Metaphysics*, 41.

97. Harman, *The Quadruple Object*, 8.

98. On "undermining" and "overmining" as strategies of reduction in philosophy, see *The Quadruple Object*, Chapter 1.

99. On this contrast, see Graham Harman, "Speculative Realism and the Philosophy of Tristan Garcia," YouTube video, 55:14, posted by Andrew Iliadis, April 13, 2013, available at <http://www.youtube.com/watch?v=71KxfHzZFnQ> (accessed October 5, 2013).

100. Graham Harman, *Skirmishes: With Friends, Enemies, Neutrals, and the Dead* (Brooklyn: punctum books, forthcoming).

5

Proliferating the Real

There comes a point when one must ask if speculative realism does not give way to the kind of unfettered philosophical whimsy targeted by Kant in the first *Critique* or, what seems worse, something akin to science fiction. After all, is it not nonfiction that realist philosophy wants, not some popular genre writing about what does not yet, or may never, exist? Does not the proliferation of objects, events, and properties that populate the pages of Meillassoux's and Harman's works risk flouting Kant's cautionary tale as well as Occam's Razor? In a sense, yes it does. But as we have seen, it is not without motivation or justification. After all, as Harman suggests, "philosophy must be realist because its mandate is to unlock the structure of the world itself; it must be weird because reality is weird."[1] What speculative realism provides in response to the rhetorics of concreteness and the Rich Elsewhere is a realism that multiplies the dimensions of reality by identifying those irreducible speculative moments of philosophical analysis that summon us to assume a realist stance because idealism, correlationism, and the linguistic turn leave us wanting. Now, the proliferation of the real is not uniformly or univocally carried out by the various speculative realists. The real is, as it were, said in many ways. Is this saying always speculative? Perhaps. But at this point it is left to be decided how, if possible, to divide the new realism into speculative and nonspeculative camps. That is a task for future studies.

This chapter gives a brief overview of the ways that realism is deployed in several contemporary thinkers, including the remaining members of the Goldsmiths cohort, Iain Hamilton Grant and Ray Brassier, as well as several figures working in what we might call the second wave of speculative realism. These include Levi Bryant, Timothy Morton, Ian Bogost, and Jane Bennett. My purpose here is to give the reader a sense of the diverse methodological approaches currently operative in speculative realism so that its future directions are apparent. In keeping with the focus of the book I have chosen to say only as much as necessary to give an account of how these approaches contrast with phenomenology. No doubt I have inevitably left out some of the nascent shoots of the rhizome that is SR.[2]

Goldsmiths 2007: The Original Speculative Realists

Speculative realism began as a foursome. Alongside Harman and Meillassoux at the 2007 Goldsmiths colloquium were Iain Hamilton Grant and Ray Brassier. Since then, Brassier, who originally suggested the label "speculative realism," has aggressively dissociated himself from the movement, saying in an interview that "I see little philosophical merit in a 'movement' whose most signal achievement thus far is to have generated an online orgy of stupidity."[3] While no doubt dismissive, it must be pointed out that Brassier's target here is not speculative realism as a philosophical position – toward which he remains committed, even if not in name – but its pronounced online presence along with the idea that it forms a coherent "movement." Brassier simply does not believe that high-quality philosophical discussion can take place through social media and blogs, nor does he think that speculative realism is as innovative as it is often made out to be. While there may be some de facto truth to this, it is not necessarily true in principle.[4] Many people ignore this point when they cite Brassier's interview. There is nothing intrinsic to social media that prevents them from advancing cutting-edge philosophical discourse. In another interview, Brassier has admitted that there is a basic unity to speculative realism in its original form: "antipathy to what Quentin Meillassoux calls 'correlationism'." Despite this unity, continues Brassier, it is also necessary to emphasize that the "alternatives to correlationism are fundamentally divergent and even incompatible in several regards."[5]

Meillassoux has likewise, albeit with less venom, distanced himself from the group. Grant remains largely silent on his affiliation. Their lower profile notwithstanding, there is a marked speculative realism in all three of these thinkers. The tendency in Brassier's work takes root in the work of continental philosophers like Deleuze, Laruelle, and Heidegger as well as the antiphenomenology of Wilfrid Sellars, Daniel Dennett, and Paul Churchland.

Grant, by contrast, is probably best known for his historical work on the German idealist F.W.J. Schelling. Not only is it difficult to disentangle his own position from his historical research, it is somewhat curious that Grant's view would ever be identified with realism. What is found in Grant's philosophy, which alchemically melds idealism and materialism into a strange metaphysics of potency and powers, is a severe complication of the line which is supposed to separate realism from idealism. This complication forces us to rethink the very meaning of both positions.

What Brassier and Grant share is an appreciation of the autonomous reality of nature, and each in his own way develops a naturalism consonant with this appreciation. Their respective positions, however, pull us in opposite directions. Whereas Brassier's strategy could be called *reductive* in that it joins forces with those who would undermine folk theory about consciousness using a more scientific physicalism, Grant's naturalist strategy is *productive* in at least two senses: first, it seeks to unearth the generative ground of being and, second, it multiplies the dimensions of nature beyond those registered by natural science. Whereas in Brassier we find a direct challenge to phenomenology, the challenge in Grant is only implied. Grant's relation to phenomenology, however, can be explicated by contrasting his and phenomenology's (especially Merleau-Ponty's) respective appropriations of Schelling's *Naturphilosophie*, as well as by retrieving Meillassoux's claim that phenomenology fails to address adequately questions about the emergence of consciousness, perception, embodied cognition, Life, *élan vital*, the flesh, Dasein, or any of the other common correlationist names. Indeed, it is this problem that holds Grant captive.

Iain Hamilton Grant

So far I have argued that phenomenology fails to deliver the reality of objects because its method confines its analyses to how objects appear for us, not how they are in themselves. In this respect phenomenology leans toward idealism, even if it never explicitly commits to it after Husserl. Defenders of phenomenology will reply to this charge in a number of ways. If they take the charge on its own terms, they will say that idealism is a misnomer for phenomenology because how things appear to consciousness just is how things are. What phenomenology does is precisely to disclose reality as it is apart from human bias, presupposition, and projection. In a certain respect, then, if phenomenology is idealist then its idealism is actually a radical form of realism – a realism whose primary obstacle is the subtraction of whatever obscures our ability to intuit the essence of objects and events. A more common defense of phenomenology's idealism exclaims that phenomenology is *beyond* the realism/idealism opposition, that realism and idealism are long-discredited categories and neither of them describe the radical mode of philosophical investigation inaugurated by phenomenology. This is a familiar line of defense in continental philosophy, but it is little more than a dodge of the problem rather than an effective dismantling. In my view, these strategies for dealing with idealism are unconvincing. After Kant, Hegel, and Berkeley there is nothing radical in saying that appearance is reality. And these days it is the rare person who is convinced by the rebuttal which insists that any criticism of phenomenology is a failure to see just how radical it is, and this failure accounts for why it is lumped in with German idealism. Not only does such a reply condescend to the critic of phenomenology, it makes a yet-to-be-realized claim for phenomenology's clean break with the history of idealism. No clean break is forthcoming, however, because phenomenology cannot escape idealism.

Although representative of the speculative realist backlash against contemporary Kantianism it is difficult to discern Grant's relationship to phenomenology because he rarely engages, or even mentions, phenomenology or phenomenologists by name. His work more often takes on the early post-Kantian philosophies, rather than those which descend from Kant's phenomenological followers. Nevertheless, it is possible to get a sense of where Grant positions himself vis-à-vis phenomenology through his work on Schelling, the philosophy of nature, and the essence of ground.[6] There are also hints in his coauthored book on the history of idealism.[7]

Not unlike Meillassoux, Grant endeavors to articulate something about the absolute. This is often framed as an analysis or investigation into the ground or emergence of being or nature, by definition a speculative endeavor. As he put it at Goldsmiths in 2007,

the philosophical problem of nature ... is a springboard for speculation – not opportunistically, but necessarily. I think that if philosophy of nature is followed consistently it entails that speculation becomes necessary, as the only means not of assessing the *access* that we have, but of the *production* of thought.[8]

Against Husserl – who, as we saw, rejects the idea that nature could precede human consciousness – Grant contends that we must assume that there is something that precedes human thought and acts as its ground. Nature can accomplish this feat because it is self-organizing; it synthesizes the real in order to yield an objectivity independent of the transcendental subject. The task of the philosophy of nature is then to articulate the "complex series of events" that conspire to generate this objectivity. Once it is accepted that there are naturalistic grounds for the production of thought, then it becomes necessary to accept that these grounds cannot be apparent to thought unless thought is conceived as part of nature. Otherwise put, the thinking of nature is nothing other than nature thinking itself. Reflection is not merely a reflection on the interiority of a subject, but objective nature reflecting on itself as producer and product of thinking. This, says Grant, is Schelling's original point.[9]

Given this starting point the task at hand is to try to describe the conditions of thought as they are produced in thought, which is the kind of thing you can see attempted in much of Schelling's philosophy of nature, and what makes his style seem so bizarre at times. The problem is that this is an impossible and inexhaustible, yet no less necessary, project. Grant characterizes this as a "necessary asymmetry ... between thought and what precedes it." Thought is by consequence different from, while at the same time dependent upon, what precedes it. It simply cannot get back into the ground of this dependence. Such is the "naturalistic" or "speculative physical" interpretation of the question of ground which Grant sees as the realist thread shared by each of the four Goldsmiths speculative realists.[10]

Following Heidegger, Grant understands the philosophy of nature as posing a distinctive problem for post-Kantian philosophy. Whereas Kant foregrounds the necessity of appearances as unconditioned, Grant follows Schelling in search of the unconditioned ground of this necessity, namely, the absolute ground of appearances. This involves a move beyond the representationalism of the Kantian philosophy and toward the "geology" of appearances. Schelling must therefore begin by overturning Kant's Copernican revolution (a gesture performed by Meillassoux's *After Finitude* as well) and reinstalling nature at the heart of philosophy, converting it into a "geophilosophy."[11]

Geophilosophy involves a descent into what, precisely, correlationism prohibits: the dynamic matter that supports and animates the correlation of thinking and being, that is, that activates the conditions of representation. The move toward geophilosophy and the interrogation of *physis*, understood not on analogy with organic nature but as the unearthing of the activity of the incorporeal ground of matter and bodies, suggests that Grant follows Schelling not toward a "neo-vitalist"[12] metaphysics, but instead toward what Schelling called *speculative physics*. Whereas most post-Kantian philosophy "has repeatedly reverted to organism, to the phenomena of *life*, precisely to head off naturephilosophical incursions," Grant critically suggests that "life provides an effective alibi against accusations of philosophy's tendency to 'antiphysics', while centralizing ethico-political or existential problematics as philosophy's true domain."[13] It is evident, especially in continental philosophy, specifically phenomenology and those works inspired by Bergson, that the concept of life functions in this way. Often when scientific disciplines are injected into the post-Kantian discussion, there has been a tendency toward "biocentrism," and this results not only for ideological reasons but for historical reasons that Grant's research into the vicissitudes of philosophy of nature after Schelling seeks to lay bare.[14]

Schelling's philosophy is for Grant a philosophy of the absolute or unconditioned through and through. The investigation of this absolute must always take place within the absolute itself because it is what we find ourselves always already in, and to this extent there is a certain truth to correlationism. To escape correlationism, however, it is not necessary to position oneself at some objective vantage point outside the correlation, which is impossible. It is also not necessary to pass through correlationism, as does Meillassoux. What is necessary is to record the "'genetic' movement of and on this world, unconditionally. Philosophy does not consist in a redescription of otherwise available phenomena, but launches 'thought-operations' in the 'medium of the universal and the impersonal'."[15] This is a "generative process" that entails an operation of nature on itself, an operation of nature as thinking subject on itself as material object. Nature is the very ground of our concept of nature, not merely conceptually, but materially as well.

The asymmetry of priority – nature as dynamic source of thought precedes thought, metaphysically speaking – means that the ground of thought enjoys a reality independent of thought. This is more than just a naturalization of (idealist) epistemology or of phenomenology, which is "conducted under the strict conditions imposed upon it by the neurophysiological constraints specific to [our] species," and "would therefore a priori fail to be an unconditioned philosophy," which is what Schelling aspires toward. The philosophy of nature for Schelling involves the creation of nature itself in the form of thought, and this means that nature as thought generated by nature "cannot be a nature restricted a priori by the particular physiological means by which it philosophizes," but "nature philosophizing must itself be unconditioned."[16]

By formulating a conception of nature as subject, Schelling ends up affirming "the *autonomy* of nature; nature, then, not as it appears to Mind, but *nature itself.*"[17] Following Schelling, Grant's position is set up in *precise opposition* to Husserl's claim in *Ideas*, echoed by Merleau-Ponty, that the nature of existence cannot be the condition of consciousness, but must be seen as the correlate of it (see *Ideas* I). Merleau-Ponty writes in "The Philosopher and His Shadow:"

> The fact that there is *no* Nature *without* mind, or that Nature may be *done away with* in thought *without* doing away with mind, does not mean that Nature is produced by mind ... Mind without Nature can be thought about and Nature without mind cannot. But perhaps we do not have to think about the world and ourselves in terms of the bifurcation of Nature and mind.[18]

This is slightly different from Meillassoux, who says that nature, as mathematical, is the unconditioned condition of knowledge of the ancestral, not the ground out of which consciousness arises. Grant's interpretation also urges us to see the realist kernel at the center of Schelling's idealism. He says, "it seems to me that idealism is committed to realism about all things, a realism that applies equally to nature and to the Idea."[19] Here Grant approaches idealism in a way very different from phenomenology, which either redefines the meaning of "real" or dismisses reality as a dusty old worry that requires little discussion.

Grant could be accused of a similar elision of the term "realism," or a sophistical conflation of realism with idealism. But we should be careful here. He, following Bosanquet, holds that logical laws like the law of noncontradiction, whether empirically or transcendentally construed, must be seen as springing from nature. Here nature is understood as a preobjective field of forces whose objectivity arises not from subjective synthesis, but from the self-objectification of nature itself. Given this premise, idealism must commit itself to realism about everything, including the ideal. "The Idea," maintains Grant, "is external to the thought that has it, the thought is external to the nature that produces both the thinker and the thought and the Idea."[20] What Grant is suggesting for realism is a complete evacuation of interiority. This is the means of escape from Kantianism. This is also what idealism is all about.[21] Its speculative edge cuts across the problem of the relation between nature as ontologically prior (what Grant calls the *prius*) to a thinking (or *posterius*) that nature necessarily depends on for its articulation.[22]

In the last analysis Grant holds that transcendental philosophy depends on the philosophy of nature for its grounding. Transcendental philosophy will resist this reorganization of priorities by claiming that if transcendental philosophy cannot enjoy priority over philosophy of nature, then "the hallmark of philosophical modernity" is lost.[23] Scientific naturalism will gain supremacy over transcendental philosophy. This worry stems, in Grant's view, from an insufficient naturalism, a deficiency for which modern transcendental philosophy is partly responsible. He writes that, for any naturalism,

> either all existents are instances of nature, or they are not. In the latter case, naturalism affirms itself ontologically parochial and so on its own testimony cannot provide a complete account of being. If it is claimed that any existent not part of nature does not therefore exist *in reality*, then such a naturalism finds itself in the odd position of affirming a domain of existents that have it in common that they do not exist. Accordingly, the only adequate naturalism must be able to account for all domains of being, including the transcendental.[24]

Grant himself rarely if ever mentions Merleau-Ponty. And yet, it would not be fruitless to compare his appropriation of Schelling's *Naturphilosophie* with Merleau-Ponty's philosophy of nature. Already in *Phenomenology of Perception* Merleau-Ponty deploys a notion of the a priori as a field of forces that are brought to objectivity by the dynamics of perception.[25] In short, he provides phenomenology with an immanent account of the transcendental, albeit not a speculative physical account. He retains this notion of the a priori in *The Visible and the Invisible* and rethinks its ground in the Collège de France courses on nature.[26] Furthermore, he frames his investigation into nature, insofar as this investigation poses the question of the division between phenomenology and nonphenomenology, precisely in terms set out by Schelling. As he writes in "The Philosopher and His Shadow:" "What resists phenomenology within us – natural being, the 'barbarous' source Schelling spoke of – cannot remain outside phenomenology and should have its place within it."[27] Whereas Grant sees the barbarous source of nature as the unconditioned and absolute ground of thinking, and therefore beyond the reach of phenomenology, Merleau-Ponty regards it as at least possibly accessible by phenomenology. His chosen metaphor for the relation between the subject and nature – the "chiasm" – gives him the means of access.

As everyone knows, Merleau-Ponty forefronts the figure of the chiasm in his descriptions of the relation between subject and world, subject and nature, sensing and sensed. The chiasm is his privileged metaphor for perception, on the one hand, and the production of nature, on the other. As Ted Toadvine writes, "The chiasm is therefore the key to Merleau-Ponty's later ontology, and in particular, to his understanding of the relationship between humans and nature."[28] The chiasm is another name for the correlation, one that seeks significantly to overcome dualism by installing an internal relationship of reciprocity, or reversibility, where the subject/object split used to be. Thus, even if Merleau-Ponty's philosophy of nature does not issue from a fundamentally anthropocentric stance,[29] it nevertheless situates the ground of nature, or what he calls "wild" or "brute" being, at the center of the human/nature chiasm. Toadvine notes that this allows Merleau-Ponty to avoid not only naturalistic approaches to nature, but also "constructivist" approaches that either regard nature as a conceptual product or situate nature in "an unknowable, noumenal alterity." Grant, following Schelling and Hegel, rejects the idea of the noumenal but does not reject the claim that nature is at bottom unknowable in itself. Toadvine continues, "For Merleau-Ponty, nature is ... not a present and objectifiable reality, but the 'auto-production of sense'; it has an 'interior' that is 'determined from within' and that precedes our reflective determination."[30] The thinking of nature is thus always undertaken from within nature itself, not from outside. But given that the sense of nature is the product of the chiasmic relation between humans and nature, even if it is prereflective, Merleau-Ponty's remains a correlationist account of nature.

To be sure, as Toadvine points out, reflection for Merleau-Ponty is not only on nature, but *of nature*. This means that reflection is conditioned by nature and, as a result, reflection "cannot exhaustively circumscribe it."[31] Whether or not this inexhaustibility is, for Merleau-Ponty, a mark of the absolutely unconditioned ground of nature as it is for Grant, or a consequence of his decision to portray the human/nature relation with the figure of the chiasm – rather than, say, a serpent chasing its tail to infinity – is an open question.

Ray Brassier

The last of the original four speculative realists, and the translator of Meillassoux's *After Finitude*, is Brassier. Although critical of speculative realism as a movement, there is little doubt that his own work – variously identified as reductive naturalism, eliminativism, transcendental or normative nihilism – fits the label, even if he no longer self-identifies as a speculative realist. In fact, few thinkers do identify themselves as such. At the end of the day, however, self-identification is just as unhelpful for locating speculative realists as it is for validating phenomenologists. What counts are ontological commitments, the assertions of existence to which a philosopher commits himself or herself.[32] To get at Brassier's realism it is helpful to ask this question negatively: what entities does Brassier deny; or, put differently, what does he want to extinguish from existence? An early subtitle of his *Nihil Unbound* was "Naturalism and Anti-Phenomenological Realism."[33] This glosses the content of the book in a much less apocalyptic tone than its published subtitle, "Enlightenment and Extinction." It also tells us more about the philosophical orientation of the book, specifically its attitude toward phenomenology, what it means by enlightenment, and what is the target of his reductionism. Given its sympathy for Wilfrid Sellars, Brassier's project is sometimes simply identified with scientific realism, but this designation misses the important eliminativist tendency in his thinking as well as his penchant for metaphysics. That said, in *Nihil Unbound* and elsewhere he provides a series of criticisms of eliminativism as well as of Sellars himself. I will say a little about these criticisms here, for they bear directly on Brassier's relationship to phenomenology.

There is something "superstitious" about phenomenology's "principle of principles" and Brassier wants to unmask it. Here he follows Dennett's suggestion that it is not entirely clear that just because appearances or phenomena are not subject to the same standards as truth claims or metaphysical judgments, that this means appearances are "absolutely transparent to us."[34] The question Brassier asks is whether or not the "non-manifest dimension of phenomenality" is something apprehensible by scientific reason or not. That is, is the excessive (or "saturated," in Marion's phrasing) phenomenon truly ungraspable or is it something that the scientific study of consciousness can apprehend? It is clear that Brassier assumes the latter and has little patience for phenomenology's attempt to articulate the excessive phenomenon with figurative or religious language so as to respect the alterity of the ungraspable while nevertheless saying something about it:

> phenomenology invariably petitions figurative language in order to carry out its descriptive task. Yet it might be better to concede that the aims of phenomenological description *stricto sensu* are best served through the artifices of literature, instead of hijacking the conceptual resources of philosophy for no other reason than to preserve some inviolable inner sanctum of phenomenal experience.[35]

In Brassier's view, the deep reality of appearances is not something that phenomenology can describe. It can only be gotten at ultimately by third-person, scientific description.

This is not to say that phenomenological or first-person description should be discarded altogether. On the contrary, it plays an indispensable normative role for an understanding of rationality. Brassier retrieves Sellars's distinction between the "manifest image" and the "scientific image" of man to illustrate this point. What Sellars calls the manifest image is the account of ourselves – our thoughts, behaviors, motivations, and so on – that we give to ourselves without appealing to theories that explain thoughts, behaviors, motivations, and so on. In other words, it is a "folk metaphysical" understanding of rationality, and one not foreign to phenomenological ontology.[36] The scientific image, by contrast, is the account of rationality that proceeds from the scientific discourses on human beings and which, at the limit, reduce human thoughts, behaviors, and motivations to a "complex physical system."[37] What Sellars shows is that the manifest image is far from theoretically innocent; in fact, it is what Brassier calls a "subtle theoretical construct" or, in other words, a concept-laden framework for explaining human behavior, one which masquerades as immediate self-knowledge. But "self-knowledge is neither internal nor absolute"; in fact, "our relation to ourselves is not fundamentally different in kind from our relation to external objects."[38] The moral of this story is that the manifest image is actually not opposed to any scientific image, but is itself an explanatory model analogous to those used by science.[39] It therefore gives us no privileged access to an understanding of either things, others, or ourselves.

What Sellars and Brassier want us to recognize about the manifest image is not just its complex theoretical character, but the *normative* role it plays in how we think about ourselves. It is what enables us to think of ourselves as a "community of rational agents" or "persons as loci of intentional agency."[40] There is, then, something indelible about the manifest image that cannot, or should not, be reduced. For it is exactly what enables us to identify ourselves as humans, as persons capable of giving, contesting, and evaluating rational grounds for believing and acting. This is why, for Sellars and Brassier, the manifest and scientific images must coexist.[41] Without the manifest image, which eliminative materialism seeks to dissolve, the norm of truth that "provides the cognitive rationale for elimination" is itself canceled.[42] Nevertheless, as we will see shortly, Brassier takes up the spirit of eliminativism.

In Brassier's eyes a lot of contemporary continental philosophy, phenomenology included, operates according to the manifest image without acknowledging its highly constructed nature. Endemic to this philosophy is what he describes as a "more or less profound hostility to the idea that the scientific image describes 'what there really is', that it has an ontological purchase capable of undermining man's manifest self-conception as a person or intentional agent."[43] Continental philosophy in general displays this in its pronounced resistance to reductivist accounts of consciousness, agency, embodiment, and so forth. This is perhaps most apparent in phenomenology's "personalism" and in philosophies that take "life" as an irreducible dimension of human existence, as in the case of Michel Henry or Bergson. These philosophies do not discount the power of science completely, but instead regard it as authoritative *only to an extent*. Just as Meillassoux draws our attention to the false modesty often displayed by transcendental philosophy when science presents it with ancestral statements, Brassier is wont to highlight the "instrumentalist conception of science" mobilized in contemporary continental philosophy. In addition to their correlationism, for example, both Heidegger and Wittgenstein exhibit

> the conviction that the manifest image enjoys a philosophical privilege vis-à-vis the scientific image, and that the sorts of entities and processes postulated by scientific theory are in some way founded upon, or derivative of, our more "originary", pre-scientific understanding whether this is construed in terms of our "being-in-the-world", or our practical engagement in "language-games".[44]

Even if it is true that the manifest image enjoys a methodological primacy insofar as the scientific image draws upon it for its analyses, this does not imply that it is ontologically or substantively prior.

The belief in our infallible, immediate knowledge of ourselves and our mental states, or what Bergson calls the "immediate data of consciousness," is undermined by Sellars's critique of the "myth of the given." Brassier paraphrases the myth as

> the claim that certain privileged experiences possess an absolute epistemic authority that does not depend upon any other beliefs. More exactly, it is the claim that all inferential knowledge rests upon a foundation of non-inferential knowledge consisting of "self-authenticating" mental episodes through which reality is directly intuited or immediately apprehended.[45]

Here Sellars appears very close to Hegel and, if Sellars is onto something, also where we glimpse the superiority of Hegelian over Husserlian/Heideggerian phenomenology. The myth of the given is effectively a commitment to the possibility of a presuppositionless science or philosophy after the manner of Husserl. The myth is not just upheld by certain empiricist epistemologies, but by transcendental phenomenology as well. Sellars's demytholo-gization of the given thus gives the lie to the view that phenom-enology can begin its investigations by attending, in accord with the dictates of phenomenological method, to the given as it is given. As Brassier puts it, "Sellars severs the intentional correla-tion between mind and world by grounding psychological inten-tionality in metalinguistic [semantic] discourse."[46] In this respect, Sellars offers an alternative deconstruction of presence to the one provided by Derrida's early work on Husserl.[47]

While Brassier warns of the danger of eliminativism for ratio-nal normativity, he also embraces some of its tenets. Indeed, he defines his own project in *Nihil Unbound* as a "metaphysical radi-calization of eliminativism" that ends in a "speculative realism."[48] What attracts Brassier to eliminativism *à la* Paul Churchland (and Dennett) is its critique of our folk psychological explanations of human thought and action. The problem with these explanations is that they do not provide a sufficient account of representation, and so they cannot adequately account for human thought and action. What can account for it, in Churchland's view, is the neu-rocomputational approach. A replacement of folk psychology by the neurocomputational approach is equivalent to a reduction of the manifest image to the scientific image of human being, and this entails nothing less than a revolution in "our understanding of ourselves as autonomous rational agents or 'persons'."[49] Being a person will still mean something, just not what we thought it meant. Eliminative materialism does not involve the elimination of meaning or consciousness, those two hallmarks of phenom-enology and postphenomenological continental philosophy, but a new, scientific explanation for their "characteristic features."[50]

One of the notable achievements of eliminative materialism, in Brassier's view, is that it has "driven an irrecusable wedge between our phenomenological self-conception and the material processes through which that conception is produced." Thus, when some-one like Husserl attempts to define the proper domain of phenom-enology – as that which is, for instance, committed to explicating the meaning of so-called originary intuitions – Churchland shows that the legitimacy of these limits are not guaranteed, or "trans-parent, since they are themselves theoretically drawn."[51] This is why Brassier remains skeptical about the value of phenomenology for realism.[52] Moreover, given its correlationist logic,[53] phenome-nology remains unequipped for acknowledging the conceivability of eliminative materialism, which is committed to the existence of a material basis for the conditions of givenness that precedes those very conditions. The presumption that phenomenal appearances are perfectly transparent to us, and therefore require no justification for truth claims made about them – for appearances are simply understood or disclosed "on their own terms" – is rendered eminently suspicious by eliminativism.[54]

Despite this suspicion phenomenology continues to insist that faithfulness to the phenomena – the "things themselves" – requires a more rigorous and elaborate description. This is what drives it to increasingly draw upon figurative and metaphorical, if not mystical and poetic, language to describe the "non-propositional dimension of 'meaningfulness' harboured by 'appearing'." Accordingly,

> much post-Heideggerian phenomenology has been engaged in an ongoing attempt to deploy the figurative dimension of language in order to sound the sub-representational experiential depths, which, it is claimed, are inherently refractory to any other variety of conceptualization, and particularly to scientific conceptualization. In this regard, the goal of phenomenology would consist in describing 'what it's like' to be conscious while bracketing off conceptual judgements about 'what it's like'.[55]

Talk of "what-it's-like-ness," as we have seen, is characteristic of the rhetoric of concreteness. What phenomenology fails to notice, however, is that the "sub-representational depths" are accessible neither to phenomenological seeing nor to its realist rhetoric. Its reality, "the *reality* of consciousness, is independent of the subject of consciousness. Only the objective, third-person perspective is equipped with conceptual resources sensitive enough to map consciousness' opaque, sub-linguistic reality."[56] This is the real that Brassier is committed to speculating about. His is a speculative commitment because it does not invest in the perfect coherence of naturalism, but gambles on the ability of metaphysical realism to render objective the *mechanisms* by which appearing is made to appear.[57]

Realism, for Brassier, cannot be dodged even by the antirealist. The really pressing question is what to be a realist about. This must be decided rationally and with an eye toward the "salient epistemological considerations."[58] Phenomenology does not meet this demand, nor does any correlationism that outlaws our commitments to the phenomenologically inaccessible on the grounds that such commitments convert the inaccessible into a correlate of thought.[59] Perhaps more fundamental, at least more curious, is the question of why phenomenology is so resistant to conferring absolute reality on the nonhuman, unconscious, and "mindless processes through which consciousness and mindedness first emerged and will eventually be destroyed."[60] That is, why is phenomenology so resistant to all-out realism?

The Second Wave of OOO

Harman's philosophy of objects has spurred a second wave of object-oriented realism in the original writings of Levi Bryant, Timothy Morton, and Ian Bogost. Each of these thinkers has articulated an original position that accepts Meillassoux's refutation of correlationism and in one way or another expands insights from Harman's work. For Bryant it is the revival of objects; for Morton, vicarious causation; for Bogost, interobject perception. This section gives a brief synopsis of their respective projects and indicates where they stand with respect to phenomenology. The section concludes with a synopsis of Jane Bennett's political ecology. Although her original position in books like *The Enchantment of Modern Life* and, notably, *Vibrant Matter* was developed independently of speculative realism and object-oriented ontology, her work has been retroactively identified with these positions. She lends an important voice to the discussion and charts a promising path toward the future. For all of the points of commonality between the second wave of object-oriented thinkers, there are notable points of disagreement. Unfortunately, these divergences are largely passed over in silence in what follows.

Levi Bryant

At one point an enthusiastic and active proponent of Harman's OOO, Bryant's work is rapidly evolving toward a materialism in the tradition of Epicurus, Lucretius, and Spinoza. His most recent book, *Onto-Cartography: An Ontology of Machines and Media*, develops what the author refers to as a "machine-oriented ontology" that does not break with the object-oriented model but modifies it in significant ways.[61] It also attempts to specify the political implications of the onto-cartographic model and what he calls "Borromean critical theory."[62] It builds on his earlier, explicitly object-oriented text, *The Democracy of Objects*, wherein we find a systematic presentation of Bryant's OOO and a robust theory of internal and external object relations.

Across all his work there is a pronounced attempt to defend a metaphysics that seeks the conditions of real existence and, it seems to me, Bryant is perpetually trying to parse the distinction between substance and aggregate, or to define "object" in such a way that does justice to the simplicity of objects while at the same time recognizing that complex networks, relations, and machines are also objects in a strict sense. In his first book, *Difference and Givenness*, Bryant provides a lucid exposition of Deleuze's transcendental empiricism and it is clear already in that text that he is concerned with the autonomy of individual objects, much more than he is in the conditions of knowing these objects. Deleuze's transcendental empiricism, he tells us, is after the conditions of real experience, not the conditions of all possible experience sought by Kant.[63] In other words, he is concerned with concrete, not abstract, universals. Indeed, this concern to draw a sharp distinction between philosophy that seeks the real existence of particulars and philosophy that seeks the conceptual means of knowing what exists continues to orient Bryant's work in SR/OOO. Here I will focus on how this concern manifests itself in contradistinction to phenomenology, in his book *The Democracy of Objects* and the essay "The Ontic Principle." Both of these texts elaborate theses in support of what Bryant calls *onticology*, the tongue-in-cheek label for Bryant's early object-oriented system.

As Bryant tells the story, the emergence of correlationism is coeval with the decline of ontology. We see this if we turn to Heidegger. It is of signal importance that we recall that Heidegger is not interested in being as much as he is interested in the *meaning* of being, or "being-*for*-Dasein," as Bryant puts it. Heidegger is not solely responsible for this shift, but, as we have seen, he has played an instrumental role in reorienting our contemporary focus from the real to the meaningful. "Ontology," as resurrected in Heidegger, "would no longer be the investigation of being *qua* being in all its variety and diversity regardless of whether humans exist, but rather would instead become an interrogation of *Dasein's* or *human* being's *access* to being."[64] For a long time now philosophy has been intent on figuring out not what exists independently of human access, but which mode of access (which correlate, as Meillassoux puts it) is the most basic.[65] Ontology becomes a philosophy of access. Or, in other words, ontological questions are reduced to epistemological questions.

Bryant rightly calls correlationism our contemporary *episteme*. It is the historical a priori conditioning and policing all questions of the form "What exists?," from Wittgenstein to Merleau-Ponty to Derrida and beyond. "Despite the vast differences and disagreements among these positions, their thought and disagreements nonetheless unfold within the horizon of the unspoken premise of a necessary correlation between being and thought."[66] Realist ontology, by contrast, makes claims about actual objects, not objects as they are for us. This does not mean that realism is antihuman or anticorrelationist, but that it begins from the assumption that humans are "among beings, entangled in beings, and implicated in other beings."[67] On the face of it, Bryant's thesis does not sound much different from Merleau-Ponty and the embodied phenomenologists. It rings of the rhetoric of concreteness. To see its difference, however, it is necessary to take a brief look at how Bryant appropriates the ontological vision laid out in Roy Bhaskar's *A Realist Theory of Science*.

Correlationism can only be escaped, ironically in Bryant's view, by transcendental means. Bhaskar begins by asking a transcendental question that is distinctly different from Kant's. Bhaskar asks: what must the world be like for science to be possible?[68] He thus begins from a question about the reality of the world, not a question about what the mind must be like in order to know this world. In other words, he "shifts the transcendental question from the domain of *epistemology* to the domain of *ontology*."[69] Bhaskar goes on to show that for scientific knowledge to be possible, there must be what he calls "intransitive" objects, or objects that are "invariant to our knowledge of them." This is not to say that they are themselves invariant, but that they do not depend on the minds of scientists for their existence or constitution.[70] These objects, along with independent "generative mechanisms," which are understood by Bhaskar as "tendencies" or "powers" of real objects, are responsible for the production of scientifically observable events and the possibility of experimental science.[71] Without this or an analogous commitment to the reality of objects and the mechanisms governing events, one runs the risk of mistaking epistemology for ontology or conflating the two in a form of cor-relationism.

For Bryant, then, realist ontology entails an a priori com-mitment to the existence of objects. This is why there cannot be a primacy of critique, cognition, or perception. When ontol-ogy is investigated through the lens of some human instrument of knowing, it inevitably results in an anthropomorphic photo-graph of being. The problem with Kant and phenomenology is that they ultimately seek "anthropological universals," which can only underwrite the possibility of *human* experience. They then illegitimately infer that experience *qua experience* is only pos-sible for humans, or that it is senseless to talk about nonhuman experience.[72] There is a strong antiphenomenology streak running through Bryant's work, and it is precisely because phenomenol-ogy consistently poses epistemological questions but then draws ontological conclusions from these questions. As such, phenom-enology is guilty of committing what Bhaskar calls the "epistemic fallacy," or "the thesis that properly ontological questions can be fully transposed into epistemological questions." It is fallacious for the following reason, given by Bryant:

> If this move is problematic, then this is because it always finds itself trapped in a self-referential paradox: to wit, it concedes the existence of at least one entity, and then uses the manner in which that entity observes the rest of the world through its own distinctions to erase the existence of other entities. Every argument of this sort, driven by how we cognize or perceive the world, will run afoul of this sort of problem.[73]

What the object-oriented ontologist does in response is not to claim that beings are given directly to us (they are always with-drawn), but to assume as a necessary premise that substances exist, for this premise is the only way to make "a whole slew of our practices" (including science) "intelligible."[74]

In "The Ontic Principle" Bryant combats what he calls the "sterility of the critical paradigm" by engaging in a curiously phe-nomenological experiment. This consists in "proceeding naïvely and pre-critically as *first philosophers*" by beginning from what is given immediately in experience.[75] Bryant recognizes the impos-sibility of such a task but thinks it worthwhile anyway. He pro-poses that we begin our inquiry into what exists by "bracketing" the project of critique and accepting the "ontic principle," or the premise that "there is no difference that does not make a difference."[76] This is what it means for something to be, for if something *is* then it differentiates itself in some way from everything else and that is how it makes itself known.

The ground of this principle is the fact that difference is given in experience as that which provokes inquiry, moves us to generalize, analyze, categorize – to think. This "pre-epistemological comprehension of difference" is presupposed by any epistemology. This implies that epistemology cannot be first philosophy. The philosophy of difference, which in Bryant's eyes is ontological in nature, must be first philosophy. It is necessary first to engage difference as such before the question of knowledge can be raised.[77] This is not to say that the experience of difference does not involve an epistemological component, but that epistemology does not tell us what difference *is*, only what difference *does* for us.[78] As Bryant writes, against Hegel as much as Husserl,

> It is only from the standpoint of a consciousness regarding objects and comparing them to one another that the differences composing objects are taken by reference to what objects are *not*. Ontological, as opposed to epistemic difference is, by contrast, positive, affirmative, and differentiated without being negative. The temperature of boiling water is not the *negation* of other degrees. Philosophy perpetually conflates these epistemic and ontological registers, requiring us to untangle them with the greatest care if we are to understand anything of the real.[79]

Onticology, premised as it is on the ontic principle, entails what we have called a flat ontology. This is not, of course, the thesis that ontology must restrict itself to the "flat" world of appearances or phenomena, which is how Bhaskar understands flatness. On the contrary, it is the thesis that "being is composed of nothing but singular individuals, existing at different levels of scale but nonetheless *equally* having the status of being real."[80] Here Bryant follows DeLanda, rather than Harman (for whom flat ontology means not that all objects are equally real, but that they are all objects). Bryant takes himself as broadening DeLanda's definition of individuals, however, for DeLanda seems to restrict individuals to natural individuals, whereas Bryant includes "signs, fictions, armies, corporations, nations,"[81] and presumably all kinds of machines, in the class of individuals.

Timothy Morton

As early as *Ecology without Nature* Morton both criticized and endorsed phenomenology for its savvy deployment of ambient rhetoric as a strategy for summoning the things themselves to language. In *The Ecological Thought* he enlisted Levinas to develop an ecological notion of otherness that he called the "strange stranger."[82] So, Morton does not position himself against phenomenology as much as he at times situates himself within it in order to perform a deconstructive adoption of this or that phenomenological tactic or concept, usually those with a polyvalent or ambiguous character. Phenomenological rhetoric cannot quite get us to the reality of interobjectivity, however. This is one of Morton's primary concerns as a member of the OOO camp. At best phenomenology can evoke "an idea of intersubjectivity, an entanglement of minds with other minds and perhaps nonmental or inanimate things."[83] The entanglement is always tinged with subjectivity, however, even when it is intensified as it is in the phenomenological animism of a work like David Abram's *The Spell of the Sensuous*. That book gives some of the most inspired, evocative descriptions of what it is like to be engulfed in nature and feel oneself absorbed into it. At times it is positively hypnotic, as are Abram's public presentations.

Abram's text is emblematic of the Rich Elsewhere rhetoric unmasked by Meillassoux as much as it is exemplary of the ambient rhetoric critiqued by Morton in *Ecology without Nature*. To see the limits of Abram's method is to see the limits of phenomenology for realism, a theme we explored at some length in Chapter 2. Morton describes Abram's style as "this weird combination of vividness and distancing, naturalness and artifice, remembering and recording, attuning and hallucinating."[84] Abram's rhetoric is a phenomenological supplement to his argument for the identity of human and environment, human and nonhuman animal, vegetable, and mineral. As much as Abrams wants to dissolve the subject/object duality of his phenomenological antecedents, this dualism is reproduced by the way his ambient poetics not only channels what it is like to be absorbed in an environment, but draws attention to "another, ghostly quality: that of *experiencing* the sensitivity of the sensory apparatus, or *appreciating* it."[85] Stubbornly, the subject just will not disappear into his poetics of place. The more the phenomenologist uses ecomimesis to shift attention to the *Umwelt*, the more the *Umwelt* feels like a Cartesian fantasy. In his reading of Abram and others Morton provides us with an indispensable tool for critiquing the limitations of phenomenology.

While he has for a long time written about objects and ecological relations, it is not until *Realist Magic* and its associated texts that Morton deliberately sits down to write an object-oriented ontology. That book is, as he acknowledges at its start, the product of his reading of Harman. Like his other texts, *Realist Magic* is written in an engaging style that is often self-referential, usually playful, and perpetually ironic. It draws references from many fields, including American pop music, children's cinema, canonical English poetry, and contemporary Australian art... as well as, of course, eastern and western philosophy. All of this is wrapped up into a single object-oriented thesis: *the aesthetic dimension is the causal dimension.*

Morton's speculative aesthetics arises out of Harman's bifurcation of the object into sensual and withdrawn objects. Objects, argued Harman, only ever touch in the sensual realm. We saw in Chapter 4 that, given this split, vicarious causation emerges as one of the chief problems of OOO. Harman's solution is to say that objects only ever make aesthetic contact. Their interactions are always a product of translation or metaphor. Morton concurs: translation is a superior way to think what causality is all about. As for the inner lives of objects, these can still only be approximated by allusions. The problem hypnotizes Morton, to the degree that *Realist Magic* can be read as an extended meditation on the utter ubiquity of vicarious relationships in every aesthetic domain, whether visual, linguistic, musical, or tactile. The book is driven by the urge to compel its reader to recognize that the world is not governed by mechanisms or efficient causes, but that interobjective causality is "a secretive affair, yet out in the open – an open secret."[86] As we saw, the real action of objects occurs at the fault line between presence-at-hand and readiness-to-hand, objective presence and objective absence. This rift is rife with ambiguity, to the extent that there is no telling what will happen there. What is more, there is good reason to second guess that what appears to happen there is what really happens there. The potential for aesthetic sleight-of-hand is immense, and Morton explores so much of it in *Realist Magic*.

If we are compelled by Morton's text, then we come to see reality as mysterious or magical, in the sense of magical realism. The mystery results, of course, from the withdrawal of real objects. The magic results from the fact that these objects somehow get in touch with each other and make things happen.

If Harman's treatment of vicarious causation has an antiphenomenological aspect, then we might say that Morton's intense focus on the aesthetic has a phenomenological touch. As he cautions, however, what we see or hear or feel about causality is akin to an illusion or magic trick – what we see is there and not there at the same time. Objects are inherently contradictory: "*All the things by which we specify the object are not the object*," he writes.[87] What we specify is the sensual, qualitative surface that we have access to – a caricature. But what we aim at is the object itself, in its infinitely withdrawn, encrypted, and unspeakable reality. An object-oriented theory of causality is needed to deal with this contradiction, which defies not only the logic of noncontradiction but also resists reduction to the laws of physics. This is because only OOO comprehends the rift in objects; it alone registers the uncanniness of this rift. It knows that all causality – and not just human consciousness – is action at a distance, a touching that is not really a touching. That things only interact in the aesthetic dimension.[88]

Here phenomenology can help a little too. Its attention to detail can draw us into the appearance of things, even if it cannot gain us admission to their hidden reality. The alien phenomenology of Ian Bogost (discussed below) will help us grasp at the "strange kind of nonhuman phenomenology" performed by things like sensors, cameras, computers, and other inanimate objects.[89]

Phenomenology eventually must be left behind. It does not deal well with interobjectivity. From the phenomenological perspective objects always appear as figures against a background. That is one of its notable findings. But the figure/ground structure is just a trick of perception, a habitual way of seeing things. It is not what is really there in front of our eyes. Background is just "an aesthetic effect – it is produced, in other words, by the interaction of $1+n$ objects."[90] This means that the aesthetic is the product of a withdrawn object entering into a relation with another, sensual object. Harman calls this intentionality. What is uncanny about intentionality, despite what phenomenology reveals about it, is that it involves a descent into the abyss. "When I reach for the coffee cup," writes Morton, "I am reaching into an abyss."[91] My causal relation with the cup makes an aesthetic appearance, but right smack in the middle of this appearance is a bottomless object (a *strange stranger*) that forever eludes my grasp. A magic trick. Levinas appreciates this kind of uncanniness. Morton calls it the "interobjective abyss." He demonstrates at length the utter weirdness and unpredictability of object-oriented causality.[92] Morton writes: "Interobjectivity means that something fresh can happen at any moment." He continues: "Interobjectivity is the uterus in which novelty grows. Interobjectivity positively guarantees that something new can happen, because each sample, each spider web vibration, each footprint of objects in other objects, is itself a whole new object with a whole new set of relations to the entities around it." Finally: "Causality is *like an illusion*. If we knew it was an illusion, it would not be an illusion, because we would be sure of its ontological status."[93] But, alas, we are not at all.

Phenomenology is also not equipped to face the problem documented in Morton's most recent book, *Hyperobjects*.[94] There he unleashes the book's eponymous concept, the *hyperobject*. These are massively distributed, truly sublime objects such as climate and the BP oil slick off the coast of Louisiana and Florida. Morton identifies them as "phenomena such as radioactive materials and global warming. Hyperobjects stretch our ideas of time and space, since they far outlast most human time scales, or they're massively distributed in terrestrial space and so are unavailable to immediate experience."[95] Perhaps, then, we should not call them "phenomena?" They are much, much larger than "middle objects"[96] like environments or horizons or *Lebenswelten*, which are phenomenologically accessible; "they are far more real than species, or atoms. They are more material than supposedly solid things."[97] They must be mapped or modeled by something other than subjective experience. As Morton writes in *The Ecological Thought*: "Learning about global warming serves to make us feel something worse than an existential threat to our lifeworld. It forces us to realize that there never was a lifeworld in the first place, that in a sense 'lifeworld' was an optical illusion that depended on our not seeing the extra dimension that NASA, Google Earth, and global warming mapping open up."[98]

Hyperobjects remind us that we are not the agents of large-scale change. We are products or victims. There is a materiality to hyperobjects that exceeds our materialism. They have something of Brassier's extinction about them, something of Meillassoux's

ancestral about them. They are of signal importance for thinking
our current ecological moment and they may very well destroy us.
To try to get a grip on them we must invest in what Bogost calls
"carpentry."

Ian Bogost

In his book *Alien Phenomenology; or, What It's Like to Be a
Thing* Bogost appears to violate one of the cardinal principles
of object-oriented philosophy in attempting a description of
how objects experience their world. This would seem to be an
obvious breach of the object-oriented approach to which Bogost
cleaves quite closely.[99] To see why it is not we must recall that for
Harman objects are always split. On the one hand, they are sensual, encountered and caricatured by other objects; on the other,
they are withdrawn from all relations, reposing in an impene-
trable reality. What Bogost's alien phenomenology attempts is a
description of how objects caricature other objects, not what it
is like to *be* an object. He is therefore engaged in an effort to
bring to light the way that objects perceive their world, the other
objects in the world, and us. He is after *their* phenomenology.
His work provides an answer to such questions as: What can we
know about interobject encounters, or "unit operations?" What
can we say about the inner lives of objects? What can we build
to display the lives of objects? All of this is conducted under the
aegis of speculation, of course, and under the assumption that the
lives of things will appear to us one way but really are some other
way. Verifying what their lives are really like is beyond the reach
of speculative realism, and arguably metaphysics as such.

Alien Phenomenology is methodologically quite fascinating.
Bogost is the only speculative realist who calls his position phenomenology, although it is not a philosophy of access. His work
is best described as *applied* speculative realism because it not only
theorizes objects, it also designs and builds them. As he sees it,
"such a method would embolden the actual philosophical treatment of actual material objects and their relations. If we take
speculativism seriously, then why might philosophy not muster
the same concrete grounding as, say, speculative fiction or magical realism?"[100] Enlisting key concepts from Harman's speculative
realism, Bogost synthesizes his background in videogame theory,
his technical knowledge of game construction, and his reading

of object-oriented ontology into a phenomenology of the alien. This is not an exercise in empathy or imagination, however. It is a hands-on platform for registering the experience of objects, or "units."[101] Bogost's idea for this emerges from his personal experience with videogame analysis and construction, as well as encounters with technical objects such as the following:

> A year before [*Racing the Beam*][102] I'd spent a consulting windfall on a Leica M8 and got back into rangefinder photography. I found myself thinking about the way different optics see a subject, the results of which photographers sometimes call "rendering" or "drawing." For example, I have a 1935 50mm f/2 Summar lens that produces images with a very particular atmosphere, thanks to a combination of factors inherent in its design. I can see how the lens sees when it exposes on emulsion or sensor, but how does the lens see without me? So, you could say that this project was borne from two parents, one a desire to concretize tool-being in some way, and the other a deep personal curiosity about the secret lives of objects.[103]

Bogost's vignette is striking because it raises a simple, almost child-like question: how does the camera see things when no one is taking pictures with it? His question is compelling because it almost forces us to admit that there must be *some way* the camera itself views the world. To conclude otherwise would seem almost silly. So, how do cameras see things?

The method of alien phenomenology involves several key maneuvers, one of which is precisely antiphenomenological. Instead of bracketing the real existence of things, alien phenomenology follows the lead of flat ontology and begins from the assumption that all things exist, even those that do not.[104] This is less of a metaphysical thesis than it is a thought-experimental methodological step almost necessary to the speculative realist standpoint. Bogost begins by assuming that there is some way for objects to experience and, with any luck, we can say something about it. He refrains from drawing the hubristic conclusion that since we cannot know what it is like to actually see like a camera, there must not be any way that the camera itself sees, or that camera vision is senseless. In order to fully understand a camera, he maintains, it is not enough to design, build, and disassemble one, it is also necessary to provide a phenomenology of camera perception. Without the phenomenology we cannot understand the machine itself, although we could provide an objective account of its operation. "The point," urges Bogost, "is this: things are not *merely* what they do, but things *do indeed do things*. And the *way things do* is worthy of philosophical consideration."[105]

Alien phenomenology borrows three strategies from Harman's arsenal: *ontography, metaphorism,* and *carpentry*. The middle three chapters of *Alien Phenomenology* develop these concepts, respectively. Harman describes ontography in *The Quadruple Object* as the practice of mapping "the basic landmarks and fault lines in the universe of objects."[106] In Bogost's hands ontography is an "inscriptive strategy," analogous to a medieval bestiary, that "uncovers the repleteness of units and their interobjectivity."[107] In its simple form it is a compendium or record of things, a list such as those "Latour litanies" scattered across the pages of works of object-oriented ontology which serve the rhetorical purpose of drawing attention away from general concepts and calling attention to the innumerable objects populating the world.[108] Ontography is not just about list-making, however; it also does the philosophical work of supplementing our "anthropocentric narrative coherence" with "worldly detail."[109] In short, it draws us into the concrete and, as such, it would join phenomenology's rhetoric of concreteness if it were put forward as something more than an aesthetic device. But it is not. Ontography does not claim to be an argumentative strategy for getting us in touch with the real, but rather a means of pulling us out of the clouds and into the thicket of objects. This is why Bogost calls ontography "a practice of increasing the number and density, one that sometimes opposes the minimalism of contemporary art."[110]

Alien phenomenology opposes the naturalistic explanation of interobjective encounters or unit operations. It instead endorses vicarious causality as a means of characterizing unit operations. Such a view is set up in opposition to the "objective phenomenology" of Thomas Nagel, which seeks ideally to describe subjective experience or what-it's-like-ness without resorting to empathy or imagination. This kind of phenomenology would be required to understand what it is like to be a bat reliant on sonar for flight navigation. Given the withdrawn nature of objects (ourselves included), alien phenomenology rejects the possibility of an objective phenomenology of object experience. The only way of accessing what-it's-like-ness is through metaphor or analogy, that is, aesthetic devices crafted to allow sensual objects to interact in the sensual ether.[111] Metaphor, of course, does not *literally* bring two objects together (which would entail reductionism). It does, however, enable us to characterize object perception, which withdraws from experience no less than the real object itself. Metaphor is what we use to understand what the camera sees. The so-called New Aesthetic tries to do the same thing by other means.[112]

Carpentry is perhaps the most distinctive element of alien phenomenology, for it is the most literally pragmatic – not that cataloguing and drawing analogies are impractical. It is the "practice of constructing artifacts as a philosophical practice."[113] Philosophers are accustomed to devising thought experiments, so why not build things that help us understand how things construct their worlds? This is what Bogost does. He makes videogames and computer software. These units enable us to see how things see. They give us a third-"person" model of first-"person" experience. They are tools for getting inside (kind of) unit operations alien to the human sensory machine. If objects only ever interact vicariously, then the best we can do is to construct models that metaphorize vicarious causality. This is the objective of carpentry. Bryant is, I think, right to be optimistic about the reach of alien phenomenology and the promise of carpentry:

> Alien phenomenology – which has been practiced under other names for a long time, though not nearly as much as it should be – provides us with a set of techniques for better encountering strange strangers and for ... developing better strategies for responding to hostile strange strangers such as corporations. It is able to integrate practices such as what people in the 60s referred to as "consciousness raising." It is able to integrate the sorts of phenomenologies of the subaltern practiced by theorists such as Sarah Ahmed. It integrates nicely with the work of queer and disability theorists who help us to explore the worlds of other bodies and how they encounter the world. It meshes smoothly with the work of the critical animal theorists, helping us to enter the worlds of animals and how the world is given to them, thereby allowing us to better attend to them. There is not phenomenology, but phenomenologies.[114]

If Bogost is right to say that speculative realism is a "philosophy *claiming that things speculate* and, furthermore, one *that speculates about how things speculate*," then there is much reason to suggest that alien phenomenology will uncover an indefinite number of phenomenologies operating within the things themselves and the lives of others. It will be impossible to verify the accuracy of alien phenomenology; it will not gain us access to the things themselves *as they are in and for themselves*. But it will, through "educated guesswork,"

> amplify the black noise of objects to make the resonant frequencies of the stuffs inside them hum in credibly satisfying ways. Our job is to write the speculative fictions of their processes, of their unit operations. Our job is to get our hands dirty with grease, juice, gunpowder, and gypsum. Our job is to go where *everyone* has gone before, but where few have bothered to linger.[115]

In other words, there is much philosophical lab work to be done.

Jane Bennett

While not a product of the speculative realist movement herself, Jane Bennett has become associated with OOO because of the warm reception her book *Vibrant Matter*, published in 2010, received from those already working from an object-oriented perspective. Bennett's work, which is perhaps more often categorized as "new materialism,"[116] aspires to provide us with a broader understanding of agency and a political ecology that takes objects to be as central to political events as human actors. Although she does not offer a rigorous philosophical argument for or against realism – given the political-theoretical nature of her work – she no doubt shares in the spirit of speculative realism. Her work is not only fascinating as a materialist ecological theory, it also has the virtue of demonstrating the political potential of object-oriented thinking.

In *Vibrant Matter* Bennett refers to her view as a *vital materialism* in order to draw it close to the materialist tradition of Lucretius and Spinoza, but also to signal a connection to vitalism, although she transcends the latter in its classical (Bergsonian) form. Instead of approaching the materialist tradition critically as many do today, her method proceeds by way of what she calls a "naïve ambition" that is realist in tendency. Against the constructivism still dominant today, vital materialism attempts to get us in touch with nonhuman vitality or what she calls "thing-power."[117] Thing-power is a polyvalent concept that invokes the *conatus* of Spinoza, the wild of Thoreau, and the absolute or outside invoked by political theology. Thing-power names the power of self-preservation inherent in every body, "the uncanny presence" of alien environments, and the limits of human construction and intelligibility. In short, thing-power is the "vitality intrinsic to materiality" "which refuses to dissolve completely into the milieu of human knowledge."[118] Thing-power sits at the heart of her realism as the force animating her posthumanist sense of agency, political power, and ethical responsibility.

Hers is not a naïve realism, however. It is naïve in the sense that phenomenology aspires to be naïve, proceeding as it does from a sense of wonder or freshness or enchantment with the everyday world. As Bennett describes it in the preface to *Vibrant Matter*, her book *The Enchantment of Modern Life* sought to explicate the ethical aspect of "the mood of enchantment or that strange combination of delight and disturbance" with which the everyday and natural worlds sometimes strikes us. Her appreciation of the power of enchantment should be contrasted with her caution about the import of "demystification" as it is deployed in a lot of critical theory, which often ends up telling us more about ourselves than it does about the materiality of things.[119] In this way she leans away from rationalism and toward a materialism attuned to the political potency of affect.

From the idea of thing-power, and with inspiration from Spinoza, Latour, Deleuze/Guattari, and others, Bennett develops a novel idea of nonhuman agency. When bodies interact with other bodies, as Spinoza showed, their power to act and exist is enhanced or diminished. When many bodies unite to form a larger body – a corporate body, military body, athletic team, or body politic – they constitute what Deleuze/Guattari (as well as DeLanda) call an "assemblage." An assemblage is an agent whose capacity or power is "distributed across an ontologically heterogeneous field, rather than being a capacity localized in a human body or in a collective produced (only) by human efforts."[120] Assemblages can be homogeneous or diverse, but Bennett is primarily interested in the latter. Significantly, they lack a centralized power source or authority. They can be comprised of human, nonhuman, living, nonliving, artificial, and natural materials.

As agential they are necessarily vibrant. She offers the example of an electrical power grid like the one responsible for the North American blackout of 2003:

> It is a material cluster of charged parts, that have indeed affiliated, remaining in sufficient proximity and coordination to produce distinctive effects. The elements of the assemblage work together, although their coordination does not rise to the level of an organism. Rather, its jelling endures alongside energies and factions that fly out from it and disturb it from within. And, most important for my purposes, the elements of this assemblage, while they include humans and their (social, legal, linguistic) constructions, also include some very active and powerful nonhumans: electrons, trees, wind, fire, electromagnetic fields.[121]

The lesson she draws from the North American blackout sums up her naïve ambition: that human will is not a necessary condition of agency. Agency is the result of collaboration, and any thing whatsoever can become a collaborator, or "actant" in Latour's vocabulary.

The agency of assemblages is positioned in contrast with the embodied agency of phenomenologists like Merleau-Ponty. For Merleau-Ponty and those influenced by him a given subject's agency is always dependent on an intersubjective field of other persons and equipment. Without these things the subject is rendered effectively powerless. Merleau-Ponty thus advances the concept of agency past the liberal, Kantian view for which the autonomous will is sufficient to grant agency; he gestures us toward the assemblage theory of agency. But even Merleau-Ponty's view is insufficient to get us to the vibrancy of matter, for it is not enough to point out the socially constituted, structure-dependent, or situated nature of embodied agency. Embodiment does not quite get us to an assemblage theory of agency, although it does form a notable impetus for Bennett's position. "In a world of vibrant matter," she insists, "it is thus not enough to say that we are 'embodied'. We are, rather, *an array of bodies*, many different kinds of them in a nested set of microbiomes."[122] To get to a vital materialist agency she suggests a "more radical displacement of the human subject than phenomenology has done."[123] This necessarily entails a move beyond the intersubjective field of embodiment toward the vital materiality of human and nonhuman assemblages. "Humanity and nonhumanity," writes

Bennett, "have always performed an intricate dance with each other. There was never a time when human agency was anything other than an interfolding network of humanity and nonhumanity; today this mingling has become harder to ignore."[124] Indeed.

Bennett is not uncritical of SR and OOP. She wonders about the "stakes" and "virtues" of privileging the withdrawn status of objects.[125] She also resists the attempt by some to privilege autonomous objects over their material substratum or the ecological system within which they operate. Although for her there is no need to take sides: all three of these levels should be regarded as interdependent. A truly flat ontology would not only treat all objects as equally objects, or all objects as equally real, but also all levels of existence as equally key for ontology. Here she follows Latour again. This kind of approach would involve a theoretical or critical modesty that parallels the ethical demand for modesty implicit in the object-oriented perspective, as she views it. After all, it seems that in addition to correlationism and the linguistic turn, public enemy number one for SR and OOO, as well as new materialism, is human hubris.[126] When it comes to combating this enemy, speculation is their weapon of choice.

Bennett's vital materialism does not operate at the deep ontological level that, say, Grant's "vitalism" does, but at a level more familiar for a political theorist. This is not to say, of course, that Bennett's view is shallow in comparison, but rather that her account is not poised as an alternative to Grant's (or any of the speculative realists, actually).[127] It is an attempt at articulating what are the practical effects of rethinking agency, neither along vitalist nor mechanist nor structuralist lines, but according to an object-oriented perspective.[128] What are the mechanisms that enable vibrant matter to "congeal" or coagulate into assemblages? What diffuses these assemblages? This is exciting work for many reasons, not the least of which is that it opens onto a landscape that speculative realism has barely glimpsed.

Notes

1. Harman, "On the Horror of Phenomenology," 336. On the problem of motivation in speculative realism, see Alexei Procyshyn, "The Epistemological Functions of Metaphysics" (paper presented at the 16th Annual Philosophy Conference, Villanova University, Pennsylvania, April 8, 2011).

2. I will not run the risk of doubly excluding an individual by naming names here.

3. Ray Brassier, "I Am a Nihilist Because I Still Believe in Truth," Interview by Marcin Rychter, *Kronos*, March 4, 2011, available at <http://www.kronos.org.pl/index.php?23151,896> (accessed October 5, 2013).

4. Bryant defends the philosophical potential of blogging in an interview with Peter Gratton. See "Interview with Levi Bryant," *Speculations* I (2010), 117–20.

5. Ray Brassier, "Against an Aesthetics of Noise." Interview with Bram Ieven, *nY* 2, May 5, 2009, available at <http://www.ny-web.be/transitzone/against-aesthetics-noise.html> (accessed October 5, 2013).

6. For a concise discussion of the "dimensions of this problem of ground," see Iain Hamilton Grant, "Does Nature Stay What-it-is? Dynamics and the Antecedence Criterion," in *The Speculative Turn*, 79–83.

7. Dunham et al., *Idealism: The History of a Philosophy*.

8. Brassier et al., "Speculative Realism," 334.

9. Brassier et al., "Speculative Realism," 334.

10. Brassier et al., "Speculative Realism," 343.

11. Iain Hamilton Grant, *Philosophies of Nature After Schelling* (London: Continuum, 2008), 6–8. For an extension of this geological metaphor, see Ben Woodard, *On An Ungrounded Earth: Towards a New Geophilosophy* (Brooklyn: punctum books, 2013). Given the influence of Deleuze on his work, Grant's philosophy could be productively explored alongside Mark Bonta and John Protevi, *Deleuze and Geophilosophy* (Edinburgh: Edinburgh University Press, 2004).

12. This is the label affixed by Morelle in "Speculative Realism: After Finitude, and Beyond?," 264.

13. The work of Michel Henry is a prime example, but also see Hans Jonas, *The Phenomenon of Life: Toward a Philosophical Biology*, new edition (Evanston: Northwestern University Press, 2011); Deleuze, *Pure Immanence*; and Leonard Lawlor, *The Implications of Immanence: Toward a New Concept of Life* (New York: Fordham University Press, 2006).

14. Grant, *Philosophies of Nature After Schelling*, 10.

15. Grant, *Philosophies of Nature After Schelling*, 1.

16. Grant, *Philosophies of Nature After Schelling*, 2

17. Grant, *Philosophies of Nature After Schelling*, 2.

18. Merleau-Ponty, "The Philosopher and His Shadow," 162.

19. Brassier et al., "Speculative Realism," 338.

20. Brassier et al., "Speculative Realism," 339.

21. As Morelle summarizes it, idealism for Grant supplies the condition of every metaphysics, every true materialism, and a non-naïve or essentialist realism. In other words, idealism is speculative realism in the form of Schellingian speculative physics. Morelle, "Speculative Realism: After Finitude, and Beyond?," 265.

22. Brassier et al., "Speculative Realism," 342.

23. Iain Hamilton Grant, "Movements of the World: The Sources of Transcendental Philosophy," *Analecta Hermeneutica* 3 (2011), 4.

24. Grant, "Movements of the World," 4.

25. See his remarks on the a priori in *Phenomenology of Perception*, 220–2.

26. Maurice Merleau-Ponty, *Nature: Course Notes from the Collège de France*, trans. Robert Vallier (Evanston: Northwestern University Press, 2003).

27. Merleau-Ponty, "The Philosopher and His Shadow," 178. See the collection by Jason Wirth and Patrick Burke, eds., *The Barbarian Principle: Merleau-Ponty, Schelling, and the Question of Nature*, (Albany: SUNY Press, 2013).

28. Ted Toadvine, *Merleau-Ponty's Philosophy of Nature* (Evanston: Northwestern University Press, 2009), 107.

29. As Bryan Bannon argues convincingly in "Flesh and Nature: Understanding Merleau-Ponty's Relational Ontology," *Research in Phenomenology* 41 (2011), 327–57.

30. Toadvine, *Merleau-Ponty's Philosophy of Nature*, 108, parenthetical citations omitted.

31. Toadvine, *Merleau-Ponty's Philosophy of Nature*, 108–9.

32. Here I am in agreement with DeLanda, "Ontological Commitments," 71, when he writes: "Any philosophy commits itself, explicitly or implicitly, to assert the existence of the entities that it intends to describe or explain."

33. Ray Brassier, email message to author, May 17, 2013.

34. Brassier, *Nihil Unbound*, 30.

35. Brassier, *Nihil Unbound*, 28.

36. Ray Brassier, "Concepts and Objects," in *The Speculative Turn*, 50, n.7.

37. Brassier, *Nihil Unbound*, 3; Wilfrid Sellars, "Philosophy and the Scientific Image of Man," in *Science, Perception and Reality* (London: Routledge and Kegan Paul), 1–40, cited in Brassier.

38. Ray Brassier, "Lived Experience and the Myth of the Given," *Filozofski Vestnik* (2013).

39. Brassier, *Nihil Unbound*, 3–5. For the story of how this construct comes to seem natural and theory-free, see Brassier's account of Sellars's "myth of Jones," and Wilfrid Sellars, *Empiricism and the Philosophy of Mind* (Cambridge, MA: Harvard University Press, 1997), 90–4.

40. Brassier, *Nihil Unbound*, 5–6.

41. Brassier, *Nihil Unbound*, 6–7.

42. Brassier, "Concepts and Objects," 50–1. "The norm of truth not only provides the most intransigent bulwark against the supernatural conception of normativity; it also provides the necessary rationale for the elimination of folk metaphysics."

43. Brassier, *Nihil Unbound*, 7.

44. Brassier, *Nihil Unbound*, 7.

45. Brassier, "Lived Experience and the Myth of the Given."

46. Brassier, "Lived Experience and the Myth of the Given."

47. Brassier, *Nihil Unbound*, 30.

48. Brassier, *Nihil Unbound*, 31.

49. Brassier, *Nihil Unbound*, 9, 10–11.

50. Brassier, *Nihil Unbound*, 17, 25. See "The View from Nowhere," *Identities: Journal for Politics, Gender, and Culture* 8, no. 2 (2011), 7–23. For more on this line of research, see Thomas Metzinger, *Being No One: The Self-Model Theory of Subjectivity* (Cambridge, MA: MIT Press, 2003) and *The Ego Tunnel: The Science of the Mind and the Myth of the Self* (New York: Basic Books, 2010). The problem with Churchland's position is that it suffers from an inadequate metaphysical naturalism. In Brassier's words, it is "inadequate to the task of grounding the relation between representation and reality."

51. Brassier, *Nihil Unbound*, 27.

52. Brassier, "Against an Aesthetics of Noise."

53. Which entails its own dubious form of reductionism. See "Concepts and Objects," 54, 57.

54. Brassier, *Nihil Unbound*, 27; "Concepts and Objects," 51.

55. Brassier, *Nihil Unbound*, 28.

56. Brassier, *Nihil Unbound*, 29.

57. Brassier's concern with and faith in scientific objectivity is evident in Brassier et al., "Speculative Realism," 323–4, 331–3. On the distinction between "is" and "seems," or being and appearing, see "Lived Experience and the Myth of the Given."

58. Morelle warns, following Harman and rightly I think, of the danger of accepting Brassier's positive conclusions too quickly ("Speculative Realism: After Finitude, and Beyond?," 263). As he says, "this method, though proving definitively powerful when it comes to refutation, appears much weaker when it comes to defending its own theses." Since *Nihil Unbound* Brassier has done a bit more to defend his own theses, and I have tried to cite some of this work in the present chapter.

59. See Brassier's discussion of the (correlationist) fallacy of "Stove's Gem" in "Concepts and Objects," 56–64.

60. Brassier, "Concepts and Objects," 64.

61. Levi Bryant, *Onto-Cartography: An Ontology of Machines and Media* (Edinburgh: Edinburgh University Press, 2014).

62. See Levi Bryant, "Borromean Critical Theory," *Larval Subjects*, February 21, 2013, available at <http://larvalsubjects.wordpress.com/2013/02/21/borromean-critical-theory> (accessed October 5, 2013).

63. Levi R. Bryant, *Difference and Givenness: Deleuze's Transcendental Empiricism and the Ontology of Immanence* (Evanston: Northwestern University Press, 2008), 3.

64. Bryant, *The Democracy of Objects*, 34–5.

65. Meillassoux, *After Finitude*, 6; Bryant, *The Democracy of Objects*, 35.

66. Bryant, *The Democracy of Objects*, 37.

67. Bryant, *The Democracy of Objects*, 40, italics omitted.

68. Roy Bhaskar, *A Realist Theory of Science* (London: Verso, 2008), 23.

69. Bryant, *The Democracy of Objects*, 43, italics omitted.

70. Bhaskar, *A Realist Theory of Science*, 22; Bryant, *The Democracy of Objects*, 45.

71. Bryant, *The Democracy of Objects*, 50–1.

72. See Levi Bryant, "Alien Phenomenology, Idealism, and Materialism," *Larval Subjects*, August 22, 2012, available at <http://larvalsubjects.wordpress.com/2012/08/22/alien-phenomenology-idealism-and-materialism> (accessed October 5, 2013).

73. Bryant, *The Democracy of Objects*, 64.

74. Bryant, *The Democracy of Objects*, 65. For a sketch of Bryant's theory of substance and relationality, see 68–71 and "The Ontic Principle," 270–3.

75. Bryant, "The Ontic Principle," 261, 262.

76. Bryant, "The Ontic Principle," 263, 264.

77. Bryant, "The Ontic Principle," 264, 265.
78. "Onticology recommends that we understand objects in terms of what they can do, that we think of objects as acts or doings, rather than as beings that possess or own properties" (Gratton, "Interview with Levi Bryant," 123).
79. Bryant, "The Ontic Principle," 266.
80. Bryant, "The Ontic Principle," 269; see also *The Democracy of Objects*, Chapter 6. For a discussion of the possible political and ethical shortcomings of flat ontology, see Peter Gratton, "Interview with Ian Bogost," *Speculations* I, 115–17.
81. Bryant, "The Ontic Principle," 270.
82. See the epigraph on page xi and 38–58 of Timothy Morton, *The Ecological Thought* (Cambridge, MA: Harvard University Press, 2010).
83. Morton, *Ecology without Nature*, 106.
84. Morton, *Ecology without Nature*, 128.
85. Morton, *Ecology without Nature*, 129.
86. Morton, *Realist Magic*, 17.
87. Morton, *Realist Magic*, 27, 36. Morton includes in his book extended discussions of the law of noncontradiction and dialetheism.
88. Morton, *Realist Magic*, 19–20, 76.
89. Morton, *Realist Magic*, 37.
90. Morton, *Realist Magic*, 64.
91. Morton, *Realist Magic*, 67.
92. Morton, *Realist Magic*, 122.
93. Morton, *Realist Magic*, 75.
94. Timothy Morton, *Hyperobjects: Philosophy and Ecology after the End of the World* (Minneapolis: University of Minnesota Press, 2013).
95. Timothy Morton, "Hyperobjects and the End of Common Sense," *The Contemporary Condition*, March 18, 2010, available at <http://contemporarycondition.blogspot.com/2010/03/hyperobjects-and-end-of-common-sense.html> (accessed October 5, 2013).
96. Morton, *Realist Magic*, 68.
97. Peter Gratton, "Interview with Tim Morton," *Speculations* I, 107.
98. Morton, *The Ecological Thought*, 56.
99. Bogost explicitly aligns himself with Harman's version of OOO. See Bogost, *Alien Phenomenology*, 5.
100. Bogost, *Alien Phenomenology*, 29.

101. Bogost, *Alien Phenomenology*, 25. He prefers "unit" to object because it is "an ambivalent term, indifferent to the nature of what it names. It is also isolated, unitary, and specific, not simply the part of a whole or ontologically basic and indivisible like an atom." See also Ian Bogost, *Unit Operations: An Approach to Videogame Criticism* (Cambridge, MA: MIT Press, 2008).

102. Nick Montfort and Ian Bogost, *Racing the Beam: The Atari Video Computer System* (Cambridge, MA: MIT Press, 2009).

103. Gratton, "Interview with Ian Bogost," 112.

104. Bogost, *Alien Phenomenology*, 11. On the other hand, Bogost says that speculation is "akin to *epoché*" insofar as it produces transcendence in the Husserlian sense (32).

105. Bogost, *Alien Phenomenology*, 28.

106. Harman, *The Quadruple Object*, 125.

107. Bogost, *Alien Phenomenology*, 38.

108. Bogost, *Alien Phenomenology*, 39.

109. Bogost, *Alien Phenomenology*, 42.

110. Bogost, *Alien Phenomenology*, 59.

111. Bogost, *Alien Phenomenology*, 64; see also Harman, *Guerrilla Metaphysics*, Chapter 8.

112. Bogost, *Alien Phenomenology*, 66–72. The "New Aesthetic" is a contemporary art movement that tries to depict what it is like for computers, sensors, and other digital technologies to perceive. Bogost, in "The New Aesthetic Needs to Get Weirder," *The Atlantic*, April 13, 2012, argues that the New Aesthetic should not restrict its scope to computers and digital devices, but should expand to include any type of object. See <http://www.theatlantic.com/technology/archive/2012/04/the-new-aesthetic-needs-to-get-weirder/255838> (accessed December 19, 2013).

113. Bogost, *Alien Phenomenology*, 92.

114. Levi Bryant, "Borromean Machine-Oriented Ontology, Strange Strangers, and Alien Phenomenology," *Larval Subjects*, July 24, 2012, available at <http://larvalsubjects.wordpress.com/2012/07/24/borromean-machine-oriented-ontology-strange-strangers-and-alien-phenomenology> (accessed October 5, 2013).

115. Bogost, *Alien Phenomenology*, 31, 35.

116. See the following collections: Diana Coole and Samantha Frost, eds., *New Materialisms: Ontology, Agency, and Politics* (Durham: Duke University Press, 2010); Dolphijn and van der Tuin, *New Materialism: Interviews & Cartographies*.

117. Jane Bennett, *Vibrant Matter: A Political Ecology of Things* (Durham: Duke University Press, 2010), 17.

118. Bennett, *Vibrant Matter*, 2–3.

119. Bennett, *Vibrant Matter*, xi, xiv–xv. See also Jane Bennett, *The Enchantment of Modern Life* (Princeton: Princeton University Press, 2001). It could be useful to compare Bennett's notion of enchantment to Harman's "allure" and Bogost's "wonder."

120. Bennett, *Vibrant Matter*, 23.

121. Bennett, *Vibrant Matter*, 24.

122. Bennett, *Vibrant Matter*, 112–13.

123. Bennett, *Vibrant Matter*, 29, 30. I offer a thorough critique of phenomenology's version of embodied agency in *Plastic Bodies: Rebuilding Sensation After Phenomenology* (Ann Arbor: Open Humanities Press, forthcoming).

124. Bennett, *Vibrant Matter*.

125. Jane Bennett, "Systems and Things: A Response to Graham Harman and Timothy Morton," *New Literary History* 43 (2012), 226.

126. Bennett, "Systems and Things," 226–31.

127. Bennett does face the same problem that Grant does, however, but at a different level. If for Grant the absolute is preobjective and therefore preformed, a plane of immanence without organization, and if for Bennett vibrant matter is the condition of possibility for assemblages which constitute themselves from diverse and heterogeneous things, then we must ask how it is that objects, in Grant's theory, and assemblages, in Bennett's, ever come into existence. See Peter Gratton, "Interview with Jane Bennett," *Speculations* I, 99.

128. To be sure, Bennett's object-oriented position draws upon Latour's concept of "actant" and for that reason invites close comparison with Harman's view.

Conclusion

After the End of Phenomenology

Hopefully the reader will not find it too crass if I end this book in the same spirit of polemic with which I began. It was a polemical affect that initiated the idea of writing it, and I would dissimulate my intentions if I were to pretend that my disagreements with and criticism of phenomenology were meant only as constructive criticism. With that said, I do want to make some suggestions about how phenomenology might live on in the future, even after it has come to an end. But first we should gather up the several senses of this end.

First, the case can be made that phenomenology never really existed. Husserl conceived it as a method for philosophy as strict science, but he could never settle on a precise formulation. Retroactively this indecision and second-guessing of himself is heralded as a mark of his deep philosophical sensibility, but it remains true that he never bequeathed a necessary set of steps for phenomenological investigation.

Second, as the years went on Husserl increasingly aligned himself with transcendental idealism, while resisting idealism's absolute and subjective forms. Reading *Ideas I* and *Cartesian Meditations*, the reader is often struck with the feeling that Husserl is finally coming around to the truth of the Kantian perspective. On this score, phenomenology could be seen as nothing other than an elaborate recapitulation of transcendental idealism, not a distinctive philosophical position with unique metaphysical and methodological commitments.

Third, many of Husserl's descendants have struggled to distance themselves from his idealism. Some, like Merleau-Ponty, prefer to call phenomenology a style of philosophy so it is not

seen as a regimented practice with formal requirements. This
suggests that anyone could easily become a phenomenologist,
and that many modes of inquiry could qualify as phenomenological. This effectively empties the meaning of phenomenology by casting its net too wide. We might recall here that when
James adopted the name of pragmatism for his work, Peirce,
who failed to recognize his philosophy in James, took up the
new title of "pragmaticism" in order to demarcate a salient difference in his methodology. Husserl might have done the same
thing. Instead of insisting on a family resemblance between the
pragmatists or the phenomenologists, so as to preserve the pre-
carious idea that the thinkers associated with each school share
a common approach or set of commitments, it might be a better
strategy to treat their *differences* as fundamental so as to dis-
sociate them. New alliances would form and entrenched ways
of thinking would be dislodged, but phenomenology might also
very well dissolve.

Fourth, given that the requirements for being a phenomenologist have loosened, it is increasingly difficult to say what it takes
to *do* phenomenology. Some think that you just have to grapple
with the meaning of Husserl's or Heidegger's main concepts, or
mobilize them in your own work, or write an early-career study
of one of the movement's canonical figures. But this cannot be
what it means to do phenomenology. Presumably, to do phenomenology requires a specific set of practices, even just one or two,
that differentiate phenomenological from nonphenomenological
philosophy. Without these phenomenology lacks a specific difference. This implies that no one has ever been, at least not for
very long, a phenomenologist. The fact that so many defenders
and proponents spill gallons of ink trying to specify what phenomenology is and should be – not to mention that it is often
defined mostly in terms of what it is *not* – indicates that even now
the very possibility of phenomenology is unapparent to Husserl's
faithful inheritors.

The new phenomenology suffers from the same incoherence
I have traced throughout this book. As the authors of *The New
Phenomenology* admit, "Whether *classical* phenomenology can be
viewed in a meaningful way as a 'school' is open to question. That
question is even more complicated for the *new* phenomenology."[1]
In order to account for their decision to collect the new phenomenologists under the same label, the authors explain that new

phenomenology is *"not united by a specific set of doctrines such that it could be considered a unified philosophical theory"* and that "new phenomenology is not clearly definable as a historical trend or movement." It is best regarded as a family resemblance term denoting a group of thinkers who draw upon the original work of Husserl and Heidegger for "inspiration." This seems reasonable, but at the same time questionable given that "the new phenomenologists are all engaged in working out what phenomenology itself requires, assumes, and supposes." If this is an open question, how are these new phenomenologists supposed to know that they are phenomenologists or that their phenomenology is new? Simmons and Benson conclude that they all share a "coherent philosophical *trajectory*," and that this is what links them.[2] But once phenomenology is reduced to a trajectory or style, it has effectively come to an end. Saying that someone shares the same "phenomenological motivations"[3] does nothing to guarantee that something called "phenomenology" can actually be kept alive. If we are still defining phenomenology negatively, we should ask if there is any sense in continuing to posit phenomenology's positive existence.

Thus, fifth, the trouble with phenomenology is that it does not have a clear principle or set of principles *animating* it. Those that once propelled it forward have been discarded or forsaken, or have withered under the sterile light of hermeneutic and deconstructive scrutiny. In response to this thesis a close friend of mine suggested that phenomenology has morphed into a "zombie phenomenology." Bogost applies the zombie label to idealism, but for different reasons.[4] There is something right, I think, about calling phenomenology undead. One is often struck by the sense that it is extremely active, but at the same time lacking philosophical vitality and methodologically hollow.

Sixth and finally, it seems to me that phenomenology has always been at its strongest when locked in a dialectical relation with scientific naturalism, and it is at its most compelling when we recall that it was generated by Husserl in reaction to a reductionist scientism that will, perhaps, always be with us. This lends a certain degree of irony to contemporary attempts to naturalize phenomenology, which seem to memorialize landmark insights from classical phenomenologists more often than they revitalize its philosophical research program.[5] Phenomenology provides a necessary corrective to the excesses of science, although these need not stand as mutually exclusive endeavors. Indeed, it is when phenomenology construes them as such that it presents itself as naïve, hubristic, or both. Phenomenology was born at a specific historical moment and in opposition to a specific mode of thinking, so we have to wonder if its force is not contingent upon historical circumstances that no longer call out for phenomenology's resources. It will contend that its method is transhistorical, if not transcendental, and therefore not dependent on history. But then it opens itself to hermeneutic criticism which arguably is sufficient to bring phenomenology to an end.

If phenomenology is to have a future, then it might present itself not as some *sui generis* ontology immune to the conceptual forces of philosophy's history, but as the irreducible supplement to natural science. It might return to the work of Husserl in order to finalize what Husserl never could: a precise phenomenological method to complement the method of science. Without this precision phenomenology will either continue to quibble over its own self-understanding or squander its rigor in the name of methodological liberation. Then again, if phenomenology agrees to become the handmaiden of science, all is lost. Phenomenology will have finally forfeited its claim to ground science, a claim that is extremely difficult to endorse in our contemporary milieu.

Another option is for phenomenology to forsake its realist aspirations and earnestly embrace its *idealist* heritage. Actually, this is not as disjunctive as it sounds. Grant has shown that idealism does not necessarily oppose realism because idealism is realist "about all things," by which he means ideas and nature. Given a proper transcendental formulation, this could once again position phenomenology underneath the natural sciences and safeguard its philosophical primacy. This may pose a problem for its theological wing, but only if idealism is incapable of demonstrating the actual, absolute existence of the divine.

In my Introduction I suggested that phenomenology has reached that Frostian point along its path where the path diverges and a decision must be made. The alternative to strong correlationism, it seems to me, is total submission to phenomenology's idealist roots. Not the transcendental idealism of Kant, however, or the neo-Kantianism to which Husserl and Heidegger were responding, but the absolute idealism of Hegel, the original phenomenology. Hegel has proven quite tenacious; he has even won over some notable analytic philosophers. A radical retrieval of the meaning of phenomenology as Hegel understood it could yield many unexpected conclusions. I am thinking particularly of the weirdness that we find in Schelling, but also the weirdness of Hegel himself and what Žižek does with both of them. Phenomenology could transform idealism into a new variant of speculative realism, and thereby forge a subterranean portal to the things themselves. This is not quite what we get in Harman. Meillassoux has said that Hegel is his "unaddressed hidden source" and, along with Marx, his "only true master."[6] If this is true, and if it is true that Meillassoux's own speculative materialism is the product of a radicalization of strong correlationism, then there is compelling evidence that phenomenology has a speculative future. Of course, it will have to redefine its method and take on some metaphysical commitments, but at least it will no longer walk the earth undead.

None of this is likely to convince the committed phenomenologist who rejects the idealist core of phenomenology and continues to insist that phenomenology transcends the idealist/realist duality; it will not convince the academic who stakes their career on phenomenology's viability. They will continue to spiral deeper and deeper into the intricacies of phenomenological description and the infinite task of describing mundane experiences or reflections on reflections on reflections on reflections. They will struggle to make sense of what Husserl, Heidegger, Merleau-Ponty, and Sartre had in mind and what the *epoché*, intuition, or the Flesh really mean. This strategy, however, presupposes that there is something called "phenomenological description" or a determinate phenomenological method that *could be* specified. It is not at all clear that there is. I have argued throughout this book that no such thing exists and, perhaps, has never existed. Husserl famously never got there, and many of his followers famously gave up on it. His major disciples all but rejected the enterprise.[7] Ironically, phenomenology as such could *never* accomplish the task of establishing its own existence: the establishment of what absolutely does and does not exist remains forever outside the purview of phenomenology proper.

At this point I am still unsure what it takes to be a phenomenologist. "Phenomenology" is on the verge of empty signification, if it has not already crossed that threshold. It is a label that we should probably apply only sparingly if we want it to actually name something. But instead, the name continues to circulate liberally and affix itself to widely diverse studies. There is still a market for monographs on the latest developments in phenomenology and handbooks for qualitative researchers. If the speculative realist critique of correlationism holds any water, however, there is yet another reason to draw phenomenology, new or otherwise, to a close.

As for the future of speculative realism, I will not make any predictions beyond what I signaled in the previous chapter. I do think Brassier is right to note that the term realism as it is applied in continental circles today must be "disambiguated." As the Goldsmiths colloquium made clear, there are many species of realism, some of them simply realist, others materialist, idealist, and naturalist. It does not seem wise to refer to every extant, nascent, or future realist position in the continental tradition as "speculative," unless it can be convincingly shown that all realism worth its salt must of necessity speculate in order to be realist. The specific difference between a realist and a speculative realist must be identified, otherwise speculative realism will meet a fate similar to phenomenology. Its methodological requirements, and consequently its meaning, remain to be decided. While I tried to indicate some likely candidates throughout this book, I have not attempted to defend them with any degree of precision. Such a defense is still called for.

For too long have we believed that phenomenology is the philosophy best equipped to deliver the things themselves. In the wake of speculative realism this belief seems more and more unbelievable.

Notes

1. Simmons and Benson, *The New Phenomenology*, 2.
2. Simmons and Benson, *The New Phenomenology*, 6.
3. Simmons and Benson, *The New Phenomenology*, 102.
4. Bogost, *Alien Phenomenology*, 133.
5. I am thinking here of the work of Shaun Gallagher, Evan Thompson, Dan Zahavi, and others. The naturalization of phenomenology does seem the best way extant to keep phenomenology alive, but again, I wonder if it keeps its method alive in any technical sense, or if it does not simply lend a cognitive-scientific authority to some of phenomenology's key ideas.
6. Harman, *Quentin Meillassoux*, 168.

7. It is, in fact, in the detailed writings of the minor and marginal figures of what Herbert Spiegelberg called "the phenomenological movement" that we find a continuation of Husserl's dream of phenomenology as rigorous science. Among these figures are Stephan Strasser, Aron Gurwitsch, Alfred Schütz, Maurice Natanson, Roman Ingarden, Mikel Dufrenne, and many others.

Index

CPSIA information can be obtained
at www.ICGtesting.com
Printed in the USA
BVHW041024200820
586901BV00012B/2232